The Gothic Fairy Tale
in Young Adult Literature

D1548211

The Gothic Fairy Tale in Young Adult Literature

Essays on Stories from Grimm to Gaiman

Edited by JOSEPH ABBRUSCATO
and TANYA JONES

McFarland & Company, Inc., Publishers
Jefferson, North Carolina

LIBRARY OF CONGRESS CATALOGUING-IN-PUBLICATION DATA

The gothic fairy tale in young adult literature : essays on stories from Grimm to Gaiman / edited by Joseph Abbruscato and Tanya Jones.

p.   cm.

Includes bibliographical references and index.

ISBN 978-0-7864-7935-1 (softcover : acid free paper) ∞
ISBN 978-1-4766-1725-1 (ebook)

1. Fairy tales—History and criticism.   2. Gothic fiction (Literary genre)—History and criticism.   3. Young adult literature—History and criticism.   I. Abbruscato, Joseph, 1986– editor.   II. Jones, Tanya, 1983– editor.

PN3437.G68 2014
398.209—dc23   2014021286

BRITISH LIBRARY CATALOGUING DATA ARE AVAILABLE

Cover image © iStock/Thinkstock

Printed in the United States of America

McFarland & Company, Inc., Publishers
Box 611, Jefferson, North Carolina 28640
www.mcfarlandpub.com

Joseph Abbruscato—
For Mom and Dad. You encouraged my curiosity,
fostered my infatuation with books,
and taught me the importance of stories.
This would not have been possible without you. I love you both.

Tanya Jones—
For the storytellers who keep fairy tales alive.
For the big bad wolf who always keeps Little Red on her toes.
And for Natalya whose fairy tale is just beginning.

Table of Contents

Table of Contents

Introduction: The State of Modern Fairy Tales

Joseph Abbruscato

One of the oldest and most well known literary genres is the fairy tale. Stemming from the oral traditions of nearly all cultures worldwide, these tales have been an integral part of children's upbringing for generations. Unfortunately, over the last 30-some years, these narratives have become ghosts of their former selves, lacking the psychic and educational importance their classic counterparts are famous for.

Filled with monsters and dragons, evil step-parents and fairy godmothers, princes and princesses, and children and adults, fairy tales are more than simple entertainment meant to pass hours in a fantasy land. These stories, "with their false brides, severed limbs" and other Gothic and fantastical elements, are used as important tools to teach children about themselves and the world around them (Bernheimer xvii). This in turn enables the audience, be it children or adults, to become productive members of their societies, cultures, and families, and able to maturely handle the crises and situations which arise over the course of their lives. These tales, according to Maria Tatar,

> are talismanic and Talmudic, volumes treasured and fetishized, ... read to pieces. Held together by rubber bands, duct tape, and rusting paperclips, they serve as companions and compass roses, offering shocks, terrors, and wonders, as well as wisdom, comfort, and sustenance [5].

Fairy tales are treasure troves stocked with everything children need to be nurtured, binding them to the stories through wondrous worlds, ancient magics, demons, and dragons. According to Hunt, these tales are "rooted in (and [have] been deliberately directed towards) stories not calculated to protect childhood from horror; or, it might be said, in expanding children's experience at too rapid a rate" (15). Traditionally, the purpose of the fairy tale has not been to mollify a child's imagination but to bolster it in ways that reality cannot. According to Kate Bernheimer, it is precisely the inclusion of such motifs that make the fairy tale world real: "It is violent; and yes, there is loss. There is murder, incest, famine and rot—all of these haunt the stories, as they haunt us. The fairy-tale world is a real world" (xxviii). The unreal, Gothic, and horrific elements of these tales are essential and necessary for children to relate to the imaginary, fantastic, and magic found in the stories to the world around them.

The interconnectedness of the real and fairy tale worlds is discussed in Bruno Bettelheim's introduction to *The Uses of Enchantment: The Meaning and Importance of Fairy Tales*. Bettelheim argues that

> an understanding of the meaning of one's life is not suddenly acquired at a particular age, not even when one has reached chronological maturity. On the contrary, gaining a secure understanding of what the meaning of one's life may or ought to be—this is what constitutes having attained psychological maturity. And this achievement is the end result of a long development [3].

Fairy tales are a necessity to a child searching for meaning in the surrounding world. Everyday occurrences excite him; there are a great number of situations which seem commonplace to an adult that are strikingly new and magical to a young child. In these ways, the real world and the fantastical world of fairy tales are seen as one and the same. Skills learned in fairy tales are applicable in the real world; both are perceived as potentially scary and awe-inspiring. Because of their content, the fears, anxieties, and situations faced by the antagonists in fairy tales are wholly relatable to the young child.

Readers depend upon fairy tales for personal growth—not as escape but as enhancement of their own lives and skills. Reading is "less a refuge from life than a quiet sanctuary, a chance to meet characters worth observing and to witness how they manage conflict, peril, and adventure" (Tatar 18). Children reading fairy tales are not searching for a way out of the reality in which they find themselves but rather for a field manual to help them understand their surroundings. In *Orthodoxy*, G.K. Chesterton succinctly states that "a child of seven is excited by being told that Tommy opened a door and saw a dragon. But a child of three is excited by being told that Tommy opened a door" (46). While the subject of the sentence stays they same (a story about Tommy), the importance lies in what children of different ages take away from the story. As the child develops his own experiences he compounds what he has learned, adding to the knowledge gained and the "exciting" moments of earlier ages. Chesterton's assertion works to show that maturation and understanding is compounding experience. As such, a child of seven years has grown past the three-year-old child in terms of maturity. He has the ability now to open doors on his own; this teaching moment has been previously internalized and can be built upon. Because of this, the teaching moment is able to serve as a platform for growth: knowledge of how to open a door enables Tommy to experience a more advanced skill, possibly breaching the doorway.

Discussing her daughter's collection of cherished tales, Tatar states that on the bookshelf are "seven tattered paperbacks, each one ... representing an important part of her identity" (5). These seven books, presumably collected over time, compound the different knowledges gleaned from the previous one. As Tatar's daughter continues to grow, age, and mature, so will her collection; more books will be added as she internalizes all she can from the previous tale; this necessitates a new one to satiate her appetite for knowledge of herself and the world around her. Had Chesterton continued with the story, describing what Tommy did next (stepping through the portal toward the dragon, closing the door), and so on, he would inevitably continue to demonstrate how the compounding of knowledge is handled by fairy tales. This intricacy of fairy tales enables a child to learn and take away new elements from rereadings of the classic tale (as well as new stories written in the classic traditions) as the child grows. Fairy tales contain both the doors and the dragons of which young children are desperately in need.

Recently, an unfortunate shift has occurred in the general population's perception of the fairy tale. The once vital stories of the type collected by the Brothers Grimm in the 1800s have become relegated to mere entertainment, being drained of the positive didactic elements and morphed to a reflection of society's view on how children's lives should be guided. Peter Hunt pinpoints this shift, stating that the last 30 years have seen an increase in reality-based stories, focusing on what adults perceive to be a child's "real life." He writes, "The 1980's and 1990's saw a vast increase in the number of books dealing with social 'realism'" (17). These books often were merely present-day retellings of classic fairy tales. "Many parents believed that only conscious reality or pleasant and wish-fulfilling images should be presented to the child—that he should be exposed only to the sunny side of things" (Bettelheim 7); gone were the terrifying aspects of dragons and monsters, abolished were the horrifying evil step-parents, non-existent were the well known motifs of "murder, dismemberment, death and sexual violence" from the traditional texts (Hunt 15). These elements were abandoned for ideals that were more easily absorbed by a general population which deemed that children needed to be protected from these horrors, and found in their stead were likable creatures deemed less traumatic for impressionable children. Fairy tales and stories have become watered-down versions of the classic forms (now devoid of their former educational value), morphed into real world-based stories that allow children no room for escape or distance from the lives they already lead. Children are more able to objectively synthesize a story involving vampires, monsters, or dragons due to the distance afforded by the fantastical elements than they are a story revolving around horrors committed by human beings. The latter describes situations that are "too close to home" in many cases. Safe versions of stories do a disservice to the child reader. They give the child no suggestions as to how life unfolds, about how he is to grow and mature; these "safe stories mention neither death nor aging, the limits of our existence, nor the wish for eternal life. The fairy tale, by contrast, confronts the child squarely with the basic human predicaments" (Bettelheim 8). The child is presented with death, elation, starvation, victories, and the entire spectrum of emotions and situations in which humans participate on a daily basis. Lacking knowledge of these experiences, the child's growth is one-sided.

The forced sanitization of fairy tales creates the illusion for children that life is completely sunny, that real life has no dragons or obstacles to overcome. This is not the case. Bettelheim explains that "in order to not be at the mercy of the vagaries of life, one must develop one's inner resources, so that one's emotions, imagination, and intellect mutually support and enrich one another" (4). Bettelheim provides here the basic elements needed for balanced growth of one's psyche: (1) the emotions, (2) the imagination, and (3) the intellect. These three elements must be fed and enriched in equal portions. When only one or two are developed and the others are neglected, there is bound to be unequal growth. The child runs the risk of maturing in an unbalanced fashion. He understands that there are obstacles to overcome, yet these new stories state that all is okay in the world, that the dragons need not be defeated. The child becomes confused; he is not groomed or taught to exercise all the faculties Bettelheim views as the key triangle to growth.

With the recent devolution in fairy tales, this equilateral growth is no longer possible.

The problematic elements of many contemporary, situational, "real life" narratives couched as fairy tales are discussed by Karen Coats. Attacking these problems, Coats states that

> twentieth- and twenty-first-century culture, however, has degraded these once psychically useful tales into little more than "a couple of rodents looking for a theme park" (*Hercules,* 1997), where ogres don't eat children as much as entertain them, an average Joe can have his princess without slaying any dragons, and a schoolgirl will be handed both her kingdom and her prince at the low cost of learning how to walk properly and style her hair. Such sanitizations render fairy tales less able to do their work ... [79].

These neutered narratives prevent fairy tales from holding the meaning and importance to children's upbringing that they once did. The challenges faced by the main characters in these modernized narratives do little to expand the reader's unconscious cognizance of real world situations. The modernization and simplification neglects the psychological importance of fairy tales. These recent imaginings of fairy tales and fairy stories may stimulate one or two of the three important areas mentioned by Bettelheim, but that leaves at least one area vital to a child's growth neglected. Bettelheim states that "the overwhelming bulk of the rest of so-called 'children's literature' attempts to entertain ... but most of these books are so shallow in substance that little of significance can be gained from them" (4). Fairy tales fill this void in children's literature; where other children's literature genres generally fall short, fairy tales excel in being psychically stimulating, helping create well-rounded, multi-intelligent children who can cope with reality.

One of the most popular stories of the past 20 years is the Harry Potter series. It includes ghosts and elves, castles and graveyards, and as such it is touted as a fairy tale. This series took years to be written and published—the better part of a decade. Rowling's narrative is more an epic series than an actual fairy tale. These tales are problematic as a child needs to read seven books, totaling thousands of pages, in order to reach the epiphanies the story holds. If the child wants to take the moral of the story to heart, he has to read many pages and will only discover the meaning later as he reads the next books in the series. In stark comparison, none of the Brothers Grimm collected tales are longer than twenty or so pages. The strength of fairy tales lies in their ability to deliver their psychically important lessons, their epiphanies and teaching moments, in as concise a package as possible.

With fairy tales, it is possible to read the tale and comprehend its importance exactly when the child needs it. If the lesson offered by a tale has already been internalized, the reader is able to build on that and advance immediately to another tale, one with more formidable challenges and lessons. To Bettelheim, fairy tales, in their traditional form, "enrich [the child's] life … stimulating his imagination; help him to develop his intellect and to clarify his emotions; be attuned to his anxieties and aspirations; give full recognition to his difficulties, while at the same time suggesting solutions to the problems which perturb him" (5). This can only be accomplished by stepping away from the false tales and holding off reading satirical versions until there is a base knowledge and internalization of the classic tales. It is vital to end the misclassification of pop culture novels as "fairy tales," and make a marked return to the original texts with all of their horrific elements.

One of the most important ways that this return to classic tales is achieved is through the re-inclusion of the horrifying, even Gothic, motifs into contemporary fairy tales. According to Coats, fairy tales are important to children's psychical development because they

> provide concrete images of villains and monsters on which to project undirected anxieties and fears so that they might be contained and dispatched, to facilitate psychic integration, and to assure the child of the possibility of happy endings when present trials are overcome [78].

These villains and monsters and kingdoms with princes and princesses are all classic elements of Gothic literature. In these stories, anxieties and fears are "transposed" (Hunt 16) into fantasy worlds where they become abstract elements that a child can apply to multiple scenarios. The knowledge gained by these transposed situations in fairy tales and fantastical adventures can be utilized in the many real-world scenarios a child finds himself, because the fairy tale is known by the child to be a vastly different place than the real world.

One such anxiety and fear that consumes many young readers is cannibalism. This concern has a long history in fairy tales, as it is a cultural taboo. According to Carolyn Daniel, stories about monsters who threaten to consume, whether they are wolves, witches, sharks, or aliens, continue to be the mainstay of much grotesque-horror fiction aimed at both children and adults. Monsters such as these act outside cultural and social prohibitions and represent the antithesis of civilized humanity [139].

This threat of becoming consumed, of personal nonexistence, or existence simply as a part of someone else, is deeply seeded in society and found in the Grimm versions of the classic fairy tales, such as "Hansel and Grethel" and "Little Red Riding Hood." The narrative of "Little Red Riding Hood" is plagued with the threat of consumption by the Wolf. Upon Little Red Riding Hoods' arrival at her grandmother's house in the woods, this fear is actualized and must be faced. The Wolf has already committed an act of cannibalism, "jumping without a word on the bed, he gobbled up the poor old lady" to trick Little Red Riding Hood in hopes of consuming her as well (Grimm's 103). Here the Wolf is personified, having "tied on her cap," donned the grandmother's clothing, and laid in her bed. As Little Red Riding Hood gazes upon the figure in the bed, she makes proclamations regarding the lupine features: "What great ears you have!… And what great eyes you have! And what great hands you have!… But, Grandmother, what great teeth you have!" (104). Each of these exclamations received a verbal reply by the Wolf, and the fourth was accompanied by the Wolf springing "out of bed, and [swallowing] up poor Little Red Riding Hood," fulfilling the fear of cannibalism (104). The series of events following the consumption of Little Red Riding Hood and her grandmother, and the subsequent killing of the Wolf, demonstrate the persistence of this fear and its continued taboo nature.

In reality, wolves do not wear clothing, lay in a bed, or speak the language of human beings. For these reasons it might be argued that the act of the Wolf eating Little Red Riding Hood is not truly cannibalism, as the Wolf belongs to the world of Animals and Little Red Riding Hood belongs to the separate world of Mankind. However, what must be taken into account is that in fairy tales, "the human and animal worlds are equal and mutually dependent. The violence, the suffering, and beauty are shared" (Bernheimer xix). Each separate world relies upon the other for existence; to deny this dependability is to rend the fabric of the tales, removing from them the ability to evenly execute Bettelheim's psychic triangle. This collapsed boundary between the human and animal worlds is vital to uphold the emotional, imaginative, and intellectual triangle.

This boundary collapse is relived again and again throughout contemporary fairy tales: the fear of being on the fodder end of the food chain is especially worrisome for contemporary protagonists. In many of these stories, the main character encounters creatures or monsters who, often under the guise of becoming new, true friends, plan on eating him and turning him into one of their kind. Just like the Wolf in "Little Red Riding Hood," these creatures do not truly belong to world of Mankind. However, they do not belong to the world of Animals either. Their existence is in an ephemeral place situated between Life and Death (which is oftentimes breached by a fairy tale hero). With the ever-present potential of cannibalization and the subsequent lack of being, these hero and protagonist identities become merged with the consumer, completely altering and eliminating their individual identity, effectively erasing him and his own story. The fears of the hero are then transmitted to the reader, who follows the tales as he too searches for identity. Children oftentimes desire to join a group that promises acceptance and identity as part of a "we," yet they are not able to understand that doing so obscures their personal identity; as individuals they become consumed. This fear of victimization via cannibalism is the fear of becoming identity-less, of losing human identity, shape, or existence. Be it evil witches, or spectral ghouls, children can place their fears of lacking an identity into the fairy tales, enabling themselves to face life around them as a maturing person. In the modernized tales, the knowledge gained is often site-specific (for example, a grade school, a suburban neighborhood, the local mall) and thus becomes grounded in that specific location for the reader. The ability use the knowledge elsewhere in their lives is eliminated.

Reintroducing these traditional elements into fairy tales is of utmost importance to bringing back the psychic enrichment that has been absent from children's literature in recent history. Coats writes of the interconnectedness of fairy tales and traditional Gothic texts:

> Traditional adult Gothic has tended to give a sinister inflection to fairy tale tropes and motifs, combining elements of horror and the supernatural to produce situations in which the humble subject can become a hero or a heroine, beset on all sides but ultimately (usually) triumphant [78].

Gothic texts were greatly influenced by the fairy tales, exaggerating, twisting, and emphasizing specific elements. While Gothic literature and fairy tales are now two distinct genres, they maintain similar tropes and motifs at their core, which stimulates all parts of a child's psyche; the emotional, intellectual, and imaginative aspects are all fed. It is because of this Coats is able to assert

> the dark landscapes, inappropriate lusts, and ravenous villains correspond to the dangerous impulses and aggressions that children actually experience as part of their own mental topographies, and fairy tales offer narratives that put those scary appetites in their proper places [78–79].

In his foreword to the contemporary fairy tale collection *My Mother She Killed Me, My Father He Ate Me*, Gregory Maguire states that "the fairy tale is about to break upon us, once and still and again" (xxv). This is both true and false. With today's popular and best selling (and psychically empty) stories being incorrectly paraded and passed off as fairy tales, this literature genre runs the risk of remaining a shell of its former self. Should this affront continue, the true Gothic- and horror-tinged fairy tales will find themselves cannibalized by popular culture, losing their identity as educational tools for both children and adults. Thankfully a handful of authors uphold the classic tropes, as demonstrated by those who submitted modernizations of classic tales to *My Mother She Killed Me, My Father He Ate Me*. This collection, while discussing the transmitting of many classic tales into a decidedly modern setting, maintains all the psychic importance found in the original stories. By hanging onto Rapunzel's hair for dear life and avoiding the cannibalistic and all-consuming wolves and witches of sterilization, the traditional themes thrive in the modern versions as deliberated upon by these authors. The following essays, like the works they discuss, encourage us to reexamine the fairy tales of our own childhood.

While each essay is unique, the essayists focused on three overarching categories of analysis: the structure of the modern, Gothic fairy tale, recurring themes and motifs, and the relationship between the reader and dark fairy tale. However, it would be impossible to claim that any single essay falls strictly under one of these specific headings, as all three categories are greatly intertwined: the themes and motifs greatly affect the relationship between story and reader, while the structures of the Gothic tales influence those very themes and motifs, and consequently have significant ramifications on the reader and audience. Each essayist's examination of the themes, relationships, and structures demonstrates exactly how the stories under investigation exemplify Neil Gaiman's assertion that "in order for stories to work—for kids and for adults—they should scare" (Gaiman qtd. in Popova). It is our hope, and the hope of all the contributors involved in this book, to shine a light into the darkest recesses of contemporary Young Adult stories, to illuminate and give form to that which both haunts and delights us.

Unfortunately, merely having a small group of writers continuing to write the genre in proper fashion does not make for a full rehabilitation of fairy tales. It is, however, a start. Only through a marked return to the classic motifs and tropes, and a rejection of the barren stories, can fairy tales truly break upon us once again as Maguire predicted (xxv). The developmental importance of fairy tales to both young and adult readers is vital for their continued survival, to enable the tales to present the dark and Gothic, the demons and dragons, and mystical worlds and fantastical creatures who are more than willing to take the fears and anxieties of their audiences onto themselves and, in return, bestow that audience with new knowledge of themselves and the world around them.

Works Cited

Bernheimer, Kate. Introduction. *My Mother She Killed Me, My Father He Ate Me*. Ed. Kate Bernheimer with Carmen Jimenez Smith. New York: Penguin, 2010. Print.

Bettelheim, Bruno. *The Uses of Enchantment: The Meaning and Importance of Fairy Tales*. New York: Vintage, 1989. Print.

Chesterton, G.K. *Orthodoxy*. New York: Dodd, Mead, 2004. Print.

Coats, Karen. "Between Horror, Humour, and Hope: Neil Gaiman and the Psychic Work of the Gothic." *The Gothic in Children's Literature: Haunting the Borders*. Ed. Anna Jackson, Karen Coats, and Roderick McGillis. New York: Routledge, 2008. 77–92. Print.

Daniel, Carolyn. *Voracious Children: Who Eats Whom in Children's Literature*. New York: Routledge, 2006. Print.

"Hansel and Grethel." *Grimm's Fairy Tales*. Ed. Elizabeth Dalton. New York: Barnes and Noble Classics, 2003. 56–63. Print.

Hunt, Peter. *Children's Literature*. Malden, MA: Blackwell, 2001. Print.

"Little Red Riding Hood." *Grimm's Fairy Tales*. Ed. Elizabeth Dalton. New York: Barnes and Noble Classics, 2003. 101–104. Print.

Maguire, Gregory. Foreword. "Drawing the Curtain." *My Mother She Killed Me, My Father He Ate Me*. Ed. Kate Bernheimer with Carmen Jimenez Smith. New York: Penguin, 2010. Print.

Popova, Maria. "Neil Gaiman on Why Scary Stories Appeal to Us, the Art of Fear in Children's Books, and the Most Terrifying Ghosts Haunting Society." *Brain Pickings*. 20 Mar. 2014. Web. 24 Mar. 2014.

Tatar, Maria. *Enchanted Hunters: The Power of Stories in Childhood*. New York: W.W. Norton, 2009. Print.

"Something like you, something like a beast"

Gothic Convention and Fairy Tale Elements in David Almond's Skellig

CARYS CROSSEN

David Almond's debut novel *Skellig*, first published in 1998, like its title character, is something of a hybrid. Marketed and categorized as a children's book (it won the Carnegie Medal for that year), it nonetheless has some more adult influences. Two of the most notable are Romantic poetry, primarily that of William Blake, who is quoted at length, and the story "A Very Old Man with Enormous Wings" by Gabriel García Márquez (Latham, "Magical Realism and the Child Reader," 1–10). The latter, according to Almond, was an initially unconscious but profound influence on his novel (Latham, 1). García Márquez's story focuses on a young couple who find the titular old winged man stuck in the mud outside their home after a storm. Bemused, they lock him up but word of the winged man spreads, and they grow rich off charging people to see him. Despite this, they are relieved when the old man escapes and flies away, as they consider him an "annoyance" (García Márquez, 193). Like the majority of García Márquez's works, "A Very Old Man with Enormous Wings" is frequently labeled magical realism, or what Stephen Hart terms "the deadpan description of uncanny, supernatural or magical events as if they were real" (129). Although this critical approach remains popular when analyzing García Márquez, there has been a recent critical backlash against the term "magical realism" when applied to his works. Some critics argue that it is overly simplistic and "obfuscates a number of important questions" (Bell, 179), as well as obscuring "the suffering of the 'subaltern' postcolonial people that they seek to represent" and that the use of magical realism ensures that "the treatment of

11

the aftermath of colonialism in [García Márquez's] writing is flippant" (Bowers, 125).

This argument is vital to mention because magical realism has—by extension—come to be the preferred critical context for discussions of the spiritual descendent of García Márquez's story: Almond's *Skellig*. Latham, in an essay focusing on both texts, argues that "while in interviews Almond has variously embraced and rejected the characterization of his work as magical realism, his novels indicate that, undeniably, he is concerned with the presence of the magical amid the mundane" (1). While this is difficult to refute, since the novel is focused on a winged man amidst the less outlandish concerns of school, moving home, and football, there are other facets to the construction of *Skellig* that the label of magical realism does not do full justice, most notably its setting, scenery, and several plot elements which will be explored in detail later in the essay. As with the works of García Márquez, regarding *Skellig* purely as an example of magical realism would be an oversimplification. That it is possible to read Almond's work as an example of magical realism is undeniable: this is not an attempt to refute this classification altogether. Maggie Ann Bowers asserts that "the variety of magical occurrences in magic(al) realist writing includes ghosts, disappearances, miracles, extraordinary talents and strange atmospheres but does not include the magic as it is found in a conjuring show" (21). The basic plot of *Skellig* seems to confirm its status as an example of magical realism: Michael, an initially unremarkable young boy, is worried for his baby sister, who is very ill in the hospital. Exploring his family's new home, he encounters Skellig, who he initially takes for a squatter but who is revealed to have wings growing under his tattered coat. With the aid of his friend Mina, Michael nurses the ailing Skellig back to health. In return, Skellig goes to Michael's sister at the climax of the novel, and mysteriously cures her of her illness.

However, it is possible to gain an equally rich and valid analysis of *Skellig* by examining it as an example of the Gothic fairy tale. When making this argument, it is important to remember that Almond's plot differs from that of García Márquez in a number of significant ways. Whereas in García Márquez's story it is suggested that the angel visited to take a child to heaven, Skellig restores a child to health and life. Moreover, it is a storm that prevents the angel from taking the child's soul in García Márquez's story—the child lives, but not through divine intervention.

It is unclear whether divine intervention saves Michael's sister, but it is apparent that something supernatural has occurred. Skellig's own return to health does parallel that of García Márquez's angel, who "not only survived his worst winter, but seemed improved with the first sunny days" (192). But whereas García Márquez's angel is connected with age, decay and death, despite his eventual recovery, Skellig is cured of his malady well before the end of the novel, allowing him to cure a child in return—a distinct contrast to the angel of "A Very Old Man with Enormous Wings," whose "only supernatural virtue seemed to be patience" (190). Almond's text clearly has very different aims and themes than García Márquez's short story. In order to more fully examine and explore these aims, an examination of how Gothic and the fairy tale are embodied in Almond's work is necessary before moving on to analyzing how defining the novel as Gothic fairy tale can offer new understanding and interpretations.

Defining the Gothic in Skellig

Defining the Gothic is at first glance an exercise in futility, not least because of the sub-genres (such as feminist Gothic and postcolonial Gothic) that have begun to appear in recent criticism, but some basic definitions are possible. For the sake of simplicity and the scope of this essay, Jerrold E. Hogle's "general parameters" (2) of the Gothic will be used in relation to *Skellig*. Among Hogle's most prominent assertions are that "a Gothic tale usually takes place (at least some of the time) in an antiquated or seemingly antiquated space" and that "within this space, or a combination of such spaces, are hidden some secrets from the past" (2). Given that *Skellig* is set somewhere in contemporary Britain, it initially appears anything but Gothic—there are no castles or mansions present in the story, and in fact the majority of it takes place on a housing estate. However, two of the most important settings in the book both consist of old, crumbling houses; one abandoned, the other left derelict after its elderly and feeble owner died. It is into the latter that Michael moves with his parents and prematurely born sister, and it is in the garage of the house that Michael first encounters Skellig. Its central importance in the narrative is emphasized in the novel's opening sentence: "I found him in the garage on a Sunday afternoon" (1). Almond is evocative in his descriptions of the place: "everything was covered in dust and spider's webs... The place stank of rot and dust. Even the bricks were crumbling like they couldn't bear the weight any more" (3). The age and decay of the garage—it is repeatedly noted to be on the verge of collapse—are its defining characteristics. It is the most antiquated space in the house, which itself is presented as being rundown and in need of extensive repair. The decay of the garage reflects Skellig's own physical and—to a large extent—emotional states: he suffers badly from arthritis and also from an unnamed mental condition, an existential despair that has resulted in what one character, Mina, refers to as "ossification" of his mind (74).

The second prominent "antiquated space" in the novel is an abandoned house left to Mina by her deceased grandfather. Though not as old and rundown as the house Michael's family moves into, the fact that it also had an elderly owner and is effectively abandoned when the story takes place, marks it as another Gothic space, what Hogle terms "seemingly antiquated" (2). Almond emphasizes the house's boarded-up windows, the bare floorboards, the family of owls that have moved into the attic, and above all the eeriness of the house at night, when the majority of the action takes place. "Our heads were filled with the darkness of the house" (108), Michael informs the reader, when he and Mina go to the house at night to tend to Skellig. The emphasis on night and darkness in this sequence is particularly interesting if considered from the perspective of Gothic criticism. The postcolonial Gothic especially has made frequent use of metaphors for darkness when analyzing "Western fears of 'primitive' religion, voodoo, idol worship and the colonial 'heart of darkness'" (Spooner, 37). Although *Skellig* cannot accurately be termed postcolonial, it makes similar use of images of night and darkness to represent the unknown and the uncanny. The inexplicable character of Skellig seldom appears in daylight or in a lit space; for example, Almond nearly always situates him in shadowy spaces, or else has Michael and Mina visit him at night. Towards the climax of the book, they try to visit him during the day, when "the sun glared over the rooftops" (138), only to discover Skellig is absent from his sanctuary in Mina's grandfather's house. This emphasis on night and darkness in relation to Skellig's character is representative of the fact that he is essentially unknowable: Almond never offers a full explanation of what Skellig actually is, and his origins remain a mystery. "Something like you, something like a beast, something like a bird, something like an angel" (158) is the only answer Skellig can give when Michael straightforwardly asks what he is. Skellig disappears at the end of the novel, and unlike in García Márquez's story, Michael and Mina do not see him leave and have no clear idea of where he has gone, although they like to believe that "someone else might find him now" (162).

Images of darkness also recur in the subplot featuring Michael's baby sister. Born prematurely, she is revealed over the course of the story to be suffering from an unnamed heart condition. A life-saving operation is scheduled for her, but the omens surrounding the baby appear ominous. Tended to by the family doctor, a man the perceptive Michael nicknames Doctor Death, the baby is linked with struggle, with images of wilderness, darkness and danger. "How can she thrive when it's all so dirty and all in such a mess?" Michael's mother cries about the house they have recently moved into (35). Michael, for his part, turns to the Greek myth of Persephone in understanding his sister's situation. He imagines Persephone struggling to find a way out of the underworld: "she squeezed through black tunnels. She took wrong turnings, banged her head against the rocks... But she struggled on" (138). The imagery present in Michael's imaginings is intensely Gothic: he imagines Persephone, and by extension his sister, both of them innocent young girls, in a dark and claustrophobic underworld, surrounded by debris of ancient civilizations. Michael pictures Persephone thus, with much emphasis on the prehistoric and the primeval surroundings: "She fought through bedrock and clay and iron ore and coal, through fossils of ancient creatures, the skeletons of dinosaurs, the buried remains of ancient cities" (138). Strongly reminiscent of Hogle's "secrets from the past" (he does actually suggest "a subterranean crypt" as a potentially Gothic space), Michael's description of Persephone is yet another example of the Gothic in *Skellig* (2). The myth in turn parallels the stories of Skellig and Michael's sister, as both are seriously ill at the start of the novel and must struggle to return to life. Though not literally trapped underground, both must struggle through darkness; literally in the case of Michael's sister, anaesthetized as she undergoes her operation, and metaphorically for Skellig. Both must also escape confinement; Skellig's hiding place in the garage and the baby's need for the machines and medicine in the hospital, before achieving health and freedom. As Anne Williams comments in an examination of Gothic spaces, "specific décor is not so important as the setting's power to evoke certain responses in the characters (and in the reader): claustrophobia, loneliness, a sense of antiquity, recognition that this is a place of secrets" (39–40). Though not a setting per se, the story of Persephone evokes concepts of claustrophobia and loneliness, with Almond emphasising her despair and weariness but at the same time pointing out her determination to escape. It also reinforces the purpose of the crumbling garage and Mina's abandoned house—to serve as places of secrets, to give a sense of age and decrepitude.

Skellig himself, despite residing in these antiquated spaces, is not quite a "secret from the past"—neither Michael nor Mina, the one person he entrusts with the secret of Skellig's existence, ever encountered him before. However, as Michael attempts to discover Skellig's origins, another theme that runs subtly throughout the novel makes its presence felt: the theory of evolution. After studying the basics of Darwinian theories at school, it occurs to Michael that Skellig might be an evolutionary throwback, a survivor from some prehistoric time when mankind had wings. Mina comments with confidence on why humans have shoulder blades: "they're where your wings were, and where they'll grow again" (50). This evoking of Darwin and the possibility of evolution (or devolution, depending on whether mankind once had wings and whether they will someday grow them again) is another indication of a well-developed Gothic tradition in *Skellig*. Victorian Gothic in particular was obsessed with the notion of evolution—or, more accurately, with the idea of devolution or degeneration. As Hurley observes, during the *fin de siècle* in particular, there was widespread cultural anxiety that

> the evolutionary process might be reversible: the human race might ultimately retrogress into a sordid animalism rather than progress towards a telos of intellectual and moral perfection [56].

Skellig, following on from this Gothic convention, offers the prospect of devolution within its pages, but also that of continuing evolution. Skellig, in keeping with the book's ambiguous nature, may be an example of either. He is indeed animalistic, feasting off dead mice brought to him by a family of owls and coughing up pellets of indigestible matter. His wings and physical structure (implied to consist of hollow bones, similar to a bird's skeleton) are a contemporary example of what Hurley terms the "abhuman" (3) in late Victorian Gothic. Hurley defines the abhuman as the body "continually in danger of becoming not-itself, becoming other ... abhuman" (4).

16

This danger, of the body becoming other, is present throughout *Skellig*: firstly in the figure of Skellig himself, secondly in two dreamlike sequences that take place in the antiquated space of the abandoned house he is moved to. It is important to remember that Skellig, in a distortion of the typical human body, has wings and can fly. Moreover, at the start of the story he is wracked and twisted with arthritis, unable to move without pain. "Turns you to stone then crumbles you away" (29) is how he describes his condition. The description suggests his body's inherent instability—like the garage he is confined in, he may crumble away at any moment. His body is rendered even more abhuman by this instability, an instability it never loses completely but which merely alters in the way it manifests. Skellig undergoes a slow and subtle metamorphosis over the course of the novel, noted by Michael, gradually appearing younger and stronger and losing all traces of his former illness. "I stared at the changed Skellig. How had this happened to him?" (126) Michael asks rhetorically, knowing he will not receive an answer. What he and Mina do receive is a mystical experience in which they link hands with Skellig, and discover how it feels to fly as their feet leave the floor and they spin in circles. It is in these two sequences that the instability and the metamorphic potential of the human body are at their strongest, as Michael describes what he sees: "each time the faces of Mina and Skellig came into the light they were more silvery, more expressionless. Their eyes were darker, more empty, more penetrating" (110). This partial, temporary transformation into creatures akin to Skellig himself is not presented as cause for terror, but for gladness, in a distinct departure from the Gothic fear of devolution.

However, Skellig's existential despair evidently has affected his mind as well as his body. Mina describes the process thus: "the mind, too, becomes inflexible. It stops thinking and imagining. It becomes as hard as bone. It is no longer a mind" (74). Skellig therefore is certainly not an example of the intellectual perfection that *fin de siècle* scientists and researchers believed mankind could one day attain, although he does eventually recover from his malaise. His state at the start of the novel is one of severe depression, sitting around "waiting to die" (72). It is this intellectual devolution, as opposed to the physical transgression into an animal, which is presented as real cause for concern in *Skellig*. As Latham observes, though essentially an uplifting story, *Skellig* also offers a critique of formal education and the British school system, most notably through the character of Mina, who is home-taught and skeptical of what Michael is learning—if anything—in school (6). Her skepticism is somewhat justified by the mocking of Michael's school friends, who call her a "monkey girl" (101) and are only interested in football, ignoring Michael's efforts to tell them about the poetry of Blake and the amazing things the world contains. Then there is the undeniable fact that the majority of Michael's learning and character development throughout the novel occur in environments other than school. He receives advice on how to treat Skellig's bodily ailments from a sympathetic doctor at the hospital where his sister is a patient (65), learns about birds, Blake and painting from Mina, and about wonder from Skellig. The danger of institutionalized education in *Skellig* is that "schools try to make everybody just the same" (100) and prevent creativity and free thinking. It is this devolution of the mind into an inert, inactive thing that is the true Gothic terror of *Skellig*, as opposed to the threat represented by the abhuman body of Skellig. Skellig is not cause for fear, but for wonderment—an escapee from a fairy tale, perhaps, something we might discover presently.

Defining the Fairy Tale in Skellig

Defining the fairy tale is just as problematic as offering a definition of the Gothic, but it is important to provide some basic parameters for use in analyzing *Skellig*. Jack Zipes, in an examination of the genre, states that

> the fairy tale demonstrated what it meant to be beautiful and heroic and how to achieve "royal" status with the help of grace and good fortune... To read a fairy tale was to follow the narrative path to happiness [*Happily Ever After*, 4].

In a later examination of the fairy tale, Zipes defines the fairy tale as a bourgeois invention that showed how "autodynamics could give rise to a new world that breaks radically with the norms of an older, more confining social order" (*Breaking the Magic Spell*, 57). Both of these definitions offer some insight into the way the traditional fairy tale narrative manifests itself in Almond's novel, which depicts Michael and Mina breaking with confining social norms and discovering a new world that contains both creatures such as Skellig and their own limitless potential as human beings. Other definitions of the fairy tale include that offered by Davidson and Chaudhri, who assert that fairy tales

> usually have a happy ending but the hero or heroine may have to overcome enormous obstacles, often by supernatural means and assisted by powerful helpers of various kinds, while other characters impose demanding tasks and threaten destruction [4].

These definitions offer a starting point for an analysis of the fairy tale elements within *Skellig*. What is notable is the emphasis on the happy ending, but also that both definitions comment on a path that must be followed, a difficult journey that must be undertaken before the happy ending can be achieved.

Both the difficult journey and the eventual happy ending are located within the pages of Almond's novel. *Skellig* does indeed follow the narrative path to happiness, shown most clearly in the recovery of Michael's baby sister, and in more bittersweet fashion in Skellig's own return to health, followed by his leave-taking. The plot of *Skellig* is remarkably similar to many traditional fairy tales: when the novel commences, Michael's family have just moved house to an unfamiliar place, a "wilderness" (35). Like the heroes of the Grimms' "The Queen Bee," who is one of several brothers (306–308) and Perrault's "Puss in Boots," another brother in a large family (115–126) the hero of Almond's tale must leave familiar surroundings for a strange country, where he must undergo trials and perform strange tasks before happiness can be achieved. Michael's own tasks may seem relatively mundane in comparison as they mostly comprise smuggling leftover food, beer and aspirin to Skellig. But even here there is a fairy tale element of working out a riddle or a puzzle: when Michael first meets Skellig, the ravenous creature asks for "27 and 53[qm] (18). Michael is baffled until he finds the menu from the local Chinese takeaway: "it was like a light went on in my head" (20). Likewise, the fairy tale convention of the animal helper—a creature aided in some way by the hero, and who eventually repays their saviour in kind—is hinted at within the novel (Davidson, 99). Mina owns a cat, called Whisper, who accompanies her and Michael when they go to visit Skellig and who keeps the mysterious creature company. As I noted earlier, there is also a family of owls that bring Skellig mice and voles to consume. Then there is Skellig himself, who though by no means is wholly animal, is closely connected to the animal kingdom owing to his wings, feeding habits, and wild nature. After having his life saved by Michael and Mina, he repays them by healing Michael's baby sister through some mysterious power. "You went to my sister ... you made her strong" (157), Michael realizes.

However, the journey towards this happiness is not an easy one. In lieu of following the tales of the two invalids directly, the story is instead told in the first person by Michael himself, and it is his dark and difficult journey that the book chronicles. In this regard, Michael is akin to many fairy tale heroes who must rescue an innocent from peril, such as the prince in Perrault's "Sleeping Beauty," and especially the Grimms' "Snow White." The baby, who spends much of the novel asleep in a plastic incubator, hovering between life and death, bears more than a passing resemblance to Snow White in a state of living death in her coffin of glass, waiting for a prince to wake her. The Grimms describe Snow White's un-dead state: "they made a transparent glass coffin so that she could be seen from all sides" (237–246). Bettelheim, in his famous psychoanalytic examination of fairy tales in Western culture, asserts that

> fairy tales deal in literary form with the basic problems of life, particularly those inherent in the struggle to achieve maturity. They caution against the destructive consequences if one fails to develop higher levels of responsible selfhood [185].

For Michael, and to a lesser extent Mina, the journey they must undertake in *Skellig* is not so much the geographical one common to fairy tales but an emotional one that involves their growing up and attaining maturity within a short space of time. And as Bettelheim observes, there will be highly destructive consequences should they fail in their responsibilities, both towards Skellig and Michael's sister. Should they abandon or somehow betray Skellig, he will most likely die or be killed. On an emotional level they, especially Michael, assume responsibility for the baby, whom Michael believes can be healed through sheer willpower— by hoping and wishing for her recuperation. "I told myself that if I listened hard enough her breathing and the beating of her heart would never be able to stop" (91), Michael tells us. This apparently childish faith in the power of hope and love to heal the sick and injured is strongly reminiscent of the heroes in various fairy-tales, such as the youngest son in the previously mentioned "The Queen Bee," who are derided for being simple and kind-hearted, yet whose faith and benevolence prove key in breaking the wicked spell or defeating the evil giant.

There is nothing childish about Michael and Mina's fairy tale quest in the novel—it is quite literally a matter of life and death. Preoccupied by juvenile concerns such as football games with friends and prone to sulking when told off at the start of the book, Michael must learn to put childish things aside and do what is needed over the course of the story. It is not an easy undertaking, and Almond does not stint in describing Michael's emotional turmoil. "And the fear just increased and increased and increased" (132) is how he describes the feeling of waiting to hear his sister's fate. But although the story starts out filled with uncertainty, images of despair and decay, and the prospect of death, by the closing chapter Michael's sister has come home, and Skellig has departed, though not without bidding Michael and Mina goodbye and offering his thanks. As Bettelheim observes, the necessary components of a good fairy tale are "fantasy, recovery, escape and consolation—recovery from deep despair, escape from some great danger, but, most of all, consolation" (143). The happy ending, the most important aspect of the traditional fairy tale, is definitely present in *Skellig*—Michael's sister, nameless for the majority of the novel, is finally christened Joy, in an expression of this exultant mood. The story's ending is not comprised of unalloyed contentment, however; there is some sadness in Skellig's eventual departure, leaving Michael and Mina behind. This is admittedly a departure from the typical fairy tale ending, in which sadness is not permitted and if bad things happen, they happen to the villains of the piece. However, the novel does follow the pattern of "recovery from deep despair," as Michael and indeed his entire family despair over the fate of his sister and eventually recover from this bleak state of affairs when it becomes clear she will live.

This journey, from selfish childhood to responsible maturity, the quest to save both Skellig and Joy, Michael's recovery from awful despair and the assistance of the animal helpers, quite clearly follows a fairy tale pattern. However, although *Skellig* follows the blueprint of a traditional fairy tale such as "Jack and the Beanstalk" or "The Tinder-Box" it is very much a modern re-working of the genre. As Jessica Tiffin notes:

> Recognition of fairy tales relies on its striking motifs and circumscribed and predictable plot structures, and also on its status as a marvellous form. Fairy-tale narratives deny reality not only in their calm acceptance of the magical

but also in their refusal to provide any sort of realistic detail or conventional causal logic to the worlds they describe [4].

One of the probable reasons *Skellig* has previously been labelled magical realism by critics is that it certainly does not deny reality, despite the presence of the fantastic; as noted in the introduction, mundane concerns such as school and moving home take up a considerable amount of Michael's narration. Realistic detail also abounds, as Almond sets his story in contemporary Britain rather than a fairy-tale world or alternate universe. Despite this, *Skellig* can still be classified as a fairy tale, albeit a contemporary re-imagining of one. Although ostensibly set in the "real world," a world that is shown to have some magical aspects, there are suggestions that Michael and Mina have left reality behind in their dealings with Skellig and entered a fairy-tale realm. In a key scene, in which they discover Skellig's wings for the first time, Michael is compelled to turn away from his discovery and creep over to a window to look out on the night. When Mina asks what he is doing, he replies, "Making sure the world's still really there" (90). Michael's evident fear that somehow the world will recede or alter (as it has, though he is perhaps not yet aware of it) suggests that reality in *Skellig* is not a fixed and immutable quantity. Like the fairy tale itself, reality is "volatile and fluid" (Zipes, *The Irresistible Fairy Tale,* 22) within *Skellig*, and although there is disagreement that "calm acceptance" becomes Michael and Mina's standard response to the wonders they discover, they come to a point where they are no longer stunned or frightened by what they encounter.

Moreover, "conventional causal logic" is distinctly absent from the section in which Skellig somehow helps Michael's sister recover from her traumatic operation. Like the case of the nameless child in García Márquez's story, it is never made clear how Michael's sister recuperates from her ill health, only that Skellig is involved in some way. "That one's glittering with life. Heart like fire. It was her that gave the strength to me" (157) is how Skellig describes it. Magical or otherwise, Skellig's intervention paves the way for the fairy-tale happy ending. Jack Zipes, in analyzing the fairy tale as told to modern children, comments on the "fairy-tale structure in which a magical transformation or miraculous event brings about a satisfying, happy ending" (*Happily Ever After,* 1). The use of the term "miraculous" contradicts Tiffin's assertion that magic and miracles are accepted as everyday events within the fairy tale, but nonetheless this is a very apt summation of *Skellig*. Worthy of marvel and amazement or not, Skellig and his deeds remain inexplicable, and it is perhaps here that fairy tale elements are at their strongest within the novel. The absence of logic as described by Tiffin and the magical transformation as described by Zipes are both present in *Skellig*, but most importantly Michael and Mina are fully aware of what an amazing being Skellig is and how miraculous the recovery of Michael's sister is. Magic is not something to be taken for granted in the conventional reality Almond creates in *Skellig*, but something to be wondered at, treasured and remembered forever. To label *Skellig* as magical realism obscures Almond's efforts to emphasise the phenomenon that is Skellig in the text. Although the author has clearly made an effort to invest Skellig with believable characteristics and detail—his light weight, his feasting off mice and insects, his dirty and unkempt appearance—Skellig is never presented as ordinary or commonplace. Whereas in "A Very Old Man with Enormous Wings," the elderly angel soon loses all fascination for his audience and becomes a mere nuisance, Skellig is a creature to marvel at, albeit only by the select few. Namely, children: whereas García Márquez's angel is merely a money-making device for his adult captors, Skellig is a continual source of wonder for Michael, Mina and the book's reader.

This stands as a contrast to magical realism as defined by Bowers: "the ordinariness of magical realism's magic relies on its accepted and unquestioned position in tangible and material reality" (24). Though Skellig's existence is accepted by Michael and confirmed for him and the audience by Mina (Latham, "Magical Realism and the Child Reader," 3), his existence and very being are the sources of continual curiosity for both the protagonists and the reader. Skellig is never ordinary, never quite loses the initial fascination Michael and Mina have for him. This is possibly because they are children and therefore still willing to believe in magic, and are unwilling to share him with a world that will try to rationalize his existence. *Skellig* in this respect is similar to other fairy-tale inspired works such as J. M. Barrie's *Peter Pan and Wendy* (1911) where only children can fly to the magical world of Neverland. Conversely, their keeping Skellig a secret is arguably a sign of maturity on their part. David Latham suggests that Michael and Mina sense that "revealing his existence will inevitably lead to his exploitation and destruction at the hands of adults" (Latham, "Empowering Adolescent Readers," 219), just as in García Márquez's story the angel becomes a source of financial gain, rather than of wonder, for the couple who capture him. Skellig never loses his wonder or secrecy for the few who know him, and therefore, I argue, is a denizen of a fairy tale.

The Gothic Fairy Tale and Skellig

Now that it has been established how the Gothic and the fairy tale manifest themselves in Almond's *Skellig*, the question must be asked— what new material comes to light in this interpretation, and what new conclusions can we draw from it? Latham, when analyzing *Skellig* as an example of magical realism, argues that Almond's aim in the novel is to show Michael and Mina "in their own way to be as extraordinary as Skellig" ("Magical Realism and the Child Reader," 6). This is a view shared by other critics such as Geraldine Brennan, who, in an analysis of several works of fiction classified as children's literature, argues that in Almond's work there is

> a common theme of young protagonists who venture where adults do not dare to tread, meddling with the forbidden, the unspoken and the forgotten. In the course of this they discover previously unknown aspects of themselves … [126].

Classifying *Skellig* as an examination of its protagonists' journey of self-discovery is not an unreasonable interpretation of the novel; the previous section made a similar assertions about Michael's emotional journey. However, when examining *Skellig* as Gothic fairy tale, one must take into account the fact that the Gothic and the fairy tale have both evolved distinct characteristics during their long cultural history and gradual transmutations over the years. Moreover, the Gothic and the fairy tale (and indeed the Gothic fairy tale) will have developed these features for a purpose. So what are these purposes, and how do they manifest themselves in *Skellig*?

Defining the central aims of both the Gothic and fairy tale depend on whether they are essentially revolutionary or conservative genres of writing—are they intended to disrupt the social status quo or to reaffirm it? Hogle's examination of the Gothic expresses some uncertainty as to whether it is a conservative or revolutionary genre, finally coming to the conclusion that "most often, though, Gothic works hesitate between the revolutionary and conservative" (13). However, Hogle also identifies the main characteristic of the Gothic as the "blurring of different levels of discourse" (9). Hogle identifies various "opposed conditions" that the Gothic takes delight in disrupting, such as "life/death, natural/supernatural, ancient/modern, realistic/artificial, and unconscious/conscious" (9). The simultaneous revolutionary and conservative potential of the Gothic is thus made apparent: it holds the possibility of being revolutionary in its disruption of borders, boundaries and more often than not social convention, but it has conformist potential also, should these borders and boundaries be reasserted and strengthened by the close of the story. For instance, in one of the most famous Gothic novels of all time, Mary Shelley's *Frankenstein*, first published in 1818, although the infamous Creature overturns all laws of Nature and religion when he comes into existence, by the close of the novel he vows to die and erase any trace of his existence, thus restoring order and balance to both the human and the natural world. The aims of the Gothic therefore, depend very much on how it manifests itself in each particular novel or story. The fairy tale, by contrast, though not without subversive potential, particularly in contemporary re-imaginings of the genre, is generally interpreted as a conservative medium. Jack Zipes, when analyzing contemporary reproductions of classic fairy tales (as opposed to revisions of fairy tales—the distinction is crucial), observes that "the consumers/ viewers want comfort and pleasure: they are not threatened, challenged, excited or shocked by the duplications. A traditional and socially conservative world view is confirmed" (*Fairy Tale as Myth, Myth as Fairy Tale*, 9). Yet Zipes also acknowledges the disruptive potential of the fairy tale, noting that it has "extraordinary power in our daily lives, and its guises are manifold" (15).

So, does analyzing *Skellig* as Gothic fairy tale reveal a conformist, middle-of-the-road sensibility or an innovative, rebellious ethos? Initially, it would appear to be the former; Skellig disappears, presumably never to return at the close of the novel, thus removing one major source of disruption from Michael's life and mostly, but not completely, eliminating the potential he brings with him as an animal/human hybrid. Again, the story follows the same plot as García Márquez's "A Very Old Man with Enormous Wings," although the reactions to the disappearance of the winged man differ wildly between the texts. Whereas the reaction in García Márquez's story is "a sigh of relief, for herself and for him" (193) Michael and Mina miss Skellig and vow to remember him. However, with the baby's return from the hospital, we see Michael's family unit—mother, father, son, and daughter—restored, all family discord forgotten, and the family settles back into a normal, comfortable existence in their new home. The garage where Skellig was first found is demolished and Mina's abandoned old house is restored by builders, eliminating any traces of Skellig. It is not quite the "and they all lived happily ever after" of the traditional fairy tale, but it is not far from it. But although Skellig leaves in a physical sense, his presence endures until the very end of the novel. He leaves behind three feathers from his wings as mementos for Michael, Mina and the baby. Michael slips one under his sister's mattress: "I smiled, because I knew she'd have the best of dreams" (167). Moreover, Michael in particular is not left unaffected by his encounter with the extraordinary creature. His friendship with Mina prompts a growing interest in nature, art, poetry and writing stories, all of which he barely knows anything at the start of the story: "we wrote stories about adventures in old houses and journeys to far-off imaginary places" (162). Though Skellig may have departed, he has not died in the gruesome method attributed to Frankenstein's monster by Shelley. He is alive and well, and disrupting someone else's life as he has done Michael and Mina's. His memory will continue to haunt and affect Michael and Mina, and it is implied that Joy, Michael's sister, will also be affected by it in a positive manner, either by unconsciously absorbing dreams and thoughts from Skellig's feather or by the stories and pictures her brother and Mina will create for her. *Skellig* cannot be termed a truly conservative work, as the disruptive figure that breaks through borders and boundaries and does not truly depart at its climax—the story's ending is certainly happy, but it is not the neat, orderly ending of the fairy tale or the conservative Gothic tale. There are hints and echoes of what has taken place: as Mina promises, "we'll remember forever" (158). Even one of Michael's school friends, Leakey, eventually realizes something noteworthy has being going on, and asks Michael for the tale. Michael responds, "Someday I'll tell you everything" (160).

 Skellig therefore cannot be termed a conservative text in the manner of the traditional fairy tale or some Gothic works: instead, it can be argued the novel utilises the conventions of the Gothic fairy tale to create a truly revolutionary vision of the world, an argument in favor of free thought. Latham observes that Almond's "narrative calls into question adult institutions like medicine and formal education" (6) but does not attach any importance to this aspect of the text. However, one of the greatest Gothic threats present in *Skellig* is not so much physical death as mental fossilisation, in which the mind stops thinking and puzzling out things for itself. Formal education in particular comes in for sustained criticism during the novel, much of which is expressed through the character of the home-schooled Mina: "we believe that schools inhibit the natural curiosity, creativity, and intelligence of children. The mind needs to be opened out into the world, not shuttered down inside a gloomy classroom" (47). Though Michael does not fully agree with this assessment, it is undeniable that his own adventurous and creative spirit strengthens over the course of the novel thanks to the influence of both Mina and Skellig. When looking at Michael's drawings after they have known one another and Skellig for a while, Mina tells him, "You couldn't have done these before … you're getting braver and bolder" (127). When he writes a particularly good story for his English teacher at school, she asks him, "You've been practising at home?" (120), acknowledging that such talent has not been nurtured at school. Michael's emotional development is strongly reminiscent of Bettelheim's assertion that, in the fairy tale, "if one wishes to gain selfhood, achieve integrity, and secure one's identity, difficult developments must be undergone: hardships suffered, dangers met, victories won" (278). Thanks primarily to Skellig, Michael escapes the threat of mental deterioration and eventual dullness and conformity, and allows his creative, thoughtful side free reign even after Skellig's departure. Moreover, he and Mina brave danger and succeed in saving Skellig, and by extension Michael's sister, lending them maturity and securing their identities by the close of the story.

Skellig's own illness is mental as well as physical, and equal importance is attached to his spiritual recovery as his bodily recovery. Mental freedom and daring are presented as the ultimate goals in the novel, and through the conventions of the Gothic fairy tale they are achieved. The hybrid monster, the dark hidden spaces of the garage and abandoned house, the quest to save Michael's sister and the children's eventual reward in the restored health of Skellig and Joy all combine to open Michael's (and the reader's) eyes and mind to a world, mysterious and dangerous, far beyond the confines of his old home and what he is given to learn in school. Although everything returns to normal outwardly at the close of the book, this return to normality is not the story's principle goal: like in many fairy tales, the purpose of their experiences is to allow them to metaphorically leave home, to enter what Tatar terms "the arena of the marvelous" (72) in which "escape from home becomes [their] sole hope and source of consolation" (72). Michael and Mina do not go on their fairy tale quest and do not brave Gothic creatures and spaces simply to return to where they started; moreover, having learned so much, going home again is impossible, at least in the metaphorical sense. Zipes, in examining the current state of the fairy tale in Western culture, highlights the importance of resistance to fairy tales that reinforce "the patriarchal and consumer tendencies of the culture industry" (*Happily Ever After*, 11). Resistance, Zipes asserts, "occurs in tales that help young people question the familiar and social standards that they are expected to accept and in tales that excite their imaginations" (11). Whether or not *Skellig* excites the imaginations of its readers must depend on the individual reading the story, but it is undeniable that Almond uses the conventions of the Gothic fairy tale not only to chronicle the character development of his protagonists but to caution against the dangers of neglecting imagination and creativity in favor of conservatism in both thought and deed. The fairy tale has been used for hundreds of years as an admonition to children to behave—stick to the path or the wolf will eat you! *Skellig* by contrast, uses the parameters of the Gothic fairy tale to deliver a very different warning—who knows what you might miss if you stick to the path your whole life? You might miss meeting something like Skellig: "something like you, something like a bird, something like a beast, something like an angel" (158), or perhaps something that simply cannot be categorized.

Works Cited

Almond, David. *Skellig*. London: Hodder, 1998. Print.

Bell, Michael. "García Márquez, Magical Realism and World Literature." *The Cambridge Companion to Gabriel García Márquez*. Ed. Philip Swanson. Cambridge: Cambridge University Press, 2010. 179–195. Print.

Bettelheim, Bruno. *The Uses of Enchantment: The Meaning and Importance of Fairy Tales*. London: Penguin, 1991. Print.

Bowers, Maggie Ann. *Magic(al) Realism*. New York: Routledge, 2004. Print.

Brennan, Geraldine. "The Game Called Death: Frightening Fictions by David Almond, Philip Gross and Lesley Howarth." *Frightening Fiction*. Eds. Geraldine Brennan,

Kimberley McCarron, and Kevin Reynolds. London: Continuum, 2001. 92–128. Print.

García Márquez, Gabriel. "A Very Old Man with Enormous Wings." *Collected Stories*. London: Penguin, 2008.186–193. Print.

Grimm, Jacob, and Wilhelm Grimm. "The Queen Bee." *The Complete Fairy Tales*. Trans. Jack Zipes. London: Vintage, 2007. 306–308. Print.

Hart, Stephen. "García Márquez's Short Stories," *The Cambridge Companion to Gabriel García Márquez*. Ed. Philip Swanson. Cambridge: Cambridge University Press, 2010. 129–143. Print.

Hogle, Jerrold E. Introduction. *The Cambridge Companion to Gothic Fiction*. Ed. Jerrold E. Hogle. Cambridge: Cambridge University Press, 2002. 1–20. Print.

Hurley, Kelley. *The Gothic Body: Sexuality, Materialism, and Degeneration at the Fin de Siècle*. Cambridge: Cambridge University Press, 2004. Print.

Latham, David. "Empowering Adolescent Readers: Intertextuality in Three Novels by David Almond." *Children's Literature in Education* 39 (2008): 213–226. Print.

_____. "Magical Realism and the Child Reader: The Case of David Almond's *Skellig*." *The Looking Glass: New Perspectives on Children's Literature* 10.1 (2006): n. pag. Web. 15 Dec. 2012.

Perrault, Charles. "Puss-in-Boots." *The Complete Fairy Tales*. Trans. Christopher Betts. Oxford: Oxford Universtiy Press, 2009. 115–126. Print.

Roderick Davies, Hilda, and Anna Chaudhri. Introduction. *A Companion to the Fairy Tale*. Eds. Hilda Roderick Davies and Anna Chaudhri. New York: D. S. Brewer, 2006. Print.

Spooner, Catherine. *Contemporary Gothic*. London: Reaktion Books, 2006. Print.

Tatar, Maria. *The Hard Facts of the Grimms' Fairy Tales, 2d ed*. Princeton: Princeton University Press, 2003. Print.

Tiffin, Jessica. *Marvellous Geometry: Narrative and Metafiction in Modern Fairy Tale*. Detroit: Wayne State University Press, 2009. Print.

Williams, Anne. *Art of Darkness: A Poetics of Gothic*. Chicago: University of Chicago Press, 1995. Print.

Zipes, Jack. *Breaking the Magic Spell: Radical Theories of Folk and Fairy Tales*. Lexington: University Press of Kentucky, 2002. Print.

_____. *Fairy Tale as Myth, Myth as Fairy Tale*. Lexington: University Press of Kentucky, 1994. Print.

_____. *Happily Ever After: Fairy Tales, Children and the Culture Industry*. New York: Routledge, 1997. Print.

_____. *The Irresistible Fairy Tale: The Cultural and Social History of a Genre*. Princeton: Princeton University Press, 2012. Print.

"Baby and I were baked in a pie"

Cannibalism and the Consumption of Children in Young Adult Literature

Tanya Jones

For countless years, wide-eyed children have been both fascinated and horrified by stories of bogeymen. Bogeys may come in many shapes and forms, but their intention is always clear: to spirit little children away for their own nefarious purposes. And, to a child, the most horrible purpose the bogeyman has in mind is to devour them. Supernatural child-snatchers have inspired a both rich and disturbing history of literature. Creatures like Baba Yaga, the demon witch who devours babies as she wanders the night on her chicken-legged throne, or the Erlking, who haunts the dark forests and kidnaps children who strike his fancy, are the antagonists of stories that have circulated in nurseries and playrooms for centuries. It is in countless works of fiction for both the young and old that the childlike fear of the bogeyman is magnified by the horror of not only the theft of a child but also the consumption of their bodies, souls, and innocence. Fairy tale villains of all types are determined to devour the hero or the innocent, as Maria Tatar notes, "giants, ogres, stepmothers, cooks, witches, and mothers-in-law all seem driven by a voracious appetite for human fare, for the flesh and blood (in some cases the liver and lungs will do) of the weak and vulnerable. The victims, both potential and real, are often children" (179–180). This essay will examine both the threat and act of child consumption, the perpetrators of such horrors, and their motives in two modern young adult fairy tales: *Coraline* by Neil Gaiman and *The Book of Lost Things* by John Connolly.

There is a direct correlation between the stolen child motif (loss of childhood innocence and illusions) and the threat of consumption by those that would steal them away. This is nowhere more prevalent than in fairy tales where children "live perpetually under the double threat of starvation and cannibalism" (Tatar 179). Though multiple theories behind the concept of cannibalism or child consumption have surfaced, the appetite defines the bogeyman in whatever form he or she chooses to take.

It is perhaps Sigmund Freud's theory regarding the act of consumption that is most prevalent in much psychoanalytic studies regarding the human psyche. Freud argues that cannibalism is an act of identification and is driven by a need to assimilate what one loves into oneself. For him, "there is … no cannibalism without love, no love without cannibalism" (Royle 208). This concept of love may be misplaced and corrupt, but Freud's suggestion of love equating to acts of cannibalism may explain the illicit implications of desire as it pertains to the possession/consumption of naïve or sexually ignorant children by those that are eager to possess them body and soul.

Though it would be hard to argue away the obvious pleasure traditionally associated with eating, cannibalism may not be all about erroneous lust or identification. Eating is also an issue regarding transference of power from the consumed to the consumer since, "[i]n primitive thought and custom, one acquires the powers or characteristics of what one eats" (Bettelheim 207). This is seemingly obvious as the act of consuming confers strength to an individual, making the process an issue of power gain and not necessarily one of food equating survival. Consider the concept of Communion: Christians participating in the Eucharist consume the body and blood of Christ the Savior in order to take him into their being. As such, they are being sustained on the life of another. This is an exchange of power, in a sense, as they are declaring themselves open to receive Christ's love by consuming him, thus completing a ritual of unity.

Still, acts of love or power exchange do not necessarily yield the only reasons for acts of cannibalism, especially in regards to the devouring of children, a fear the fairy tale highlights. Yet again, the covetous masticating imagined by the cradle-snatchers may also be in response to their misplaced lust for a child of their own as "the act of eating represents an inverted birthing: biological ownership through incorporation" (Warner *NGB* 56). One could argue this theory is a union of both an inappropriate love and a need to gain a semblance of power. Regardless of the intent behind the practice of consumption or the form the bogey takes, the underlying threat of the act inspires a deep fear in the child who waits nightly for the creature in the dark to finally come and gobble him up.

Of all fairy tale or folk lore bogeys, no character has a darker history than the evil witch or substitute mother figure. In the fairy tale tradition, not only are these characters often malevolent and manipulative, but they frequently seem to be driven to feed their victims and feed *off* of their victims. While the mother often represents the primary source of food for her family (breastfeeding, cooking meals, etc.), especially her children, fairy tale mothers are often just as prone to eat their children as they are to feed them. Neil Gaiman's 2002 fairy tale novella *Coraline* gave readers just such a witch-mother in the form of the Other Mother or Beldam. The Other Mother seeks to possess Coraline for her very own, urging her to abandon her world and her real parents (especially her real mother) in favor of the Other Mother's love, which comes at a price.

The story is, in a sense, akin to "Hansel and Gretel" penned by the Grimms. Having been abandoned in the woods by their stepmother, who manipulates their father into participating in the evil deed against his better judgment, Hansel and Gretel come across a house of gingerbread, cake, and sugar in the woods. As the children were abandoned due to the stepmother's oral greed and fear of starving herself, an entire shelter constructed of food and sustenance is exactly what the siblings would believe they required. Gaiman's *Coraline* centers on his titular character, Coraline Jones, and similar themes of neglect, abandonment, and oral obsession.

Coraline opens with our heroine suffering from boredom. Though this is not necessarily suggestive of neglect, Coraline's demeanor suggests that she feels a semblance of neglect or abandonment by her parents. Repeatedly in the first chapters, Coraline seeks out her parents as they are working, and she demands entertainment. Time and again, she is "rejected" and left to entertain herself, though her parents offer her half-hearted suggestions of fun things to do. Ultimately, however, they seem indifferent to their young daughter and urge her to find amusement elsewhere that will not bother them or create messes that they would need to clean up. Gaiman writes,

Coraline went to see her father.

He had his back to the door as he typed. "Go away," he said cheerfully as she walked in.

"I'm bored," she said.

"Learn how to tap-dance," he suggested, without turning around.

Coraline shook her head. "Why don't you play with me?" she asked.

"Busy," he said. "Working," he added. He still hadn't turned around to look at her [Gaiman 20–21].

This ambivalence towards their ten-year-old, again, may not appear to be an issue of abandonment, but the repeated instances of being ignored by both her father and mother leave Coraline feeling sorry for herself and abandoned *emotionally*. It is in this emotional state that Coraline finds herself when she encounters the Other Mother for the first time.

Coraline's Other Mother, whom she finds after crossing into a Secondary World, the portal of which is a sealed door in her flat, is seemingly the perfect solution to Coraline's feelings of deprivation. This new mother has created an entire world under the guise of pleasing her potential daughter, insisting that she will do anything Coraline desires, unlike her real parents. The Other Mother tells Coraline, "Perhaps this afternoon we could do a little embroidery together, or some watercolor painting. Then dinner, and then, if you have been good, you may play with the rats a little before bed. And I shall read you a story and tuck you in, and kiss you good night" (Gaiman 94). To reinforce her position in the hopes of claiming Coraline for herself, she steals Coraline's real parents away in the hopes she can make Coraline feel abandoned, just as if Coraline were Hansel or Gretel deposited in the woods and left to fend for herself: "Whatever would I have done with your old parents? If they have left you, Coraline, it must be because they became bored with you, or tired. Now, I will never become bored with you, and I will never abandon you" (73).

However, the principle tool this Other Mother seems to utilize against Coraline is food. Coraline's first venture into the Other Mother's world begins with a special dinner in Coraline's honor, and treats are consistently used to entice her. Food is made all the more tempting because, at home with her real parents, Coraline adamantly refuses to eat things her parents have prepared for her dinners. Though she has not been made to starve as Hansel and Gretel were, she feels as if her parents are actively intent on denying her food items she desires, paralleling her feelings of emotional neglect. This tactic of denying food is easily perceived as acceptable by child readers who may both resent their own parents attempts to "force" them to eat food they do not care for and see Coraline's food denial tactics as a way to demonstrate their independence in an attempt to gain power over their families. Unlike Hansel and Gretel who were starved because their family could not provide food, Coraline goes hungry out of protest for what she is being provided, turning herself into a martyr young readers can sympathize with.

With such an emphasis on food, we can see the correlation between Gaiman's modern fairy tale and the classic story of "Hansel and Gretel." This focus on food places Coraline directly in the position of Hansel and Gretel and makes her an easy target. Maria Tatar's analysis of the witch in the story of "Hansel and Gretel" is easily adapted to fit Coraline's situation, as she claims while the real mother is at home, "providing neither food nor nurturing care, the witch in the forest initially appears to be a splendidly bountiful figure, offering the children a supper of pancakes with sugar, apples, and nuts and putting them in beds so comfortable that they feel as if they are 'in heaven'" (181). Coraline's real mother may be providing food, but it is not the food Coraline wants and this is, in her mind, another indication of neglect, making her an easy target for a witch to manipulate and spoil.

It seems that, for the Other Mother and many other fairy tale witches, food is a bargaining tool. The Other Mother tells Coraline, "We're ready to love you and play with you and feed you and make your life interesting" (72). Like the witch in "Rapunzel" that offers food in exchange for a baby or the White Queen in *The Lion, the Witch, and the Wardrobe* that seduces Edmund with promises of Turkish delight and his favorite delectables, Gaiman's witch-mother is determined to win Coraline's heart through her stomach. The Other Mother's house, though not made of gingerbread or cakes, is filled with delicious smells and tasty treats the Other Mother cooks to delight Coraline. Each dish, whether chicken (34), chocolate (51), cheese omelets with bacon (108), or fresh orange juice and hot chocolate (111), is designed to deceive Coraline into believing she is safe, when she is actually being made more and more vulnerable to attack. These are comfort foods with predictable tastes, far removed from the "recipes" of Coraline's father which involve spices she is unfamiliar with which—in her mind—renders them inedible. Bettelheim suggests that when children in fairy tales focus so on food and oral desires, they are putting themselves on the path to destruction:

> When the children give in to untamed id impulses, as symbolized by their uncontrolled voraciousness, they risk being destroyed. The children eat only the symbolic representation of the mother ... the witch wants to eat the children themselves [162].

It is immediately recognizable to the reader that the Other Mother seems to have both maternal and cannibalistic designs on Coraline. Initially, Coraline cannot seem to place what it is about the Other Mother that makes her uncomfortable, regardless of her overly affectionate demeanor. It is only later she realizes that the look behind the Other Mother's button eyes is one of hunger: "As she ate, her other mother smiled at her. It was hard to read expressions into those black button eyes, but Coraline thought that her other mother looked hungry, too" (Gaiman 111). This fear is confirmed when she encounters the ghost children left abandoned behind the mirror.

Though the Other Mother promises she will love Coraline forever and never abandon her, it would seem that promise had been made and broken several times before. Behind the mirror in the Other Mother's home, three ghost children have been left to be forgotten, becoming little more than shadows. When Coraline speaks to them, they tell her of how the Other Mother took them and of how she "stole our hearts, and she stole our souls, and she took our lives away, and she left us here, and she forgot about us in the dark" (100). The ghost children are the embodiment of Coraline's fears of abandonment as they have been forgotten and left alone in the dark, regardless of the Other Mother's promises.

There is also still the threat of consumption by this witch-mother bogey. The truth behind this threat is corroborated by the ghost children when they explain how the Other Mother did more than just forget them. She left them in the dark and, as they tell her, "she kept us, and she fed on us, until now we've nothing left of ourselves" (101). The Other Mother's inappropriate preoccupation with Coraline (previously the ghost children) and almost desperate need to provide her with food as a form of affection turns her into a vampiric cannibal, for "the smothering mother ... provides food that inevitably poisons the eater in some way, draining them of vitality/power/subjectivity, which she absorbs, so that instead of feeding, it is she who consumes" (Daniel 103). Thus, she really has drained the lives of her previous false children and left them as empty husks. How she has actually done this is never revealed, but she does insist that "the proudest spirit can be broken, with love" (Gaiman 92).

This Other Mother is just as desperate to have Coraline love her as she is to devour her. A great deal of time and energy on the Other Mother's part goes into the creation of the Secondary World where Coraline finds herself. Not only is the food delightful, but every aspect of this spider-web world is meant to lure and enchant her prey. Great care went into this creation and time is only spent on things someone would actually care about. Though her love is twisted and corrupt and certainly not maternal, there does seem to be genuine emotion on the part of the Other Mother. This is remarked upon by the cat when Coraline questions the Other Mother's reasons for desiring her:

> "Why does she want me?" Coraline asked the cat. "Why does she want me to stay with her?"
> "She wants something to love, I think," said the cat. "Something that isn't her. She might want something to eat as well. It's hard to tell with creatures like that" [78].

The question is best answered by a closer look at her obsessive and destructive nature. Considering her preoccupation with her false daughter's love, one can assume that this Other Mother is, in fact, desperate for a child of her own, but she seems unable to understand *how to* love, thinking that love and possession is the same thing. Coraline recognizes this even when the Other Mother does not: "It was true: the other mother loved her. But she loved Coraline as a miser loves money, or a dragon loves its gold ... Coraline knew that she was a possession, nothing more" (127). As suggested by Marina Warner, when witches in domestic settings "prey on the young, their malignant envy of others who have and can bear children may appear to be their underlying motive for raiding cradles and devouring infants" (*NGB* 28). Similar to the child envy portrayed in the witches from "The Snow Queen" and "Rapunzel," the Other Mother hopes to steal Coraline away from those that love her and possess her totally.

However, unlike the Snow Queen and Rapunzel's witch-mother, Coraline's Other Mother has designs are Coraline's flesh as well as her affection. The Other Mother literally follows through with a favorite nursery game—and playful threat—between mothers and their offspring: eating the baby. Mothers (and fathers) often pretend to nibble on their children's toes or fingers in a sort of play. This is a common enough game implying that parents love their child so much that the children are good enough to eat and when "a mother squeezes her child and murmurs, "'Mmm, you're so good I'm going to eat you,' she's using the same imagery of union, of total commingling intimacy," as if she could form a more literal bond with her child through ingestion (Warner *SMT* 88).

The Other Mother has kidnapped several children in the hopes that they will love her, but her covetous love ends in their destruction. This is another clue to her identity as a cannibalistic figure who eats to possess and possesses to eat. The ghost children refer to her as the Beldam. An archaic term for witch, *beldams* or *belles dames sans merci* have an eerily similar literary history to the fairy tale witch (OED Online). Most commonly associated with the Keats poem of the same name, *belles dames sans merci* are women known for luring their prey into their clutches with their charms and promises of love. But they are, as their names suggest, without mercy and, in a sense, feed off the sacrifice of those that succumb to their temptation, destroying that which they love.

A similar character is seen in John Connolly's young adult/adult crossover novel, *The Book of Lost Things* along with other cannibal villains. The novel focuses on the plight of twelve-year-old David, who, after losing his mother to illness, is transported into a world of fractured fairy tales. Hunted by several cannibalistic creatures, young David must make choices that affect not just him but the family he left behind, and the world he is trapped in.

One of Connolly's cannibalistic bogeys appears as a corrupted version of Perrault's princess from "The Sleeping Beauty in the Wood." In later versions of the story, like the one penned by the Brothers Grimm, the princess became Briar Rose and all instances of cannibalism were removed. In Perrault's tale, however, the princess is awoken by the prince, bears his children, and is subjected to the threat of consumption at the hands of her queen mother-in-law (Bettelheim 229). The queen—believed to be part ogress—demands that her chief cook prepare the finest meals using the flesh of her son's wife and children, whom she both envies and covets, so that she may partake of the fare in an act of incestuous cannibalism. In *The Book of Lost Things*, Connolly combines elements of both tales to envision his Sleeping Beauty: a vampiric horror who preys upon the knights and princes that attempt to free her.

Connolly's Sleeping Beauty, like her fairy tale counterparts, is imprisoned behind the walls of a creeper and ivy covered fortress. David and his knight companion Roland come across the fortress while seeking out Roland's lost friend (and lover). As in the original Perrault tale, the creepers melt away at their approach, allowing them access to the inner castle. Yet, quite unlike the earlier stories, Connolly's palace is not dotted here and there with the prone bodies of the sleeping servants and animals caught up in the same spell that caused their princess to fall into a hundred year sleep but with the dismembered bodies of those knights and princes that had crossed the threshold before. The perceived threat of violence in the original tales is made explicit in Connolly's revision.

David, lured to the top of the fortress by the voice of his mother ringing in his ears, finds the Sleeping Beauty sleeping on a raised dais, just as she is in many versions of the tale. Drawn to her side, he sees her as his dead mother. Suffering beyond measure at her untimely passing, David is unable to see past the trap he finds himself in, so focused is he on the return of the mother figure who, he believes, has called him into this Secondary World as her knight to save her from enchantment. Though he is surrounded by the bodies of the fallen, including Roland whom he sees impaled upon a giant thorn, David is captivated and unable to resist the allure of this false mother, especially as she begs of him to awaken her in the typical fairy tale fashion: "'*Kiss me,*' David heard her say, although her mouth remained still. '*Kiss me, and we will be together again*'" (Connolly 234).

It is after David awakens this false mother/Sleeping Beauty with a chaste kiss on the cheek that he realizes his mistake. The image of his mother melts away, changing into the guise of his stepmother, Rose, though David also recognizes that she is "Not-Rose. She was night without the promise of dawn, darkness without hope of light" (236). Likely a play upon the name of the Grimm princess Briar Rose, Not-Rose is anything but a princess. Described as something akin to a stereotypical vampire with teeth that were "very white and very sharp, the canines longer than the rest" and a pale, alabaster neck dotted with blood "like a necklace of rubies frozen upon her skin," Connolly's Sleeping Beauty is out to harm the hero, not act as his prize (234).

Surrounded by the dead she has lured to her chambers, she reveals little to David, but enough for the reader to realize that she is another vampiric *belle dame sans merci*. Coming across the body of a beheaded knight, David notes the curious lack of blood and the even more curious fact that "the knight's remains had been reduced to a husk inside the armour, rotting away to almost nothing so quickly that the flower he'd wore, perhaps for luck, had not yet had time to die" (228). Preying upon blood, the cannibalistic vampire *belle dame* is driven to consume her saviors.

Though we are unsure as to the effect the consumption of another has on her, we are aware that, like with the Other Mother, a misplaced sense of love is attached to her feeding rituals. She pursues David through the tower, demanding that he kiss her, likely how she draws the life from her prey into herself. We can safely assume that it is specifically his blood she is after and not necessarily the kiss itself, "for she had no blood in her veins" (236). Regardless, this Not-Rose is insistent in her pursuit for both David's blood and affection, as she tells him, "[Y]ou are mine. I will love you and you will die loving me in return" (237). Her need for approval and affection seems to be just as important as the actual act of feeding, as she is desperate for David (a young boy) to look upon her with desire. To David, her demeanor changes as she notices his retreat, as if she was genuinely shocked and wounded by his rejection of her: "'Am I not beautiful?' she asked. Her head tilted slightly, and her face looked troubled. 'Am I not pretty enough for you?'" (235).

Here again, a child is confronted with the smothering attentions of a corrupted mother figure. Depicted as both his deceased mother and his step-mother, this vampiric figure plagues David both with the conscious horror with the threat of consumption and the unconscious emotional trauma he has already been made to suffer as he struggles with feelings of abandonment by his biological mother and resentment towards his step-mother. These distresses are made all the more horrible by the incestuous implication of the life-sucking creature posing as both of David's mother figures as she tries to seduce him with compliments: "'Never hassss one ssso young come ssso far. Sssso young, and ssso beautiful'" (236).

While the Other Mother and Connolly's own *belles dame sans merci* are driven by equal parts love and hunger, some cannibalistic bogeys are driven to consume children for other reasons. A second group of carnivorous villains in *The Book of Lost Things* is the pack of Loups. Drawing upon stories of "Little Red Riding Hood," Connolly's Loups are akin to werewolves, half-man and half-wolf creatures lusting for blood and flesh. This comparison to the ancient werewolf figure is fitting when one considers the first cannibal werewolf tale is the story of Lycaon, the Arcadian king that kills a man, cooks him, and eats him and, as punishment, is turned into a werewolf (Warner *NGB* 36). Scholars have also examined the nature of the wolf in "Little Red Riding Hood" stories from the 16th and 17th centuries and argue the likelihood that is was Perrault that changed the villain into a wolf while "the original villain in French folklore was probably a werewolf," considering the "virtual epidemic of trials against men accused of being werewolves … charged with having devoured children" (Zipes 19). It is also unsurprising that Connolly would use the wolf figure in his novel of fractured fairy tales since "they are the most familiar predators, an actual danger in times of famine … but straddling the realms of reality and fantasy" (Warner *NGB* 37).

The Loups, spawned from the union between human females and male wolves, stalk the forests of the Secondary World David finds himself in. The story of the Loups begins quite similarly to the Perrault tale of "Little Red Riding Hood," a cautionary tale of sexual domination. However, Connolly's Little Red is not the innocent girl seduced by the wolf into bed to be devoured. Instead, like Connolly's predatory Sleeping Beauty, *she* is the pursuer and beds the wolf willingly, "for there are … women who dream of lying with wolves" (Connolly 80). The Loups both envy and hate humans because that is what they wish to truly be, but their appetites tend to take over: "for in time the Loups turned on those who had created them and they fed upon them in the moonlight" (80).

Though part human, the Loups are abominations and despised for both their existence and their nature; they violate natural laws, as Connolly writes, "'Man does not eat man,' said the Woodsman in disgust" (74). This puts the creatures in a very precarious position. Driven by hunger and hatred, the Loups consume that which they desire most to be: humans. Betrayed by their very nature, they are unable (or possibly unwilling) to conquer their instincts. The pure wolves, controlled by the Loups, "were cannibals, content to feed upon their own kind, but the appetites of the ones who resembled men were much worse," likely because David feels that by being self-aware, they should have control over their baser instincts (75). Instead, this self-awareness has given rise to a different form of cannibalism, one fueled as much by hatred as it is by starvation.

Though they claim that their primary goal is to kill the King and take over his rule, the Loups—especially their leader, Leroi—are just as obsessed with David. The reasons behind this are unclear, but they are not able to disguise their hunger for his flesh and demand the Woodsman hand David over to them as an obvious offering of sacrifice: "'You cannot keep the boy safe.... Give him to us, and we will offer him the protection of the pack.' But the wolf-man's eyes gave the lie to his words, for everything about the beast spoke of hunger and want" (74). A wolf may kill to feed itself, naturally, but asking for a token in the form of a child is a far cry from hunting. It is only after David and the Woodsman make their escape that the actual hunt begins.

This provides us with a new look at the cannibalistic nature of the creatures. Where animals, like wolves, kill out of simple survival, the Loups commit conscious acts of cannibalism to both eat and destroy. Hunting for food is not an act of malice, but the Loups have turned their hunt into a sport—a very human act. This is made all the more terrible since it is David—a child—that they are targeting before they reach the King's castle. The self-awareness that David recognizes the creatures possess and their perversion of man's nature is terrible enough, but their preoccupation with a child's flesh makes them all the more horrific as predators.

They are certainly not the only creatures hunting David, but Connolly's main antagonist is not out to consume David. Instead, he is out to devour David's baby brother, Georgie. While David's pursuers are interested in his flesh and blood, Georgie's hunter suggests a different kind of cannibalism all together. The Crooked Man, the story's primary villain, is the cannibal as child abuser, his whole being devoted to the capture and consumption of young children. Basing his character on stories of tricksters—most notably the fairy tale of "Rumpelstiltskin"— the Crooked Man stalks David in both the Primary World and the Secondary World, using his despair at the loss of his mother and his jealousy of his father's new family to manipulate him, hoping to convince him to sacrifice his younger brother to the Crooked Man's vile appetites. Likely the most horrific of Connolly's cannibals, the Crooked Man is not only interested in the consumption of children but takes delight in making them suffer.

David, having suffered a most significant loss for a child due to the loss of his mother, is vulnerable because of his emotional trauma. As "many fairy stories begin with the death of a mother ... the death of the parent creates the most agonizing problems, as it (or the fear of it) does in real life" (Bettelheim 8), which is David's state at the beginning of *The Book of Lost Things*. Like Coraline, David suffers from feelings of abandonment by his mother (who is dead) and his father (who has remarried and has a new son). Yet, unlike Coraline, David's abandonment issues are more easily justified. Bettelheim writes of such abandonment issues:

> There is no greater threat in life than that we will be deserted; left all alone. Psychoanalysis has named this—man's greatest fear—separation anxiety; and the younger we are, the more excruciating is our anxiety when we feel deserted, for the young child actually perishes when not adequately protected and taken care of [145].

David, still quite young, is plagued by this very anxiety. He is also undergoing feelings of extreme guilt, as he believes that, in some way, he is responsible for his mother's untimely death since he was unable to look after her as he thinks he should have: "David, ashamed of his failure, began to cry" (Connolly 5). These feelings, of course, are unfounded, but their existence is no less real to David, and it is this sense of guilt that the Crooked Man uses as one of his manipulative tools, speaking to David in his dreams using the voice of his dead mother: "She called to him out of the darkness. She called to him, and she told him that she was alive" (48).

David's feelings of abandonment and his misplaced sense of guilt regarding his dead mother are not the only tools the Crooked Man uses against him. Like the Other Mother, the Crooked Man plays upon David's fears of being forgotten by his one remaining parent, adding to his feelings of abandonment:

> David saw his father, and Rose, and baby Georgie. They were all laughing, even Georgie, who was being tossed high in the air by his father just as David had once been.
> "They don't miss you, you know," said the old man. "They don't miss you one little bit. They're glad you're gone.... He has forgotten you, just as he has forgotten your mother" [158].

This manipulation plays upon David's feelings of abandonment by his father, sure enough, but also upon new anxieties fostered by fears of isolation in the new family structure and envy caused by sibling rivalry. Georgie's unhindered place in the family, as son of both David's father and his new wife, is possibly the most damaging influence on David's fragile psyche because "something tore inside [David] each time he saw his father holding the new arrival. He was like a symbol of all that was wrong, of all that had changed" (39). It is this jealousy-fueled hatred that the Crooked Man needs to encourage.

The Crooked Man's consumption of children is akin to transubstantiation. By devouring children, the Crooked Man has kept himself alive, dealing for their lives in order to enhance his own. These acts of cannibalism result in not necessarily a power exchange but a shift from one individual to another, because "the child's lifespan would become the Crooked Man's" (274). Like the Christian Eucharist, the Crooked Man is seeking his salvation—immortality—through acts of cannibalism. Thus, a perversion of that tradition results in a twisted and corrupt magic.

It is the child's heart that the Crooked Man must consume in order to obtain the lifespan of his prey. Again, this is akin to the Christian Eucharist, in which the devout consume the body and blood of Christ the Savior in order to form an eternal and sacred bond through sacrifice. The heart—both the source of life and blood functions—is the organ of choice for cannibals in several fairy tale adaptations like "The Juniper Tree," "Snow White," and "The Robber Bridegroom." So, whereas the Christian Eucharist is consumption resulting in completeness and unity through faith, the fairy tale tradition of "body and blood" consumption is one of theft, possession, and death. The Crooked Man's method of ingestion is through torture, whereupon he forcibly rips the hearts from his child victims while they live, in order to cause them as much physical pain as he can, enjoying their torment as he steals their lives: "'He put his hand inside me, tearing at me with his nails, then pulled it out and ate it in front of me,' she said. 'And it hurt, it hurt so much'" (265).

This need to inflict pain seems to be at the core of the Crooked Man's nature as child abuser and cannibal. And though the Crooked Man seems to be sexually indifferent to his prey, he still maintains an air of lechery and uses sexual knowledge on the innocent to devastate them emotionally. As such, he is a modern day bogeyman, appearing as not only a child abuser but also a pedophile. This fact is not lost on David or the reader. Shortly after learning about the existence of the Crooked Man, the reader hears of the abduction of children by strange men. David, remembering an instance prior to his mother's death and

43

his parents insistence that he never talk to male strangers, recalls a boy who had disappeared on his way home from school. Later, his body was found—naked—by some railway tracks and "David knew from the way they were talking that something very bad happened to Billy before he died, something to do with the man from the clean little house" (41). David is warned again by his mother to never talk to strange men and to certainly never go with them anywhere regardless of what they said. David, still thinking of the Crooked Man from his dreams, wonders if perhaps such a man kidnapped the children Rose told him of from her family and took them, like Billy, to some railway tracks, "[a]nd there, in the darkness, he had played with them, in his way" (41).

What David does not know is that the Crooked Man did indeed take the children, though not for the same reasons that David imagines. However, the threat of pedophilia is still inherent in the Crooked Man's cannibalistic desires. Not only does he see Georgie as a source of food, his unconscious actions—as interpreted by the reader—seem to be indicators of a more sexual infatuation at times, such as when he hears Georgie crying in the nursery and his "fingers extend into the air, as if Georgie were hanging before it like an apple ready to be plucked from the tree" (48). There are also other instances of a similar nature: holding David's pajamas up to his face to smell them (89), licking his lips while singing nursery rhymes to himself (250), and insisting to David that he prefers soft creatures to dine upon (207).

It is also through sexual innuendo that the Crooked Man destroys innocence in order to both devastate and possess his prey more completely. Repeatedly throughout the course of the novel, the Crooked Man tries to convince David that his traveling companion—Roland—sees David as more than just a child, suggesting that the grown man watches David while he sleeps and thinks him beautiful (208). Though the implication throughout the story regarding Roland's homosexuality is later confirmed as fact, Roland is certainly not the one that regards David as anything more than a friend. It is only the Crooked Man who has evil designs on David, but, by planting the seed of doubt in the young boy's mind, the damage is done, and David begins to suspect Roland, though he later dismisses the thoughts as absurd.

By exploiting the vulnerability of children, the Crooked Man feeds on, not only their flesh, which gives him life, but their fears, which give him pleasure. Thus, he uses carnal knowledge as a torture device. In his lair beneath the King's castle, he has a room devoted entirely to the corruption of children by exposing them to sexual knowledge. Though the children are not violated physically, they are traumatized emotionally:

> A bedchamber contained a naked woman and a naked man, and the Crooked Man would bring children to them … and the man and the woman would whisper things to them in the darkness of their chamber, telling them things that children should not know, dark tales of what adults did together in the depths of night while their sons and daughters were sleeping. In this way, the children died inside. Forced into adulthood before they were ready, they had their innocence taken from them and their minds collapsed under the weight of poisonous thoughts [272].

By deliberately using the idea of sex to harm the children he takes, the Crooked Man is the personification of the modern day cannibal bogeyman, manifested in "the threat posed by serial killers and paedophiles" (Warner *NGB* 384). Therefore, the Crooked Man is not only a physical cannibal of children, but an emotional vampire as well, draining the innocence from his victims.

Oddly enough, it is through the vocalization of names that the Crooked Man obtains his victims and is able to possess them body and soul. He is unable to simply consume a child as an ogre; he must have the child offered as a sacrifice by having his or her name spoken aloud as a ritual. This is, of course, a fractured version of the "Rumpelstiltskin" story. In the popular fairy tale penned by the Brothers Grimm, it is the trickster's name that must be spoken in order to save a child from the trickster. The idea of names having power is a standard one in literature, but the notion that the bogeyman can only devour that which is sacrificed by name is remarkably less so. In this manner, the Crooked Man makes a bargain, giving him consent to both eat the child's body and possess his or her soul, similar to metaphoric deals with demons and devils. This is also akin to a devil's tithe, in which fairies were believed to offer the souls of human children in order to gain immortality or pay a debt to Satan.

Though each of the aforementioned cannibals all have their own appetites, so to speak, the very nature of their desire for the flesh, blood, or soul of child is what makes them monstrous and, as Carolyn Daniels suggests, "represent the antithesis of civilized humanity" (139). The obsessive pursuit of affection by the Other Mother at the cost of destroying what she longs to possess is as damning to Coraline as the perverse desires of the vampiric dual-mother are to David. And though they may have different motives, both the Loups and the Crooked Man are cannibals fueled by hatred and greed. Such creatures make a mockery of traditional social and cultural norms by their deliberate and concentrated efforts to prey upon children.

What is interesting to note is that in both traditional and modern day fairy tales, it is the emotionally frail or damaged child who is most likely to be the target for the cannibal figure. This is not surprising, as the very nature of the predator is to find the weakness in its prey. Both Coraline and David are targeted because they believe they have been abandoned and fear that they are insignificant. It is this fear that allows them to become targets for their own bogeys and it is only the conquering of this fear and acceptance in their own self-worth that allows them to escape being consumed.

Regardless of the reason behind the act itself, the cannibalistic nature of the bogeyman and his/her proclivity towards consuming children has a place in literature for the young, both old and new. Whether with misguided acts of love or selfish pursuits of pleasure, the child cannibal plays upon the fears and anxieties of the innocent in order to possess his/her victims and consume their flesh. It is only when the child begins to mature and reflect that they are able to escape the threat of nonexistence.

Works Cited

"beldam, n." OED Online. April 2013. Oxford University Press. 5 April 2013. http://www.oed.com/view/Entry/17334.

Bettelheim, Bruno. The Uses of Enchantment: The Meaning and Importance of Fairy Tales. New York: Vintage, 1975. Print.

Connolly, John. The Book of Lost Things. London: Hodder and Stoughton, 2006. Print.

Daniel, Carolyn. Voracious Children: Who Eats Whom in Children's Literature. New York: Routledge, 2006. Print.

Gaiman, Neil. Coraline. New York: Harper Trophy, 2002. Print.

Royle, Nicholas. The Uncanny. New York: Routledge, 2003. Print.

Tatar, Maria, ed. The Classic Fairy Tales: Texts & Criticism. New York: W. W. Norton, 1999. Print.

Warner, Marina. No Go the Bogeyman: Scaring, Lulling, & Making Mock. New York: Farrar, Straus and Giroux, 1998. Print.

_____. Six Myths of Our Time: Little Angels, Little Monsters, Beautiful Beasts, and More. London: Vintage, 1994. Print.

Zipes, Jack, ed. The Trials and Tribulations of Little Red Riding Hood. New York: Routledge, 1993. Print.

Orson Scott Card's
Ender's Game
Authoring Home in Fairyland

ERIN WYBLE NEWCOMB

As winner of the 1985 Nebula Award and the 1986 Hugo Award, *Ender's Game* often gets slated as genre fiction—an excellent text, but one primarily categorized as a work of science fiction. Yet within a broader realm of speculative fiction, *Ender's Game* engages with tropes of both science fiction and fantasy literature, and uses those to transcend genre and address issues of heroism and utopianism more broadly. Much of the scholarship on *Ender's Game* grapples with relationships between children and adults, deconstructing the myth of childhood-as-utopia[1] and highlighting the abusive contexts that enable Ender's monstrosity. While no other critic has dealt as extensively with Fairyland as I will do here, there is critical consistency on Ender's ambivalent characterization. Elaine Radford's polemical review "Ender and Hitler: Sympathy for the Superman" posits Card's work as an apologia for Hitler's life and philosophies. John Kessel's "Creating the Innocent Killer: *Ender's Game*, Intention, and Morality" questions Card's authorial intent in a text that asks readers to like Ender so much that we overlook the title character's destructiveness. Carl Malmgren takes a similar tack, asserting that Ender's imaginativeness makes him empathize with the "Other" so completely that he "reconceives the Other as a Self," illustrating the extent to which Ender is both insider and outsider, hero and monster (20). Writing about *Ender's Game* and Card's later companion text and parallel novel *Ender's Shadow* (which follows the character Bean) Christine Doyle claims Ender's superior empathy makes him adopt the healing role of "Speaker for the Dead" but also prohibits him from returning to the earth he helped catapult into chaos ("Orson Scott Card's Ender and

47

Bean"). With Susan Louise Stewart, Doyle further considers the instrumentation of children, imploring readers to envision children as complex persons—beyond the simplicity of the stereotypically-innocent child (200). Further questioning that childhood innocence, Melissa Gross reads *Ender's Game* (like many critics) as a story of grotesque abuse, where Ender's only refuge is Fairyland, a place to struggle with "a choice between his own grisly death and an even worse murder" (Card, qtd. in Gross 122). Though each of these scholars approaches *Ender's Game* differently, all seem to share the perception that Ender as a character is both disoriented and disorienting; he is difficult to read precisely because he blurs the boundaries between childhood and adulthood, innocence and depravity, hero and monster. There is no easy place for Ender—not in scholarship and not in the worlds of his novel. He finds solace in the computer-simulated mind game called Fairyland, where Ender encounters fairytale tropes like a giant, wolves, a serpent, a dragon, a unicorn, a bottomless well, and a magical mirror; each trope illustrates a psychological issue Ender struggles with in reality as well as in the narrative of the mind game. As Ender asserts authorship in Fairyland, his world becomes increasingly complicated, and the alternative space of the mind game demonstrates that there is no easy working out of the categories Ender straddles. There is no simple passage through worlds polluted by abuse and warfare, no graceful transition from child to adult in contexts that use children as tools and scapegoats. Yet Ender's imagination never fails, and it is his creativity in both the dystopian worlds of the military schools and Fairyland that ultimately renders him author and destroyer, hero and monster. It is through his creative cartography within Fairyland that Ender authors an alternative home for himself, a home that, in spite of its violent formation, ultimately offers Ender his own hope of redemption.

Dislocating and Disorienting Homes

Ender's authorship in Fairyland, his desire to map out a terrain familiar to him both literally and metaphorically, originates from his pervasive sense of homelessness. As Dink, one of the older boys at the Battle School, laments, "Hey, I know nobody's supposed to talk about home. But we came from somewhere" (Card 109). That "somewhere" is as nebulous as the traditional fairy tale beginning that orients readers in a land once upon a time and far, far away. Even in the physical space of his parents' house, Ender is not at home; he is displaced as a Third child in a world of strict population control (15), and the Battle School commander reasons with Ender, "I know you, Ender. I've been watching the monitor disks for some time. You won't miss your mother and father, not much, not for long. And they won't miss you long, either" (21–2). Twice Ender cries in the night, like so many of the children at the school, "I want to go home" (44, 93), but by morning, "[h]ome was merely a dull ache in the back of his memory. A tiredness in his eyes" (93). When his family moves while Ender is away at school, his sister Valentine wonders, "How would Ender find them here, among these trees, under this changeable and heavy sky? He had lived deep in corridors all his life, and if he was still in the Battle School, there was less of nature there. What would he make of this?" (123). Later, as Ender gains prestige at the Battle School (and his tormentors ratchet up their bullying), he acknowledges a fear that reminds him uncomfortably of home (187). Throughout the text, Ender's associations with home are predominantly negative: sadness, fear, rejection, discomfort, abuse. As a Third, Ender lacks a place in the world of earth. As a superior student, he lacks a place in the Battle School; thus the loss of gravity as he transitions from earth to space symbolizes a much deeper disorientation. Ender is rootless, set adrift, dislocated, homeless.

It is no wonder, then, that Ender is irresistibly drawn to the mind game Fairyland, where he, as centuries of readers before him, starts to make a home for himself. In "Children, War, and the Imaginative Space of Fairy Tales," Donald Haase envisions fairy tale texts as "an imaginative geography that lends itself to the representation and mapping of wartime experience" (361). Using Freud's theory of the uncanny as his foundation, Haase further asserts "[w]hen violence upsets their familiar environment, the children are physically dislocated and forced into exile, into a defamiliarized perception of home. In typical fashion, their displacement is followed by relocation to a secure or familiar environment— that is, home reconstituted on a new plane" (364). Ender's discussion of home represents that displacement, the removal from his earthly home of origin (where he was abused by his older brother Peter, bullied at school, and neglected by his parents and other authority figures) to the Battle School (where peer-abuse and authoritative neglect continue).

Ender's world is upset by the violence following the first bugger invasion globally and the sadistic fraternal relationship personally. Violence characterizes his home as well as the school where he begins to feel at home, and violence likewise characterizes the Fairyland game, in which Ender can only win or move forward by violence. When he finally defeats the Giant who guards the entrance to Fairyland, Ender admits, "He hadn't meant to kill the Giant. This was supposed to be a game. Not a choice between his own grisly death and an even worse murder. I'm a murderer, even when I play. Peter would be proud of me" (Card 65). The reconstituted home and imaginative geography of Fairyland reenact the violence characteristic of the only homes Ender has ever known. He establishes himself within the familiar terrain of violence, where he feels securely unsecure, familiarly at home with violence and abuse yet longing for an alternative choice.

Ender's attraction to and eventual manipulation of Fairyland signal Freud's definition of the uncanny, which, translated from the "unheimlich" or "unhomely," Freud defines as "that species of the frightening that goes back to what was once well known and had long been familiar" (Freud 124). Contemporary fairy tale scholar Jack Zipes expands on Freud's work, stating, "We can see that instinctual drives are conditioned and largely determined through interaction and interplay with the social environment" (*Fairy Tales and the Art of Subversion* 48) and "The more social relations make us discontent and feel as though we were objects alienated from our own communities, the more we seek a haven in mental projections of other worlds" (*Why Fairy Tales Stick* 106). Zipes' commentary on Freud's work and the utopian appeal of fairy tales (however much constructed by social factors) highlights the ways in which Ender's violent contexts at home and school project onto Fairyland. Ender's Fairyland is a landscape marked by violence, beginning with his own multiple virtual deaths in the Giant's game and proceeding from the eventual murder of the Giant. Describing the game and his reactions to it, Ender explains, "He never guessed right. Sometimes his head was dissolved. Sometimes he caught fire. Sometimes he fell in and drowned. Sometimes he fell out, turned green, and rotted away. It was always ghastly, and the Giant always laughed" (Card 63). In spite of his evident frustration and the Giant's sadism, Ender returns, irresistibly drawn to the Fairyland game: "The game was rigged but still the Giant talked about Fairyland, some stupid childish three-year-old's Fairyland that probably had some stupid Mother Goose or Pac-Man or Peter Pan, it wasn't even worth getting to, but he had to find some way of beating the Giant to get there" (64). Conflating video games and traditional fairy tales, Ender assumes in his description that the game is childish and therefore worthless, perhaps because his society continually tells him that childhood is worthless unless it can be used for some larger military purpose. Despite his frustration, Ender pursues the game, obsessed with passing the Giant and gaining entrance into Fairyland, where, maybe at some subconscious level, he hopes to reconstruct and reorient himself in an imaginative space of utopian childhood—safe, secure, loved, and belonging. Ender cheats to pass the Giant, showing a disregard for the standard Fairyland script; in his rejection of the established modes of play, Ender asserts himself as author, limited not by the rules of the game but only by his own (seemingly boundless) imagination.

Fairyland represents, for Ender, a final frontier, a last opportunity to orient himself within a world free from strife. As fellow student-soldier Dink explains, "I've got a pretty good idea what children are, and we're not children. Children can lose sometimes, and nobody cares" (Card 108). Dink's knowledge, ironically, comes from old library books, since none of the children in the Battle School has ever experienced that kind of childhood. When Ender finally defeats the Giant and enters Fairyland, he finds a playground; unlike the children he discovers, though, Ender cannot use the playground equipment. He falls through the physical space of the slides and the other children gather around to bully him (71), recalling scenes of his home and school lives, in both earth and in space. There is no play within Ender's world. As Ender wanders further into Fairyland, past the playground, the children reappear: "Out of the woods emerged a dozen slavering wolves with human faces. Ender recognized them—they were the children from the playground. Only now their teeth could tear; Ender, weaponless, was quickly devoured" (72). He returns to the game and destroys the children, who, like the Giant, do not reanimate upon his reappearance in Fairyland (117). Ender finds the same cruelty and violence in Fairyland that he knows too well outside of it. Fairyland is not a utopian space, just as childhood is not a utopian space, and Ender's movements through the game assert again and again the brutality of the worlds authored for him. He continues to travel through Fairyland, down a well, past a table of jewels and a feast, to a place marked "THE END OF THE WORLD."

The well, jewels, and feast are all typical fairytale landscape features, and each poses its own possibilities and dangers: the bottomless wishing well that sends Ender into freefall instead of offering a refreshing drink; the riches he ignores that surely entice players to temptation, theft, and retribution; the food that looks alluring but poisons or ensnares the eater for life. Every element in Fairyland trains the Battle School's students to anticipate peril even where there seem to be gifts, and so the commanders prompt children to kill by teaching them that the world is teeming with dangers in disguise—just like Fairyland itself. Ender leaps off the edge of the world's end and finds himself in a room where "the small rug before the fire unraveled itself into a long, slender serpent with wicked teeth. 'I am your only escape,' it said. 'Death is your only escape'" (73). Ender, apparently, is the first player ever to reach this stage of the game, demonstrating his relentless creativity. At that instant, the Battle School commanders override the game, interrupting Ender's journey in Fairyland to tell him to go to his barracks. As soon as Ender begins to assert control of Fairyland, it seems, the adults disrupt his imaginative cartography and emphasize their power over his movements. They can disconnect the game and order Ender to move from one space within the Battle School to another; they monitor his movements within the game and outside the game, and just as Ender discovers something of Fairyland that he alone owns, the authority figures interrupt him and reassert their dominance.

Ender's assertion of authorship in Fairyland disturbs the hierarchy within the Battle School in much the same way that child and adult readers struggle for power over the interpretation of fairy tale texts. As critic Maria Tatar claims, "It is important to remember that what we produce in our retellings and rereadings discloses more about an adult agenda for children than about what children want to hear. Thus fairy tales may not offer much insight into the minds of children, but they often document our shifting attitudes toward the child and chart our notions about childrearing in a remarkable way" (*Off with Their Heads!* 20). In her text *Enchanted Hunters*, she also states, "In real life, children are far more like silenced subalterns than imperial adventurers and conquistadors. For them, mobility comes in the form of books, and reading oddly becomes akin to an exercise in moving from that position of silenced subaltern to sovereign imperial subject" (137). As Tatar's research indicates, reading is not a neutral activity but (often) a struggle for autonomy.

Fairytale historians like Tatar illustrate the ways the genre has morphed over the centuries, moving from an adult audience to a child audience in order to establish authority over each new generation. Still, children's readings cannot be completely controlled, and the contested space of fairytales tells us what adults want for children, as well as what children want—mobility and power. To an extent, Ender possesses both in Fairyland, yet the adults of the Battle School ultimately permit freedom for Ender's imagination only insofar as it is useful to their cause. Ender pushes for authorship in Fairyland and the commanders push back, making even his creative rendering of Fairyland's geography a tool of military might.

That is not to say that the adults are unconcerned by Ender's manipulation of Fairyland's space, a space they erroneously believed to be controlled by their computer system. Ender, it seems, is the first player of Fairyland to reach "THE END OF THE WORLD" because he created it himself. As he continues his travels through Fairyland, the adults discuss his maneuvers; tellingly, these conversations take place apart from the body of each chapter, in bolded text, disembodied from the primary story of Ender in the same way that its speakers—those in charge of the Battle School—maintain their distance from Ender. The originator of the game, Major Imbu, explains, "The End of the World in the game isn't necessarily the end of humanity in the bugger wars. It has a private meaning to Ender" (Card 121). Pursuing this line of thinking further, Major Imbu continues, saying,

> You've been isolating the boy. Maybe he's wishing for the end of *this* world, the Battle School. Or maybe it's about the end of the world he grew up with as a little boy, his home, coming here. Or maybe it's his way of coping with having broken up so many other kids here. Ender's a sensitive kid, you know, and he's done some pretty bad things to people's bodies, he might be wishing for the end of *that* world.... The mind game is a relationship between the child and the computer. Together they create stories. The stories are true, in the sense that they reflect the reality of the child's life. That's all *I* know [121].

Imbu's explanation returns to a sense of home, though it's evident that the violence and neglect of the Battle School mirror Ender's family. Imbu's discussion also compares the game to a story, mutually authored by Ender and the computer, and at the end of his speech, the Major acknowledges that he has little control over either author. It would seem that the commanders, Ender, and the computer all play a role in defining Fairyland, with no one party exercising complete control. That shared authority leaves the adults of the Battle School in unfamiliar territory, unsure how to interpret Ender's obsession with "THE END OF THE WORLD." As Ender explains it, "It was the one dangerous place left. And Ender, however often he vowed that he would not, always went back there, always killed the snake, always looked his brother in the face, and always, no matter what he did next, died" (141). The commanders' ignorance of how the computer retrieved a current picture of Peter, mingled with Ender's insistence on virtual suicide missions to look in the mirror at his brother, present significant interpretive challenges for the Battle School's mission. Ender, absorbed in the reflection of Peter, becomes useless in the bugger wars. Fairyland, then, represents Ender's withdrawal from military demands and the conflicted school setting, but he moves from one danger to another, replacing reality's horrors with virtual and psychological torments. The reflection of Peter in Fairyland prepares Ender to face the evils within him, and his suicidal obsessions fit his eventual role as a commander who must sacrifice human lives to win the bugger war. What these images further reveal, however, is Ender's struggle to independently map out a safe space for himself, in spite of his creative genius.

Mapping beyond Mirror, Mirror

Even in the Fairyland of his own authorship, Ender must contend with the reflected image of Peter. Ernst Bloch writes about the symbolism of the mirror image within fairy tales. In "The Fairy Tale Moves on Its Own in Time," he states "the mirror of the fairy tale has not become opaque, and the manner of wish-fulfillment that peers forth from it is not entirely without a home. It all adds up to this: the fairy tale narrates a wish-fulfillment that is not bound by its own time and the apparel of its contents" (163). Indeed, Ender's past and present are consumed by the concern that he is like his sociopathic brother Peter. Ender's continual visits to the mirror and the steadfast reflection of Peter project, if not a "wish-fulfillment," then perhaps a self-fulfilling prophecy where Ender, despite his desire to save the world from bugger violence, becomes the perpetrator of even greater violence. A return to Freud's "uncanny" makes sense at this juncture. Discussing the *"Doppelgänger,"* Freud writes,

> a person may identify himself with another and so become unsure of his true self; or he may substitute the other's self for his own. The self may thus be duplicated, divided and interchanged. Finally there is the constant recurrence of the same thing, the repetition of the same facial features, the same characters, the same destinies, the same misdeeds, even the same names, through successive generations [142].

That Ender sees Peter within himself is unsurprising; both brilliant children, Peter was deemed too cruel even for the military program, yet it is Ender who murders other children along his ascent to military prowess. On Earth, Peter ultimately gains political office and secures world peace, whereas Ender, meanwhile, is unable to return to Earth because he nearly exterminates the bugger race. While those events exist in Peter's and Ender's futures, even their mild-mannered sister Valentine (yet another brilliant child) must rally herself to insist, "Ender is not like Peter! He is not like Peter in any way! Except that he's smart, that's all—in every other way a person could possibly be like Peter he is nothing nothing nothing like Peter! Nothing!" (Card 148). Valentine's insistence is qualified, and stated from a distance; at the time of this statement, she is physically and emotionally close to Peter, but she has not seen or heard from Ender in several years. She calls Peter "the worst person I know" (148), yet her dramatic denial of her brothers' likeness just might betray her own anxieties about the shared genes, similar intelligence levels, and potential for evil inherent in all three children. Ender sees his affinity with Peter from the beginning: "Take my monitor away, and I am just like Peter" (8). The monitor remains, metaphorically speaking, in that the adults running the Battle School are still supervising Ender's actions within and outside Fairyland without his knowledge. Whether Ender is like Peter in intentions or morals becomes nearly irrelevant because Ender sees Peter's violence in his own actions, just as Kessel points out in his essay regarding the characterization of Ender as an "innocent killer." Kessel calls Ender "the murderer as scapegoat. The genocide as saviour. The exterminator as Christ Redeemer" (93) and questions Card's narrative tactics that distance both readers and Ender from his own acts of violence. The mirror image in Fairyland illustrates the extent to which Ender identifies with Peter, no matter how emphatically Valentine declares their differences.

At the "END OF THE WORLD," Ender throws the snake at the mirror and shatters the glass, causing the emergence of "dozens of tiny snakes, which quickly bit Ender's figure again and again. Tearing the snakes frantically from itself, the figure collapsed and died in a writhing heap of small serpents. The screen went blank, and the words appeared PLAY AGAIN?" (Card 118). Once again, Fairyland seems to require Ender to perpetuate violence, if not against others, then against himself. The choice between murder and suicide haunts Ender in the Battle School itself and in Fairyland, because both spaces orient him by acts of violence. In this instance, he watches from a distance, regarding his virtual double destroyed because of decisions made by his non-virtual self. Ender watches the screen where his avatar gazes at a mirror reflection of Peter; he is doubled, and doubled again, witnessing and effecting violence in a cycle that seems unbreakable even when Ender authors the story himself. To this brutal mind game, Ender responds, "What difference does it make that when the little serpents killed me in the game, I agreed with them, and was glad" (119) and eventually reasons, "I'm trapped here, Ender thought, trapped at the End of the World with no way out. And he knew at last the sour taste that had come to him, despite all his successes in the Battle School. It was despair" (141). He ultimately concludes, "Only the game was left to him" (151). Ender's response to his *Doppelgänger*, the image of Peter reflected in the mirror and his actions, is both destructive and creative. His despair prompts the urge to end the world of the Battle School and its attendant sufferings and sadisms, but it also propels Ender toward creativity within the game. Fairyland becomes the singular space where Ender can orient himself, as opposed to the drifting planet and shifting habitation of his earthly family or the gravity-manipulated Battle School. Ender's use of Fairyland coincides with the literary usages of the fairy tale genre. As Zipes writes in *The Irresistible Fairytale*, the stories "originated and derived from wish fulfillment coupled with a desire for other moral worlds. They had always been told, serving to compensate for the impoverished lives and desperate struggles of many people. Whatever the outcome of a fairy tale, there was some sort of hope for a miraculous change" (155). Ender seems to hold the same hopes for Fairyland; despite his resistance to and frustration with the game, he returns to it again and again, perhaps because it seems like the only space over which he can exert control, the only unchartered terrain where he can potentially locate both hope and home.

Other scholars agree with Zipes regarding the inherent hopefulness of the fairy tale. G.K. Chesterton concludes, "I came to feel as if magic must have a meaning, and meaning must have someone to mean it" (*Collected Works* 268) and "morality can be enjoyed because it puts us in fairyland, in a world at once of wonder and of war" (*All Things Considered* 109). C.S. Lewis discusses the "special kind of longing" awakened by fairy tales (30) and reasons, "For in the fairy tales, side by side with the terrible figures, we find the immemorial comforters and protectors, the radiant ones; and the terrible figures are not merely terrible, but sublime" (32). Both Chesterton and Lewis discuss the ways that fairy tales—and their readers—construct meaning; there are dramatic extremes in the fairy story, they reckon, yet the narrative logic balances the evil with the good and imbues all things with a meaning and a force behind the meaning: a Maker. For Ender, neglected and abused by parents and teachers alike, the stability of authority (however illusory) in Fairyland must have exerted considerable pull. Beyond the despair of the Battle School and the perpetual disorientation of his young life, in Fairyland Ender discovers and makes meaning for his life. After reading his sister Valentine's letter that had been engineered by the commanders to push Ender forward in his education, Ender, in his misery, returns to the game. He looks in the mirror, and instead of trying to eat or kill the snake, he kisses it: "the snake in his hands thickened and bent into another shape. A human shape. It was Valentine, and she kissed him again. The snake could not be Valentine. He had killed it too often for it to be his sister. Peter had devoured it too often for Ender to bear it that it might have been Valentine all along" (Card 152). Instead of trying to devour or destroy the snake, Ender embraces it with an act of love and affection. He, like the symbolic snake, comes full circle, envisioning the snake as that which he most fears (his brother Peter) and that which he most loves (his sister Valentine). The Fairyland mirror allows Ender to see what the earthly letter cannot, that Ender is a mixture of profound evil and profound good, and that perhaps his brother and sister are, too. Ender's love for Valentine prompts him to respond to the snake differently, not with cruelty but with kindness. The snake, so often destroyed, is resurrected each time Ender returns to the game, signaling hope restored by his sister's love. Peter may be Ender's double, but Valentine is as well. For Ender, Peter represents "the terrible figures" of his childhood and Valentine embodies "the immemorial comforters and protectors, the radiant ones" (Lewis 32). It is the Fairyland mirror which reflects Ender's realization that both the terrible and the good exist within him too. As Chesterton and Lewis point out, the structure of fairytales balances evil with good, creating a kind of logical morality. Until Valentine's appearance, Ender has only seen the evil within Fairyland and within himself. Her emergence along with the unicorn suggests hope and the potential for redemption in Ender's story-world.

That intermingling of evil and good presents itself in the new reflection conjured in the Fairyland mirror. The snake morphs into Valentine and

> they stood before the mirror, where instead of Peter's cruel reflection there stood a dragon and a unicorn. Ender reached out his hand and touched the mirror and so did Valentine.... Tears filled his eyes, tears of relief that at last he had broken free of the room at the End of the World. And because of the tears, he didn't notice that every member of the multitude wore Peter's face. He only knew that wherever he went in this world, Valentine was with him [Card 152].

Freedom comes for Ender in finding a home—not a stable, inanimate home, but a shifting one personified by his beloved sister. She joins him in Fairyland and holds his hand, illustrating that even in this uncharted territory she is with him, metaphorically if not literally. She reinforces his resolve to save the world for her sake, because she is the only thing he considers worth saving. The evil that Peter represents (and that Ender continues to see within himself, in the form of the Dragon) still surrounds him, but it is balanced by Valentine and the unicorn. The dragon's power is symbolized by solitude, danger, destruction, and greed, while the unicorn's power represents purity, beauty, healing, and innocence. Ender's *Doppelgänger*-reflection is itself multiplied, with the visage of Peter reproduced all around him and the reflection itself depicting two creatures instead of one. Ender seems more at peace with himself and his world in this state of fragmentation than he did when gazing upon the singular image of Peter. The images multiplied are set against the positive power of Valentine and the unicorn. There is evil, yes, profound and terrifying, but there is also good, profound and terrifying. In Fairyland, and nowhere else thus far, Ender discovers the sublime morality that Chesterton and Lewis depict, and the one that makes all worlds livable. Ender finally transcends "THE END OF THE WORLD," not with violence but with love, and the despair that drove him to suicide (even virtually) is dispelled by the radiating hope Valentine represents. By casting his sister as his feminine home, Ender acknowledges their parents' negligence and his refusal to accommodate to the adult world; his sister as his primary love affirms his longing for that elusive state of childhood innocence and confirms his mistrust of adults who are assigned to care for him. Her letter may be fabricated by the military authorities, but Ender weaves his sister into his imaginative mapping of Fairyland, finding at last both hope and home.

Authoring "Secondary Worlds"

Ender acts as author in Fairyland, particularly at "THE END OF THE WORLD." The Fairyland story is framed by Ender's larger story within the Battle School, which is itself framed by the disembodied and removed dialogue of the commanders overseeing Ender's life. Fairyland is a place removed, if not initially by space, at least by imagination and time, and it serves as an escape for Ender just as literary fairy tales offer readers a utopian vision of moral clarity. J.R.R. Tolkien describes the creative authorship required by fairy tales in his text *Tree and Leaf.* He dismisses the concept of "suspension of disbelief" and argues that great art offers, instead, "a Secondary World" as an alternative to the real, or "Primary World" (36–37). Creating a true "Secondary World," Tolkien asserts, is "a rare achievement of Art: indeed narrative art, story-making in its primary and most potent mode" (48–49). Ender achieves that art, employing the powerful creativity his commanders view as his greatest asset in the Battle School. The same creativity that makes Ender the savior of the human race makes him the creator of the "Secondary World" which helps him escape, psychologically and later physically, from the devastation caused by his military prowess. Escapism, Tolkien writes, is one of the strongest incentives for creating a "Secondary World": "There are other things more grim and terrible to fly from than the noise, stench, ruthlessness, and extravagance of the internal-combustion engine. There are hunger, thirst, poverty, pain, sorrow, injustice, death…. There are profounder wishes: such as the desire to converse with other living things" (65–66). There is, further, "the oldest and deepest desire, the Great Escape: the Escape from Death. Fairy-stories provide many examples and modes of this—which might be called the genuine escapist, or

(I would say) fugitive spirit" (67). Ender seems to embody Tolkien's "fugitive spirit," pushing himself to the world's end in search of escape from the array of conditions just listed. He finds not just escapism but communion, with Valentine and ultimately with the buggers' Queen, whose species he sought to destroy. Tolkien concludes that "every writer making a secondary world, a fantasy, every sub-creator, wishes in some measure to be a real maker, or hopes that he is drawing on reality: hopes that the peculiar quality of this secondary world (if not all the details) are derived from Reality, or are flowing into it" (70). That hope seems almost necessary to Ender's survival. His childhood has been marked by abuse, neglect, and intentional isolation. Fairyland provides a psychological refuge from those traumas, but it also, at times, mirrors those traumas. Not until Ender incorporates Valentine into Fairyland does it become a place of communion, a real home, where the purpose is not to escape evil but to foster good. By the conclusion of *Ender's Game*, he has been tricked into xenocide, the near-extermination of the buggers, yet his military success and his character are questioned back on earth; as throughout Card's text, there seems to be no stationary home for Ender, no place of return, and Valentine's arrival does not ground Ender but sends them both further into orbit, nomads in search of a new home. Not until Ender and his sister depart does he realize the extent of his authorship—that his Fairyland home exists in space as a product of communion and a symbol of hope.

Ender's "Secondary World" creation extends beyond the psychological space of Fairyland, though he is not at first aware of that. His desire to escape the terror and despair of the military school system couples with his unique military genius to help him empathize with the enemy, the buggers, more than any human. The entire bugger war, Ender learns afterward, was predicated on miscommunication; as Graff (finally, after the xenocide, accessible to communicate with Ender) explains, "If the other fellow can't tell you his story, you can never be sure he isn't trying to kill you" (Card 253). Ender, however, earlier explained to Valentine that he does understand the buggers, that it is his deep understanding that gives him the tools to destroy them:

> The moment when I truly understand my enemy, understand him well enough to defeat him, then in that very moment I also love him. I think it's impossible to really understand somebody, what they want, what they believe, and not love them the way they love themselves. And then, in that

very moment when I *love* them…I *destroy* them. I make it impossible for them to ever hurt me again. I grind them and grind them until they don't *exist* [Card 238].

Ender is as skilled in warfare as he is in art. The same child who creates new worlds in Fairyland destroys old worlds belonging to the buggers. Throughout Card's story, Ender deconstructs the boundary lines between child and adult, artist and military mastermind, creator and destroyer. The imagery of Valentine and Peter, the unicorn and the dragon, within Ender's imagined mirror reflects the reality that Ender is both hero and monster, a human and super-human capable of profound love and ultimate destruction. Following the bugger war and subsequent human wars on earth, Ender laments once more, "I want to go home … but I don't know where it is" (302). Valentine appears and urges Ender to explore the cosmos with her, the two of them finding home not within a place but within their relationship. She asserts the allure of authorship to persuade him, justifying the conquest of the buggers' former home worlds with the conclusion, "In all the bugger worlds, there was never more than a single story to be told; when we're there, the world will be full of stories, and we'll improvise their endings day by day" (Card 312–3). Even near the conclusion of the novel, Ender's home is deferred; he is offered, instead, the opportunity to create, to author more stories, more "Secondary Worlds" as he seeks, once again, to escape the chaos and danger that would await him on Earth. Ender's home, it seems, is in the telling, the making.

Ender wanders the universe and stumbles upon a world that looks strangely familiar. A feeling of déjà vu occurs and Ender recognizes the remains of the Giant. In that instant, he realizes the extent to which he authored his "Secondary World": "The Giant's corpse. He had played here too many times as a child not to know this place. But it was not possible. The computer in the Battle School could not possibly have seen this place…. The buggers built it for me" (317). Fairyland, constructed initially in Ender's mind as a means of escape and a psychological home for a child endlessly adrift, has come to fruition as a physical place. Ender's empathetic communion with the buggers was mutual, and they expressed themselves by constructing the place that once existed only in his mind. Again, this narrative turn recalls Freud's depiction of the "uncanny," where, Freud argues, "if someone dreams of a certain place or a certain landscape and, while dreaming, thinks to himself, 'I know this place, I've been here before,' this place can be interpreted as representing his mother's genitals or her womb. Here too, then, the uncanny [the 'unhomely'] is what was once familiar ['homely,' 'homey']. The negative prefix *un-* is the indicator of repression" (151). Home is defined here as a distinctly feminine space, and Ender's life is notably lacking in feminine influence (his neglectful mother, the predominately-male population in the military). His singular previous experience of home is feminine—his sister Valentine—giving credence to Freud's interpretation that the uncanny space of Fairyland is anchored in Ender's continually-deferred quest for the nurturance he associates (though perhaps only subconsciously) with embodied femininity.

This interpretation is supported by what Ender discovers behind the mirror in the buggers' rendition of Fairyland; the snake, once animated, is reduced to a rug, and Ender opens up the mirror to discover the egg of the Hive Queen, the last hope for the buggers. Encompassed within the feminine pupae is Ender's ultimate creative prospect, the discovery and authorship of a new world for the buggers to redeem the race he nearly destroyed. Yet the discovery of the Hive Queen still does not give Ender the chance to rest. It makes him more restless, as he feels compelled to search the universe to find a home, not for himself, but for the Queen. With Valentine and the Queen, Ender continues to wander, relinquishing the name affiliated with violence and taking on the title "Speaker for the Dead," a position that defines his life by authorship, telling stories of and for those who cannot speak for themselves. Just as Ender revises the rules and the landscape of Fairyland, he re-imagines the definition of home, not as rest and stagnation but as creation and storytelling.

Redeeming Stories

The nomadic conclusion to *Ender's Game* is not a happily-ever-after ending but a new beginning and a quest for redemption from Ender's war crimes. The monster Ender ultimately discovers in Fairyland is not the Giant or the buggers, but himself. Ender's simultaneous heroism and monstrosity is consistent with scholarly claims about the purposes of fairy tales. Sheldon Cashdan sees fairytale monsters as opportunities for child-readers to engage with the evil within themselves: "Children need opportunities to become conversant with parts of themselves they are going to have to deal with for the rest of their lives" (252). Bruno Bettelheim asserts, "We want our children to believe that, inherently, all men are good. But children know that *they* are not always good" (7, original emphasis). Based on that premise, Bettelheim recommends fairy tales with real moral struggles, because "the monster a child knows best and is most concerned with [is] the monster he feels or fears himself to be, and which also sometimes persecutes him" (120).

The slippage between hero and monster is characteristic of the postmodern fairytale, explains Maria Nikolajeva (147), and Marina Warner agrees: "[r]elations with such enigmas, with monsters real and imaginary, call into play the very concept of metamorphosis, as both natural event and metaphorical transformation. Metamorphosis entails a fluidity of categories" (25). That "fluidity of categories" is represented in Ender's relationship with Fairyland, which becomes, in some ways, another kind of double. It bears the scars of Ender's violence without erasing the evidence of his atrocities, a monstrous history that Ender carries with him for the rest of his life. It likewise contains his creative potential, his ability to commune and communicate with others, to build relationships and map out safe spaces in a life and a world defined by trauma. Fairyland exhibits Ender's destructiveness, because the place that serves as a haven for the Hive Queen exists as a direct result of Ender's martial prowess. But through Fairyland, Ender also becomes what Tolkien terms "a real maker" (70), an author whose "rare Art" (48–49) transcends the initial world and inspires a "Secondary World" that gives hope to Ender, Valentine, and the Hive Queen. Through stories of his own making, Ender reorients the patterns of violence that characterize his life and conjures a real future in a land far far away; for Ender, the Xenocide, there is no happily-ever-after, but for Ender, "Speaker for the Dead," the hope of redemption is rekindled in each tale, each story that blazes the trail from his dystopian origins.

Note

1. For further discussion of this construct, see the introduction to Carrie Hintz's and Elaine Ostry's 2009 text *Utopian and Dystopian Writing for Children and Young Adults*.

Works Cited

Bettelheim, Bruno. *The Uses of Enchantment: The Meaning and Importance of Fairy Tales*. New York: Vintage, 1989. Print.

Bloch, Ernst. *The Utopian Function of Art and Literature: Selected Essays*. Trans. Jack Zipes and Frank Mecklenburg. Cambridge: MIT Press, 1989. Print.

Card, Orson Scott. *Ender's Game*. New York: Macmillan, 1992. Print.

Cashdan, Sheldon. *The Witch Must Die: How Fairy Tales Shape Our Lives*. New York: Basic Books, 1999. Print.

Chesterton, G.K. *All Things Considered*. CreateSpace Independent Publishing Platform, 2011. Web.

_____. *Collected Works*, vol. 1. San Francisco: Ignatius Press, 1986. Print.

Doyle, Christine. "Orson Scott Card's Ender and Bean: The Exceptional Child as Hero." *Children's Literature in Education* 35.4 (2004): 301–318. *Academic Search Complete*. Web. 11 Jan. 2013.

_____, and Susan Louise Stewart. "Ender's Game and Ender's Shadow: Orson Scott Card's Postmodern School Stories." *The Lion and the Unicorn* 28.2 (2004): 186–202. *ProQuest*. Web. 9 Jan. 2013.

Freud, Sigmund. *The Uncanny*. Trans. David Mclintock. New York: Penguin, 2003. Print.

Gross, Melissa. "Prisoners of Childhood? Child Abuse and the Development of Heroes and Monsters in *Ender's Game*." *Children's Literature in Education* 38.2 (2007): 115–126. *Academic Search Complete*. Web. 11 Jan. 2013.

Haase, Donald. "Children, War, and the Imaginative Space of Fairy Tales." *The Lion and the Unicorn* 24.3 (Sept. 2000): 360–377. *ProQuest*. Web. 11 Jan. 2013.

Hintz, Carrie, and Elaine Ostry. Introduction. *Utopian and Dystopian Writing for Children and Young Adults*. Eds. Carrie Hintz and Elaine Ostry. New York: Routledge, 2003. 1–22. Print.

Kessel, John. "Creating the Innocent Killer: *Ender's Game*, Intention, and Morality." *Foundation: The International Review of Science Fiction* 33.90 (2004): 81–97. Web. 11 Jan. 2013.

Lewis, C.S. *Of Other Worlds: Essays and Stories*. New York: Mariner Books, 2002. Print.

Malmgren, Carl. "Self and Other in SF: Alien Encounters." *Science Fiction Studies* 20.1 (1993): 15–33. *Humanities International Complete*. Web. 11 Jan. 2013.

Nikolajeva, Maria. "Fairy Tale and Fantasy: From Archaic to Postmodern." *Marvels and Tales* 17.1 (Apr. 2003): 138–156. *Project Muse*. Web. 11 Jan. 2013.

Radford, Elaine. "Ender and Hitler: Sympathy for the Superman." *Fantasy Review* 102 (Aug. 1987): 7–11. Web.

Tatar, Maria. *Enchanted Hunters: The Power of Stories in Childhood*. New York: W. W. Norton, 2009. Print.

_____. *Off with Their Heads! Fairy Tales and the Culture of Childhood*. Princeton: Princeton University Press, 1992. Print.

Tolkien, J.R.R. *Tree and Leaf*. Boston: Houghton Mifflin, 1965. Print.

Warner, Marina. "Metamorphoses of the Monstrous." *Fairy Tales, Monsters, and the Genetic Imagination*. Ed. Mark W. Scala. Nashville: Vanderbilt University Press, 2012. 24–36. Print.

Zipes, Jack. *Fairy Tales and the Art of Subversion: The Classical Genre for Children and the Process of Civilization*, 2d ed. New York: Routledge, 2006. Print.

_____. *The Irresistible Fairytale: The Cultural and Social History of a Genre.* Princeton: Princeton University Press, 2012. Print.

_____. *Why Fairy Tales Stick: The Evolution and Relevance of a Genre.* New York: Routledge, 2006. Print.

Being Nobody
Identity in Neil Gaiman's The Graveyard Book

Joseph Abbruscato

Many fairy tales begin in far away places, with castles, princesses, and other standard motifs (as exemplified in "Cinderella," "Sleeping Beauty," and "The Three Feathers," among many others). The hero or heroine, in search for an identity, voluntarily leaves home to find themselves in the wild world. These adventures often took place on the open road, through varying idyllic wildernesses and forests, quaint villages, and ancient castles. This path does not serve a modern audience as well as it once did, as the landscape of society has changed, leading young readers to be more familiar with expansive city-scapes, complex societies, and paved highways, as opposed to the dusty roads, thatched roofs, and wooded paths of the traditional tales. Explained by Jack Zipes in *The Irresistible Fairy Tale*, "fairy tales embody worlds of naïve morality that can still resonate with us of their underlying dramas are re-created and re-designed to … collide with out complex social realities" (136). As such, Neil Gaiman's young adult novel *The Graveyard Book* takes this quest motif and transposes the classic locations, motifs, lessons, and structures, into to a current social setting. This "collision does not … end in destruction"; this combining of classic tale structures with modern locations known to today's child readers are "necessary to shake up the world and sharpen our gaze" (Zipes 136). *The Graveyard Book* does not appear, at first glance, to fit the idea of a "fairy tale," being a full length novel. However, all chapters within the book are able to stand alone as their own tale independent of each other, each utilizing various fairy tale structures, ideas, and motifs. These elements are detailed throughout this chapter, further exploring the intersection of traditional and contemporary fairy tales. Opening the tale with the bloody, brutal murder of his entire family, the then-infant protagonist Nobody Owens escapes by the fabric of his diaper and is forced to begin his search for identity before he can even take care of himself. According to Bruno Bettelheim, "Fairy tales, unlike any other form of literature, direct the child to discover his identity and calling" (24). Unlike many fairy tales where the protagonist has an idea of their identity (replete with name, a family, etc.), Bod, reminiscent of Mowgli from *The Jungle Book,* is identity-less from the start: he has no name, no family, and effectively, no home to which he can return. Consequently the novel follows his fairy tale quest to discover his name and identity.

Escaping the house where his family is ruthlessly killed, the infant Bod, who has yet to receive a name, stumbles and toddles to the titular graveyard, where he goes through what can be seen as a naming ceremony. When he is first discovered by the denizens of the graveyard (ghosts for the most part, with the exception of one mysterious "Undead" gentleman), they gather, argue and bicker about what the child's name is to be. Voiceless, the infant Bod is subjected to who each of the ghosts believe him to most closely resemble from their own lives, with potential names (and with them, histories and identities) ranging from Marcus, to Stebbins, to Harry. It is not until "Mrs. Owens, who has agreed to care for the boy, says, firmly 'He looks like nobody'" (Nilsen, 79) that his name is agreed upon: "Nobody Owens," which is shortened to the familiar "Bod" or sometimes "Boy," depending upon who is addressing him. This identity place holder "Nobody" is integral to his growth while in and about the graveyard. It is a blank slate for him to inscribe various aspects of identity upon, adding, and removing when necessary, different components as he grows and matures. As there is no name, and consequently, no histories associated with him, he is able to truly grow into whoever he is supposed to be.

The name "Nobody" also serves as a bit of grim irony, because when broken down into its two root parts, his full first name reads "No" and "Body." As the only human in the graveyard, Bod happens to be the only inhabitant of the graveyard who does in fact have a body (while the Undead gentleman Silas does have a body, the fact remains that he is undead, and as such, disparate from Bod and human beings). This irony is useful in eliciting laughter from the reader, who on the first page of the novel is greeted by a blood dripping knife held by the hand of a meticulous, silent killer, and subsequently ghosts and the undead. Karen Coats comments on the use of humor in Gaiman's works:

> Gaiman's device of treating what could be a horrible situation with a humorous twist is a move that empowers young readers.... It is the unexpectedness of the turn-around and its successful outcome that release psychic tension and results in laughter [82].

Young readers, confronted with this brutal beginning, a graveyard full of ghosts, and an undead gentleman, need this twisted word play as comic relief in order to relieve the fear and tension that has built up inside of them. Bod, too, feels relief at this point: "It was then that, as if responding to the name, the child opened its eyes wide in wakefulness" (Gaiman 25). This realization can be viewed as an early revelation on Bod's behalf of his ultimate association with this identity (though it will take many years to fully come to terms with it). In fairy tales and real life alike,

> children are searching for the solutions to the first and last questions—"Who am I? How ought I to deal with life's problems? What must I become?"— they do so on the basis of their animistic thinking. But since the child is so uncertain of what his existence consists, first and foremost comes the question "Who am I?" [Bettelheim 47].

In order to help protect Bod on his quest to find meaning and identity, he is given the Freedom of the Graveyard by The Lady on the Gray, who ferries everyone to their final resting place. Despite not being dead, this gift is given to Nobody in order to assist the ghosts in protecting him. Ultimately, it effectually alters who and what he is for the time being, enabling him to survive and grow up in the graveyard. Through numerous gifts awarded with the title, Bod becomes an amalgamation of human and ghost, while being not quite either: despite being alive and corporeal, he is given the ability to see and interact as easily with ghosts as he can with "normal" humans. Also, he is provided with ghostly attributes such as "Fade," "Fear," and "Dream-walking." These abilities cannot and do not last forever; however,

> the fairy tale ... projects this acceptance of reality for the child, because while extraordinary transfiguration's in the hero's body occur as the story unfolds, he becomes a mere mortal again once the struggle is over. At the fairy story's end we hear no more about the hero's unearthly beauty or strength [Bettelheim 57].

This is true in the case of Bod and *The Graveyard Book*. At the end of the story, Bod ultimately embraces his identity as Nobody Owens, including official documentation of it from Silas: "You have a passport in the inner pocket of your suitcase. It's made out in the name of Nobody Owens" (Gaiman 304). Serving as a rite of passage, this official government document validates Bod's identity and humanness, not just for himself, but for anyone who would dare question his identity. With this internalization of his identity and the official human documentation of it, Bod must lose the supernatural ghostly abilities which had carried him through the challenges of his youth. He slowly loses the ability to see his ghostly neighbors, while graves become solid where he once could pass through them. Signifying his re-transformation into a completely human person, Bod must leave the graveyard, knowing it is no longer his home. This does not scare Bod, however; being Nobody is nothing to be afraid of. For

> once the fairy-tale hero has achieved his true identity at the story's ending (and with it inner security about himself, his body, his life, his position in society), he is happy the way he is, and no longer unusual in any respect [Bettelheim 57–58].

Gaiman depicts this fairy hero perfectly in the books final paragraphs:

> There was a passport in his bag, money in his pocket. There was a smile dancing on his lips, although it was a wary smile, for the world is a bigger place than a little graveyard on a hill; and there would be dangers in it and mysteries, new friends to make, old friends to rediscover, mistakes to be made and many paths to be walked before he would, finally, return to the graveyard or ride with the lady on the broad back of her great grey stallion.
> But between now and then, there was life; and Bod walked into it with his eyes and his heart wide open [Gaiman 307].

This ending depicts a fairy tale hero who has fully synthesized all of his knowledge and experiences into one complete identity. He understands that there are dangers in the world, as he has already met his own share of them; he knows that there will be friends to be made and decisions to be thought upon, as he already has firsthand knowledge of such dealings. Bod is a young man prepared to face his life, having finally reached a point in his journey where he knows who he truly is.

This search for, and ultimate acquisition and integration of, his name and identity does not happen overnight, however. It takes Bod approximately 13 years before he can fully identify himself as Nobody

Owens, and it is only through taking complete inventory of the years he lives in the graveyard is he able to grow and mature properly. At each stage of his development (demarcated in the book by approximately two years time passing between each chapter) there is a new challenge which must be faced and overcome. These obstacles come in various shapes and sizes, increasing in difficulty as Bod ages.

Followed by calm periods of life growth not portrayed in the novel, these challenges which Bod must face build upon each other, each necessitating the repetition of particular problem solving methods he previously was forced to learn. Classically, fairy tales deal heavily with the concept of freedom versus imprisonment or isolation. These periods of isolation are vital to a hero's growth (though the hero may not recognize this at first). These periods of isolation or imprisonment often are positive in the long run, aiming to protect the hero, and in turn enabling the possibility of a new life, a new identity, or both (von Franz 88). Such acts of isolation can be seen in "Sleeping Beauty," where Sleeping Beauty is isolated and imprisoned in a magical sleep, protecting her from death until a new life is available to her (Perrault 3–21). This motif of isolation and protection also appears in *The Graveyard Book*. Bod's growth appears at times when he begins to feels overly trapped within the graveyard and fights against his isolation and imprisonment to explore, not realizing the dangers and potential cost such actions and explorations could have. The first of these occurs in Chapter Two, "The New Friend," after Bod meets a young girl named Scarlett. Sent on an assignment by Silas to complete grave rubbings of the letters of the alphabet, Bod meets Scarlett and the two begin talking about the oldest person in the graveyard. This conversation culminates in an attempt to find him. While this quest does not lead them outside of the physical boundaries of the graveyard (which Bod is forbidden to cross), it does leads the two deep under it, far below the old mausoleum on the hill in the graveyard. Once inside, the two children run across two obstacles, the first of which is the Indigo Man. Furthering the idea that Bod is the only human denizen in the graveyard, the Indigo Man seems to be more of a projection of a human covered in indigo tattoos than something which was an actual person. Despite being a projection, the Indigo Man has the power to instill fear within anyone who stumbles down into the cavern, and Bod realizes this through careful observation of his surroundings:

> Bod looked at the remains of the gentleman in the brown coat. There was a lamp beside him, broke on the rocky floor. "He ran away," said Bod aloud. "He ran because he was scared. And he slipped or he tripped on the stairs and he fell off" [Gaiman 53].

Recognizing the disastrous end results of being scared of the Indigo Man, Bod internalizes this, and builds upon an earlier reference and description of the usefulness of scarecrows made by Scarlett. Using her explanation of a scarecrow's purpose of being scary but harmless, Bod continuously repeated that there was nothing to be afraid of in the Indigo Man. Putting this knowledge to use is what permitted them to evade the Indigo Man, who had, amongst other things, threatened to feast on their livers. Controlling their fear and not letting it influence their decisions permitted Bod and Scarlett to continue through the cavern to face their next challenge: the Sleer. An unseen force, the Sleer repeats its desire for its Master (presumably a druid from pre–Roman times, who left the barrow and never returned), urging Bod to succumb to its want. The Sleer attempts to persuade Bod through fear, as well as appeals to multiple aspects of Bod's desires, specifically the chance to have an identity as the Sleer's new Master. This is not the identity Bod wants, and through the knowledge gained from facing down the Indigo Man, Bod and Scarlett are able to control their fear in front of the Sleer and safely make their way back up to the surface of the graveyard. This encounter with the Indigo Man and the Sleer occurs multiple times over the course of the book. In subsequent chapters, the Sleer's desire for its Master's return becomes more and more persistent, and more ominous.

This section of the text was vital to the growth of Bod as a character and as a person. He is faced with fantastical beings from a time before recorded history, learns how to control his fears when necessary, and internalizes the wonders of the Sleer, the Indigo Man, and the hill (the ancient brooch, knife, and cup, the Sleer is guarding) for future use. Whereas in the first chapter the humorous naming ceremony is used to feed the emotional portion of the readers psyche, this adventure feeds the imaginative and the intellectual portions. The child reader, along with Bod, is given the chance to imagine a people older than the oldest person in the graveyard and older than the Roman Empire, they are led to imagine a people unlike themselves who were covered in blue paint. For a young reader, this departure from the "normal" look of people is exciting and wondrous. Readers are also taught here the importance of the utilization of their surroundings to feed and expand upon knowledge of a situation in which they may feel trapped, which in Bod's case is being trapped by the Indigo Man and the Sleer. When entering the Sleer's barrow, and encountering the Indigo Man for the first time, Bod takes note of the dead body of a man next to the stairway. This man presumably turned and attempted to flee the Indigo Man due to his fear of this creature. In the process of succumbing to his fear, the man fell and died, his body preserved and serving as a warning to others entering the Sleer's barrow. Bod notices the body, and through his observation and internalization of the scenario which must have led to the man's death, Bod is able to outwit the Indigo Man by not giving into fear, and thus survive the challenge.

Bod's next adventure and difficulty which he must overcome are the Ghouls from Ghulheim. At the onset of this chapter, a new character is introduced to Bod: Miss Lupescu. As his teacher and interim guardian while Silas is away, Miss Lupescu teaches Bod (an unwilling student, which many young readers will be able to relate to), key phrases in every language that exists, including Night-Gaunt. Night-Gaunts are the beasts which fly high above Ghulheim and terrify the Ghouls who reside there. Despite his stubbornness and highly vocalized doubt that he would ever need to use such phrases, he reluctantly learns them. It is after these lessons one day that Bod runs across a cadre of humorously named characters, and in an irrational and emotion-driven fit of feeling unloved (a mark of adolescence and part of the maturation process of all children), Bod agrees to embark on a trip with these Ghouls, who are humorously named "The Duke of Westminster," "the Honorable Archibald Fitzhugh," and "the Bishop of Bath and Wells." They are later joined by "The Emperor of China," "the 33rd President of the United States," and the "Famous Writer Victor Hugo" (Gaiman 74). The Ghouls are not, of course, these people, but rather have taken on their names after consuming them. These characters ultimately turn out to be the very ghouls of which Miss Lupescu warned him. They teach him to open and close the Ghoul-gate (which will come in handy for Bod later in the text), and it is not until this group is on their way that Bod realizes their true intentions: the trip is merely a ruse, and they are really attempting to kidnap and bring Bod to Ghulheim, where they plan on consuming him. This devouring will turn Bod into one of them, depriving him of an identity. Calling out in Night-Gaunt from the back of one of the ghouls, the very languages and lessons begrudgingly learned from Miss Lupescu turn out to be his saving grace, and he is rescued from certain death (and transformation into a ghoul).

This again serves as a lesson for Bod and the child readers, specifically on the importance of nurturing the intellect of the child. The rescue is due, in part, to his observation of his surroundings, which was learned previously in his encounter with the Indigo Man and the Sleer. Using a screw from a piece of broken coffin, he is able to break through the canvas sack the Ghouls trapped him in. Escaping from the sack enables Miss Lupescu and the Night-Gaunts to bring him to safety. For the child readers, repeating the idea of understanding one's surroundings reinforces the necessity of maintaining one's wits in serious situations. Also, while Bod is reluctant to participate in his lessons (a feeling which readers will be familiar with), the importance of learning them is demonstrated through the extreme occurrence of kidnapping and the use of this new knowledge to escape successfully.

However, it must be observed that Bod was careless and left with the ghouls willingly before he knew their true identities. At a time when he was tired of the lessons by Miss Lupescu, the seemingly uncaring attitude of his adoptive parents, and what he thought of as abandonment by Silas, all Bod wanted to do was enjoy himself and have a good time. Child readers are going to recognize this feeling inside of themselves, as it is a universal part of growing up. As such, they will be able to recognize, and internalize the importance of Bod's actions in these situations. Seemingly a merry bunch on first meeting, the Ghouls represent the psychological id, seeking pleasure at all cost (for young children, this a very familiar feeling, as they often want to do nothing but play and revel in the pleasure they receive from doing so). The Ghouls fight each other constantly, both physically and verbally, want only to eat and drink, are seemingly appreciative of each of the other ghouls, and despite their physical appearances, are strong and supposedly fearless. Tempting Bod with visions of a "city of delights, of fun and magic, where [he] will be appreciated, not ignored" and where "the food's the best in the whole world," they eventually dare him to join them on an adventure (Gaiman 77). All of this helps persuade Bod to travel with them to Ghulheim, as at the moment he irrationally desires only hedonistic, pleasurable, and exciting things. Child readers will empathize with Bod, knowing that from time to time they feel neglected as well (Bettelheim 72).

While in the midst of the trip to Ghulheim, the Ghoul's true intention of eating him comes to light and triggers Bod's understanding of his traveling companions' true identities. The fear of being on the fodder end of the food chain is especially worrisome for Bod. According to the ghouls, upon his cannibalization and transformation into a ghoul, he will become "a nameless ghoul, and would be named as they had been" (Gaiman 85). Bod is spoken to by the group of ghouls transporting him to Ghulheim:

> "Don't take on so," said the Duke of Westminster. "Why you little coot, I promise you that as soon as you're one of us, you'll not ever remember you even had a home."
> "I don't remember anything about the days before I was a ghoul," said the Famous Writer Victor Hugo.
> "Nor I," said the Emperor of China, proudly.
> "Nope," said the 33rd President of the United States [Gaiman 86].

This erasure of Bod's past and surrogate home is the complete antithesis of what he is searching for: an identity. Should he become one of the ghouls, he would have no chance at discovering himself and his purpose. As the other Ghouls, his physical self and identity would be stolen and transformed, his emotional self would be completely erased, and what was left of "him" would ultimately steal the name and "identity" of another. He learned something from his prior experiences, from facing the Indigo Man, to learning his alphabet from grave rubbings, and speaking multiple languages from Miss Lupescu. All this would be for naught if he were eaten. Bod's fear is transmitted to the reader, who is following Gaiman's tale as they too search for their own identity. Children are oftentimes desirous of joining a group which promises acceptance and identification as part of a whole, yet are not able to understand that doing so obscures their personal identity; as individuals they become consumed.

The threat of becoming consumed, of personal nonexistence, or existence simply as part of somebody else, is both deeply seeded in society and found in the classic fairy tales, particularly the tale of "Little Red Riding Hood." The narrative of "Little Red Riding Hood" is plagued with the threat of consumption by the Wolf. Upon Red Riding Hood's arrival at her grandmother's house in the woods, this fear is actualized and must be faced. Cannibalism has a long history in fairy tales, being a cultural taboo for centuries. According to Carolyn Daniel,

Stories about monsters who threaten to consume, whether they are wolves, witches, sharks, or aliens, continue to be the mainstay of much grotesque-horror fiction aimed at both children and adults. Monsters such as these act outside cultural and social prohibitions and represent the antithesis of civilized humanity [139].

The Wolf has already committed an act of cannibalism and acted "outside cultural and social prohibitions" (Daniel 139): "jumping without a word on the bed, he gobbled up the poor old lady" in order to trick Little Red Riding Hood in hopes of consuming her as well (Grimm's 103). As the Ghouls are personified with the names of famous people, here the Wolf is personified as well, having laid in her bed, donned the grandmothers clothing, and "tied on her cap." As Little Red Riding Hood gazes upon the figure in the bed, she makes proclamations regarding the lupine features: "What great ears you have! … And what great eyes you have! And what great hands you have! … But, Grandmother, what great teeth you have!" (104). Each of these exclamations received a verbal reply by the Wolf, and the fourth was accompanied by the Wolf springing "out of bed, and [swallowing] up poor Little Red Riding Hood," fulfilling the fear of cannibalism (104). The series of events following the consumption of Little Red Riding Hood and her Grandmother, and the subsequent killing of the Wolf, demonstrate the persistence of this fear and its continued taboo nature.

In reality, wolves do not wear clothing, lie in beds, nor speak the language of human beings. For these reasons it might be argued that the acts of the Wolf eating Little Red Riding Hood and the Ghouls consuming Bod are not truly cannibalism, as the Wolf belongs to the world of the animals, the Ghouls to the world of the Undead, and Little Red Riding Hood and Bod belong to the separate world of Mankind. However, what must be taken into account is that, in fairy tales, "the human and animal worlds are equal and mutually dependent. The violence, the suffering, and beauty are shared" (Bernheimer xix). This fear of participation in cannibalism, either being eaten or being the eater, "in terms of Western philosophy, means to literally dehumanize one's self," to shed oneself of humanity and cross into the animal or undead worlds (Daniel 162). Each separate world relies upon the other for existence; to deny this dependability is to rend the fabric of the tales, removing from them the ability to evenly execute Bettelheim's psychic triangle, which states the need for the equal growth and maturation of a persons imagination, intellect, and emotions. This collapsed boundary and the relationships forged in fairy tales between the human and animal and undead worlds is vital to uphold the triangle. Maintaining the crossing between human and animal, dead and undead, enables readers to utilize all areas of their psyche, as the intellectual side is utilized through the hero interacting with other human characters and overcoming obstacles, the imagination through a heroines relationship with talking and personified animals, and emotion through confronting death or the undead. Cannibalism in fairy tales intertwines all areas of this, as readers will internalize a hero's use of intellect, imagination, and emotion in the challenge of avoiding being eaten. Be it personified Ghouls or Big Bad Wolves, children can place their fears of lacking an identity into the fairy tales, enabling themselves to face life around them as a maturing person.

It is vital that Bod continue to experience these challenges. While he does so, the child reader learns that reasoning must be based upon the use of all three elements of the psyche: he needs a proper balance of imagination, emotion, and intellect. This combination of psychical elements is first truly demonstrated when Bod makes the conscious decision to do a good deed for a friend. When Bod is about eight years old, he, for the first time, meets a member of the unconsecrated grounds bordering the graveyard proper. Elizabeth (Liza) Hempstock, a witch-girl burned at the stake and buried without a headstone to mark her resting place, tells her story to Bod. Taking it upon himself to purchase Liza a headstone, Bod leaves the safety for the Graveyard in an attempts to sell a brooch found in the Sleer's cave at a local pawn shop to raise the money needed. This is his second encounter with the Sleer, and Bod yet again is reminded of the Sleer's wish for its Master's return. Bod's adventure to the pawn shop is his first trip outside of the graveyard since his entrance as an infant. He makes use of items and articles of clothing found within the graveyard to pass himself off as a "normal" boy, and ultimately makes his way into the grasps of the treacherous Abanazer Bolger, who plots to sell Bod out to the man Jack, his family's murderer. Abanazer represents the classic fairy tale villains, who, according to Bridget McGovern, "often talk in unhelpful platitudes, dispense dubious advice, and exhibit a penchant for being utterly pigheaded at times" (*New Gaiman*). Pretending to be his friend, Abanazer goads Bod and finally convinces him to step into a back room in his shop, where he locks him away. Bod yet again finds himself trapped, helpless to escape

76

by himself. Eventually, he is aided by Liza who comes to his rescue. After she helps him finally and successfully to Fade, Bod is able to escape by ingeniously knocking the key, absently left in the locked door, out and sliding it inside of the room, using it to free himself. Yet again, Bod triumphantly escapes by utilizing his surroundings.

Bod's repeated use of his surroundings is important in the fact that it reemphasizes resourcefulness. It must be noted that Bod has never been alone, despite how he may have felt. Through each challenge, Bod is accompanied by someone who is able to help him, be it Scarlett on his first encounter with the Sleer, Miss Lupescu on the road to Ghulheim, or Liza in Abanazer's pawn shop. However, "the fairy tale suggests that merely repeating the same things with variations is not enough … a new and different achievement not relying on chance is needed" (Bettelheim 110). In "Nobody Owens' School Days," the chapter leading up to the final encounter with the Jacks of All Trades, Bod decides it is time to attend school in the real world and gets himself in trouble with the school bullies. This time, Bod makes use of his surroundings, but he has little in the means of help in getting himself out of this new trouble. This new challenge is human, with no connection to the man Jack, and as such no graveyard denizens can assist him. Realizing this, Bod uses his intellect to show the other students that they do not need to pay the bullies their lunch money. He then lures the bullies to a chapel graveyard by the school. It is only once he is there that he is able to utilize all of the abilities granted by the Freedom of the Graveyard. Employing the Fade and Fear abilities to scare the bullies trying to evoke an extreme emotional response), Bod masters, and uses, Dream Walking (the act of entering into a persons dreams to influence them in some way) to truly stop the leader of the bullies from picking on his fellow students. He also must use his sharp intellect to get himself out of the grasp of the police. This chapter of Gaiman's fairy tale demonstrates Bod's non-reliance on chance due to the full integration of his psyche. Bod uses all the lessons previously learned to aid himself in overcoming his final obstacle, gaining freedom from the Jacks of All Trades.

Once Bod has taken what he can from his experiences through the challenges placed before him, he is able to fully and psychically integrate them into himself in order to completely overcome the final obstacle: freeing himself from the danger imposed by the ever present Jack and the Jacks of All Trades. He has discovered the value of relying upon others in times of distress, as well as how to fend for himself and utilize his surroundings to his greatest advantage; he also has learned how to read, as well as mastered the gifts given to him through the Freedom of the Graveyard. Only once he has these fully under control can he be resourceful enough to defeat the man Jack and the Jacks of All Trades who are out to kill him. The repetition and structure of fairy tales demonstrate psychic integration through "a hero who encounters these various tendencies one at a time and builds them into his personality until all coalesce within him, as is necessary for gaining full independence and humanity" (Bettelheim 97). Bod has done just this. By pulling together and internalizing all of the lessons learned from the experiences and challenges he has faced, he enables himself to face the Jacks of All Trades.

In his final test, Bod exemplifies numerous fairy tale motifs, but first and foremost is the use of trickery to escape dire circumstances. When children read or are read fairy tales, they take delight in the trickery used to defeat adult characters, most especially the evil ones. Adults do not "want to accept how easy they [children] think it is to fool us, or to make fools of us, and how delighted they are by this idea" (Bettelheim 27). Looking to the classic fairy tale "Hansel and Grethel," the children are ultimately able to free themselves from the evil witch's clutches by tricking, and subsequently pushing her, into the very oven which she had prepared to cook them in (62). Bod excels in this trickery, and uses it to manipulate the Jacks of All Trades out of his way as he attempts to defeat the man Jack. Ironically, it is the man Jack who teaches the use of trickery to Bod by using it first on him and Scarlett; disguising himself as one "Mr. Jay Frost," the man Jack moves into Bod's old home, where he ultimately lures the two young people in an attempt to kill Bod. Jay Frost's moving into Bod's old home is another classic fairy tale motif, where the rightful home of the main character is, temporarily, usurped by the evil doer (Bettelheim 9). While Bod's surrogate home has become the Graveyard, he is still the rightful resident of the house in the world of the living. This is the one part of Bod's life, and as such, identity, that he has ever known. Even though Bod was only there a short time, it is where he spent the beginning of his life, and the house is a part of his identity. The house becomes a microcosm for the entirety of Bod's story: he is attacked by, and escapes, the man Jack both inside the house and outside of it. It serves as both protection and as threat. The house represents "a variety of relationships between ... itself and the characters of the novel…. It can threaten, resist, love, or confine, but in all these actions, it stands as a total environment in one-on-one relation" with Bod; the house "becomes the entire world" of possibilities for him (Holland and Sherman 283). He is innately familiar with the attic where his nursery was and the stairs he once slid down, and as such, Bod is finds himself able to utilize his connection with the house to evade the man Jack's clutches once again, escaping and preventing the man Jack away from tainting this surviving element of his identity. Classically, fairy tale usurpers are unable to control a residence taken by force or trickery for an extended amount of time. Similar to Bod, in *Snow White,* Snow White is driven from the castle she rightfully belongs in by her evil stepmother, and is able to regain her rightful position with her mother's ultimate defeat. While Bod does not retake control of his house, this serves to demonstrate that in fairy tales, the place in which a protagonist lives becomes a part of them, once which is not conquerable by any usurper or villain. By retracing the very steps he took as an infant, Bod retreats from attic room, runs down the stairs he once toddled, and once again makes his way to the safety of the graveyard, where he has been forming his identity ever since the murder of his original family.

Once they escape to the safety of the graveyard, where Bod is most truly at home, he must rectify his family's murder by defeating the Jacks of All Trades, and doing so systematically. None of the Jacks of All Trades are directly killed by Bod, but the reader is left to assume this is what happens to them. Bod tricks the Jack called Ketch into falling into a deep grave (where Silas later goes to find him) (Gaiman 272), and using knowledge learned from the Ghouls who threatened him with being consumed, he reopened the Ghoul-Gate, ridding himself of Jack Tar, Jack Nimble, and Jack Dandy by sending them tumbling towards Ghulheim (273). Harkening back to Coats' mention of the humor involved in Gaiman's writing, these tricks, while conveniently devastating for the Jacks of All Trades, leave a smile upon the reader's face, particularly the image of Mr. Nimble's (whose own name is a bastardization of the nursery rhyme character Jack B. Nimble) unfortunate leap over the ghoul gate, being halted at its zenith, as if he had hit a wall, and subsequently being sucked down the passage towards Ghulheim.

With four Jacks of All Trades dispatched and out of the way, Bod travels deep into the hill, back to the home of the Sleer where he knows the man Jack awaits him. This final encounter with the man Jack utilizes everything that Bod has learned about himself and his surroundings. On Bod's fourth journey to the Sleer's cavern (the stealing and return of the brooch can be counted as one complete encounter), he is now reminded for the third time that the Sleer desires a master. The fact that Bod has had three previous complete interactions with the Sleer falls directly in line with a traditional fairy tale structure: the repetition of an act three times, followed by an alternative (fourth) variation (von Franz 64–65). In the case of the Sleer's cavern, Bod's first visitation was with Scarlett, his second encounter was to steal/return the brooch, the third was to seek out the Sleer's advice, and the fourth was to attempt to defeat the man Jack. During the first two encounters, the Sleer bemoans its desire for its Master's return. During the third visit Bod asks the Sleer for advice on how to proceed with the man Jack, being told to "FIND YOUR NAME" (Gaiman 322), which reaffirms in Bod his search for his identity. The fourth visit is where everything changes. Marie Louise von Franz explains this classic sequence: "in fairy tales, there are often three steps and then a finale…. Wherever you look you will see that this is a typical rhythm in fairy tales. There are three similar rhythms and then a final action" (64). This cycle can be seen in classic fairy tales such as "Cinderella," "The Three Spinsters," and "The Three Feathers." Bod's fourth trip into the Sleer's cave unfolds as follows: the Sleer makes known, for the third time, its desire for a master. It is also at this moment that Bod vocalizes the internalization of his identity, announcing to the man Jack, "I know my name[…]. I am Nobody Owens. That's who I am." By stating this out loud, claiming his identity as "Nobody Owens" validates all of the learning, peril, and challenges Bod has passed through over the course of the story. In a final act, Bod appeals to the man Jack's vanity and hubris, offering him the "opportunity" to become the Master of the Sleer. The man Jack, desiring the power to finally do away with Bod, agrees to be the Sleer's master, and with encouragement from Bod, the Sleer promptly sucks the man Jack through the wall where it can protect him forever. At the moment when Bod actualizes himself and truly become Nobody Owens, the man Jack fatally fulfills both his wish for power as well as the Sleer's wish for a Master, which in turn marks losing his identity. Bod's identity is solidified, and the man Jack's is literally dissolved. Falling in line with von Franz' theory, this is completely different outcome than the previous visitations completed by Bod. Glibly put, von Franz argues:

The three are always clear units: 1, 2, 3, with a certain similar repetition, which is why the fourth is so often ignored, for the fourth is not just an additional number unit; it is not another thing of the same kind, but something completely different. It is as if one counted, one, two, three—Bang! [65].

Here, the "Bang!" is the Sleer finally getting its master. Whereas Bod's previous encounters with the Sleer left the creature master-less, the Sleer's wish and desire is finally fulfilled. Having someone to protect, the Sleer takes advantage of the man Jack's impromptu claim as Master and immediately absorbs him into the cavern walls.

Bod's search for and the actualization of an identity necessitated many challenges, pitfalls, and dangers. While there was the constant opportunity for Bod to simply identify himself as the Sleer's master, he realized the need to be nobody before he could become Nobody. This can be seen in parallel for man Jack's wish for complete power. Wishes in fairy tales are common place, occurring in many tales, and are made by adults and children alike. However, the result of wishes made by adults and children vary greatly. The man Jack, never before having been in the Sleer's cave, had no idea of the Sleer's power and ultimate goal, whereas Bod had previous experience in the cave and the Sleer. Bod's experience provides him with an awareness of the dangers associated with the Sleer. Lacking this experience, the man Jack irrationally proclaims his wishes to be the Sleer's master: "Of course. It's been waiting for me. And yes. Obviously, I am its new master" (Gaiman 283). This claim to the false identity as the Sleer's master is fulfilled, being disastrous for him and freeing for Bod. Bettelheim states that "it is as if the fairy tale … expects only adults to have sufficient self-control not to let themselves get carried away, since their… wishes come true" (72). Bod had very viable reasons for desiring the strength and protection of the Sleer, but he opted to not irrationally take advantage of this opportunity. Relying upon his strong intellect, emotions, and imagination, Bod laid claim to an identity that was years in the making through trial and error. He found within himself "a single and stable personal identity," one of which he had control over making and to which, via the use of his passport, he could assert and "present to the world and to others" (Zipes and McCallum 68). Nobody but Bod, the story demonstrates, could become Nobody Owens.

Works Cited

Bettelheim, Bruno. *The Uses of Enchantment: The Meaning and Importance of Fairy Tales.* New York: Vintage, 1989. Print.

Bernheimer, Kate. Introduction. *My Mother She Killed Me, My Father He Ate Me.* Ed. Kate Bernheimer with Carmen Jimenez Smith. New York: Penguin, 2010. Print.

Coats, Karen. "Between Horror, Humour, and Hope: Neil Gaiman and the Psychic Work of the Gothic." *The Gothic in Children's Literature: Haunting the Borders.* Ed. Anna Jackson, Karen Coats, and Roderick McGillis. New York: Routledge, 2008. 77–92. Print.

Daniel, Carolyn. *Voracious Children: Who Eats Whom in Children's Literature.* New York: Routledge, 2006. Print.

Gaiman, Neil. *The Graveyard Book.* New York: HarperCollins, 2008. Print.

"Hansel and Grethel." *Grimm's Fairy Tales.* Ed. Elizabeth Dalton. New York: Barnes and Noble Classics, 2003. 56–63. Print.

Holland, Norman N., and Leona F. Sherman. "Gothic Possibilities." *New Literary History* 8.2 (1977): 279–294. *Jstor.* Web. 13 Apr. 2013.

"Little Red Riding Hood." *Grimm's Fairy Tales.* Ed. Elizabeth Dalton. New York: Barnes and Noble Classics, 2003. 101–104. Print.

McGovern, Bridget. "New Gaiman: *The Graveyard Book.*" Torwww. Tor Publishing. 7 Oct. 2009. Web. 24 Feb. 2010.

Nilsen, Don. "The Graveyard Book." *The Journal of Adolescent & Adult Literacy* 53.1 (2009): 79–80. Print.

Perrault, Charles. "The Sleeping Beauty in the Wood." *Perrault's Fairy Tales.* New York: Dover, 1969. 3–21. Print.

von Franz, Marie Louise. *Interpretation of Fairytales.* Dallas: Spring, 1982. Print.

Zipes, Jack. *The Irresistible Fairy Tale: The Cultural and Social History of a Genre.* Princeton: Princeton University Press, 2012. 1 October 2013.

_____, and Robyn McCallum. *Ideologies of Identity in Adolescent Fiction: The Dialogic Construction of Subjectivity.* New York: Routledge, 1999. Print.

"She would not think of it"

Surviving Incest in
Robin McKinley's Deerskin

Sarah R. Wakefield

The specter of father-daughter incest lurks in collections by the most famous European fairy-tale writers: Giovanni Francesco Straparola, Giambattista Basile, the Brothers Grimm, and even Charles Perrault. Perrault published "Peau d'Âne," or "Donkey Skin," at the end of the seventeenth century. His story features a beautiful queen whose dying request is that her husband's second wife be her superior. The narrator assures the readers, "Her confidence in her own matchless gifts made her regard such an undertaking deftly obtained by a kind of ambush, as a solemn oath never to remarry" (Lawrence 103). Her plan backfires horribly when the king chooses his daughter to be his next bride. Blessed with pluck and a fairy godmother, the princess demands three fantastic gowns—the color of the sky, the moon, and the sun—and finally the hide of her father's magical donkey, the source of all his wealth, to discourage his advances. The impassioned king agrees to every request, and, left with no other choice, his daughter disguises herself in the filthy donkey skin and flees to a neighboring farm, where she cleans the pigsty.

A prince likes to visit the exotic animals on the estate, and one Sunday he peeks through the keyhole of the heroine's bedchamber, where she stands, resplendent in her dress more brilliant than the sun. Now dying of love, the king's son demands a cake made by Donkeyskin, and while she is baking, her emerald ring falls into the batter (the narrator suggests "she dropped it in on purpose"). Declaring he will marry only she whose finger fits the tiny ring, the prince finds his beloved, who emerges in radiant beauty from the grimy donkey hide. The couple weds in the presence of the princess's proud father, who "had banished all criminal desires, and the small trace of that odious flame which remained, merely strengthened his paternal love" (112). Fast-forward to 1993, when fantasy writer Robin McKinley published her young-adult novel *Deerskin*. Rather than avoid or excuse the incestuous plot of Perrault's tale, *Deerskin* explores what happens when an unwilling daughter gets swept up in her parents' Oedipal drama and is raped and almost killed. It eloquently explores the aftermath of childhood neglect and incest, from post-traumatic stress to acceptance, but happy-ever-after remains elusive. Princess Lissla Lissar learns to nurture herself and others, survives three battles with monsters, falls in love, faces her father, and goes through two rebirths, yet all she can promise her prince is to *try* to stay with him. The psychological scars never go away, but for Lissar, "she was winning; she was here and she was not mad, and she remembered" (225).

Memories of incest are a loaded issue in psychoanalysis. In 1896, Sigmund Freud published three papers discussing early childhood sexual abuse that his patients repressed, creating neuroses, but just one year later he abandoned what is now called "seduction theory." Instead he argued that his female clients, driven by Oedipal fantasies, invented their sexual stories. As he wrote in a letter to colleague Wilhelm Fliess, "it was hardly credible that perverted acts against children were so general" (qtd. in Diamond 423). Freudian scholar Bruno Bettelheim embraces the Oedipal complex in his classic fairy-tale study *The Uses of Enchantment*. He argues repeatedly, "A child not only dreams about marrying his parent of the other sex, but actively spins fantasies around it ... what the child needs most is to be presented with symbolic images which reassure him that there is a happy solution to his oedipal problems" (39). So what to do with "Donkey Skin"? The princess *wants* to marry her father, Bettelheim writes, but feels guilty about her desire because "deep down a child who knows that she does want her father to prefer her to her mother feels she deserves to be punished for it—thus her flight or banishment, and degradation" (246). To extend his logic, *Deerskin* shows the negative consequences of Oedipal fantasies realized: brutal rape, so the daughter can deny any responsibility, and premature (and psychologically damaging) entry into sexual maturity.

For young female readers who have suffered incest, the idea that they unconsciously "asked for" the rape is repugnant. Several decades after Freud's death, psychiatrists shared what they saw in their practices regarding women actually molested in childhood. For example, a 1986 survey of 930 women found that 16 percent endured sexual abuse by male family members (Diamond 426). Incest is a frightening reality for too many girls, and novels like *Deerskin* refute the Oedipal complex and acknowledge the devastating, life-changing effects of a father's sexual attention. Perhaps more important for the average teenage reader, Princess Lissla Lissar's story shows that recovery, while slow and stumbling, is possible for trauma survivors.

Psychoanalysis does not offer the only explanations for avoidance of intrafamily sexual relations. In *The Elementary Structures of Kinship*, Claude Levi-Strauss concludes, "The prohibition of incest is in origin neither purely cultural nor purely natural, nor is it a composite mixture of elements from both nature and culture. It is the fundamental step because of which, by which, but above all in which, the transition from nature to culture is accomplished" (24) and, further, "the incest prohibition expresses the transition from the natural fact of consanguinity to the cultural fact of alliance" (30). In a patriarchal society, a father needs to marry his daughter to another man, preferably from another clan or tribe, in order to create alliances.

Yet some men are reluctant to part with their daughters, no matter how grand the alliance. In *Deerskin*, Princess Lissla Lissar hears one such fairy tale repeatedly in childhood. It is the kind of story that Bruno Bettelheim says helps a *little boy* deal with his unconscious Oedipal issues, the rescue of an imprisoned maiden by a clever hero, and it tells how the heroine's parents were married. Six powerful kings, as well as the crown prince of the wealthiest kingdom nearby, want the heroine's mother for their wife. But no one wins the prize easily, Lissar's nursemaid tells her, "for such a joy was the daily presence of your lovely mother that her father was not eager to part with her. And so he looked to drive her suitors away, or to lose them on topless mountains and in bottomless valleys or upon endless seas" (4). Setting tasks for suitors occurs frequently in world folklore. To win Michal's hand in the Bible, David must bring King Saul the foreskins of 200 Philistines; in the *Odyssey* Penelope puts off her hundred wooers by demanding that they use her missing husband's bow to shoot an arrow through twelve axes.

Deerskin sets its prince the impossible task of fetching "a leaf plucked and unfallen from the tree of joy, which grows in the farthest eastern edge of the world, and an apple plucked and unfallen from the tree of sorrow, that grows at the farthest western end of the world" (4–5). Confident in the quest's impossibility and pleased by his daughter's refusal to choose a husband until the prince returns, the old king believes that he will keep her forever. Indeed, "so terribly did he want to keep her" (6) that we wonder if this fierce love crosses the line into incest, foreshadowing the cycle of abuse that continues in the next generation. The prince comes back a year later but tosses the precious apple and leaf into the fireplace. Rather than set an additional task, as he threatened, the old king relents and dies just eight months after the wedding.

Free of her possessive father, the nameless, beautiful queen entrances everyone. All praise her modesty: "the queen spoke little, but few words of her were necessary, for the wonder of her presence was enough" (8). She sees herself so completely as an attractive body that when illness steals a shadow of her charms, she wears a veil and gloves, even in the presence of her husband, who grovels at her bedside like a distraught toddler; indeed, he sits with "his knees drawn up like a little boy's who is being scolded" (21). If anyone suffers from unresolved Oedipal issues in *Deerskin*, it is the king. He screams and raves when she requests a final portrait of herself in her former glory, to be hung above her husband's throne for all visitors to see, and wills herself to die. The queen makes the fairy-tale request that her successor be as lovely as she, and "there was a strange tone in the queen's voice; were it not so sad an occasion and were she not so weak, it might have been thought that the tone was of triumph" (20). Minutes later, she is dead. It appears that McKinley's queen, like Perrault's, believes herself so exceptional that her widower never can remarry.

Everyone, especially the childish king, is so distraught that no one thinks to tell the princess of her mother's passing. No one thinks of Lissar at all, really, and at age fifteen (her recent birthday forgotten by all), she lives in the nursery, four flights of stairs up from the rest of the palace. Her situation contrasts sharply with the many "Donkey Skin" variants, where "in all stories the heroine at first enjoyed love and high esteem" (Bettelheim 247). Even worse is how the kingdom rationalizes its disregard for the heir:

> The king and queen had absorbed all their people's attention for as long as they had been king and queen; there had never been anything left for the princess. That there might be something odd about this, even wrong, occurred to no one; their king, their queen, were too glorious, too luminous,

too superb, for there to be anything wrong with them. That they forgot their child themselves, and distracted their people into forgetting her also, was merely a natural result of their perfections [23].

Notice how the subjects excuse and glorify their monarchs, a dark presentiment of their reaction should their "perfect" king propose to his daughter. For her part, Lissar does not grieve her loss. Far from the "good mother" of classic fairy tales, who dies a benevolent saint, this Queen is a vicious-tempered, inattentive parent.

Lissar would go on, unremembered, if Prince Ossin, heir in a neighboring kingdom, did not send a fleethound puppy to console her. The princess barely remembers how to get to the palace's receiving-hall, a sign of how little she goes there. Then "she went up to the dais and curtseyed to the floor, to her father; and looked up, and met his eyes. The blankness there parted for a moment and she saw—she did not know what she saw, but it made her cold all over, suddenly, so cold that the sweat of terror broke out on her body" (27–28). With his beloved mother-wife dead for only a few weeks, the king turns lustful eyes on the daughter who can remember no time he looked at her before. For the next two years, she avoids him, haunted by nightmares in which the king simply gazes on her.

For emotional satisfaction, the princess dotes on her new fleethound, Ash, who stays constantly by her side as a physical and psychological guard. Ash is well named, since Yggdrasil, the World Tree of Norse mythology, typically is represented as a massive ash tree, and the dog binds together the heroine's universe completely. Happily covered in fur, Lissar goes everywhere with her elegant hound, like a mother who can't be parted from her child (a far cry from her own relationship with the queen). By devoting herself to the dog, the princess also starts to act for herself, choosing her own living quarters and pastimes. Boys hold no interest, however, except as a way out: "She did not look forward to her inevitable marriage, but she thought of it in terms of being sent away from her father, and this she found hopeful" (47). Unlike the king, who harbors lingering Oedipal feelings for his mother, the princess welcomes any love-object who is *not* her father. Lissar meets some potential husbands at dinners, where "her brevity of speech, in a princess of such tender years, was accounted modesty, and applauded" (40). People also applauded Lissar's mother as modest for her few words. Again we wonder about the queen. Did she welcome suitors to escape an incestuous father and choose the handsomest, or, even worse, unconsciously gravitate towards one who resembled her abuser?

As Lissar blossoms beyond adolescent awkwardness, the kingdom throws a ball in honor of the princess's seventeenth birthday, and she knows very well that "she was now old enough to be auctioned off in marriage to the alliance best for her country" (47), just as Levi-Strauss would predict for a patriarchal culture. She enters her birthday ball flinching at the touch of the king's hand and likely unaware his blue velvet suit is her dead mother's favorite color. Then "she looked briefly into his face and saw there the look she had spent the last two years eluding; the look she found treacherous but with no word for the treachery. She had the sudden thought that these last two years of her life had been pointless, that she had learned nothing that was of any use to her, if she still could not escape that look in her father's eyes" (53). Everyone whispers in admiration about Lissar's beauty, so like her mother's, but the eyes in the dead queen's portrait are merciless, for they "knew the truth, and hated it" (55), both the truth of her surpassed attractions and her widower's intentions.

Here the princess stands, an attentive father on her arm and a furious mother looking down in disapproval: the young girl's Oedipal drama realized. But by bringing the queen back into the fairy tale, McKinley reminds readers that the true struggle lies between the parents—between a mother-wife determined to be peerless and a child-husband desperate to satisfy both her demands and his desires. Lissar clearly is an unwilling pawn in these Freudian games. Even at the Cinderella-hour of midnight she is trapped by the king, who sees his mother / wife / child as a possession to *keep*, not to trade in alliance. "She is my daughter, and I can do with her as I please" (57), the king informs his uncomfortable ministers. Still in denial, Lissar finally escapes her party and thinks, "How could she have hated her seventeenth-birthday ball? No reason, no reason. No reason to hate and fear her father. No reason" (65).

The next morning, the king summons the entire court, including Lissar, for a special proclamation. His manic glee disturbs the assembled nobility, and even *before* his announcement, they recast their withdrawn princess as a flirtatious Electra, living proof of Freud's theories about little girls. There is no other way for them to explain their perfect king's behavior:

Every girl wants her father to herself. Look at her now, pretending to be so bashful, so shy that she cannot open her eyes, as if she did not like being the center of attention. Look at her, half-swooning, making sure by her weakness that her father will stand close, will hold her, protect her, not take his eyes off her. She probably has a hundred little petting, luring ways with him when they're alone together [69].

The princess is terrified, not shy, and she and the king never are alone together, since Lissar wants her father nowhere near her. She faints when she hears her father means to marry her, while the court blames the victim even more, asking, "What has she done to him, this witch-daughter, that he should desire to devastate his country and his people this way?" (73) and saying, "How evil the girl must be" (74). No one stops to think that the proposal results from the obsessive absorption of the royal couple; the king remains so tied to the dead queen for an identity that marrying her double is irresistible. Except for Lissar herself, not a soul steps forward to object to the incestuous alliance. She dully contemplates suicide or escape, but shock sets in and her mind starts to disintegrate. Unlike in "Donkey Skin," this heroine has not yet met a fairy godmother to help her invent reasons to delay the wedding.

And the king cannot wait to satisfy his lust. "The king symbolizes a person completely dominated by his id because his ego, due to severe disappointments in life, has lost its strength to keep his id in bounds" (88), writes Bettelheim about the murderous King Shahryar of *Thousand and One Nights*, in words that apply perfectly to McKinley's monarch. His first queen defied him by refusing to live; therefore, he decides to satisfy every desire, and, we might conjecture, to make sure no woman / mother ever leaves him again. He comes to his daughter's bedroom late that night and the next, pounding in frustration on the locked door, while Lissar wanders in and out of awareness. On the third night, he enters through the adjacent garden, flings Ash against a window, and brutally beats his screaming daughter until she is close to death. When her voice finally fails, "her father was satisfied, and he ripped off the remaining rags of her shift, and did what he had come to do" (83), leaving the princess in a bloody heap. Later, we learn that he "raped his daughter once, twice, three times, for the nights that she had locked her door against him, for he was her father and the king, and his will was law" (296). *Deerskin* clearly shows that Lissar did nothing to cause the assault, which has nothing to do with love. Rape involves power and control, something a young female reader needs to understand.

The novel holds nothing back regarding the aftermath of incest. Suffering from a severe concussion, bruises from head to toe, and fractures to her ribs, pelvis, and left arm, Lissar dissociates into a fugue state. As two psychologists note about incest victims, "Although a child can manage considerable denial of the parents' badness or failures, she cannot avoid the information gained through the violation of her body … the child knows it is the parent who is the agent of violation" (Grand and Alpert 333). Avoidance requires extreme psychiatric responses, sadly common in cases of familial rape, as the earliest non–Freudian researchers discovered. A benchmark 1980 literature review of 33 different psychiatric studies identified incest as a consistent cause for dissociative identity disorder (Rosenbaum and Weaver), while the 1986 study still considered foundational revealed that 83 percent of 100 patients with multiple personality disorder had a history of sexual abuse, and among the women in the sample, 68 percent were victims of incest (Putnam et al.). Even Bruno Bettelheim acknowledges that in myth "oedipal difficulties are acted out and in consequence all ends in total destruction, whether the relations are positive or negative" (198). There should be little hope for Princess Lissla Lissar.

But Lissar has Ash to anchor her in the world. Drawn back from death by the frantic licking of her pet, "Lissar knew they dared not stay where they were. They dared not because … no, they simply dared not. She need not remember why; the instant choking crush of panic told her as much as she needed to know" (89). Unable and unwilling to recall what has happened, the princess dresses, takes her dog, and begins to walk, in and out of consciousness, until finally the pair finds a deserted mountain cabin. She thinks she is an herbalist's apprentice, thanks to dim memories about gardening. She learns to butcher and cook the game that Ash brings home. In fact, Lissar relearns everything: focusing both eyes on a single object, eating, drinking, walking, and finally bathing. For a rape victim, "a new, more complete reinhabiting of the bruised and humiliated body she feared and tried to ignore" (107) can be traumatic, and the heroine almost blacks out when her arm brushes against her breast. But she steadies herself, and the descriptions of her determination are worth quoting:

Slowly, slowly, slowly, she made her other hand approach her body and ... touch it, touch her own body, stroke her own skin, as if it were some wild beast she hoped to tame, or some once-domesticated beast whom she could no longer trust.... I have less charity for you, my own poor flesh, than I do for Ash.... This is my body. I reclaim my own body for myself: for my use, for my understanding, for my kindness and care [106].

Today, a clinician might diagnose Lissla Lissar with post-traumatic stress disorder. According to criteria proposed for the newest revision of the Diagnostic and Statistical Manual of Mental Disorders (DSM-5), PTSD includes four diagnostic clusters with a total of 20 symptoms. The disorder starts with a stressor, threatened death or real injury—the heroine's incest certainly qualifies. Afterwards, the person experiences long-term intrusive memories, dreams, or flashbacks of the event, if she remembers it at all, and shuns anything that might trigger recollections ("effortful avoidance"). The PTSD sufferer struggles to feel a range of emotions, lives on high alert, and cannot see a future for herself, symptoms that prevent the individual from functioning day to day (Miller et al.). Lissar wakes screaming from nightmares and embraces avoidance, saying to herself whenever something causes her to panic, "No, she would not think about it" (89) or "No, she would not think of it" (90). She is unaware of *why* these flashes of memory hold such terror, but several months later, denial fails to protect her from the past.

Lissar starts to worry about her bloated stomach. This new awareness of her body allows memories to smash through, including a vivid flashback to her rape. As if the incest were not harrowing enough, she is five months pregnant with her father's child, the final Oedipal triumph in the unconscious of a little girl but nothing short of horror for a seventeen-year-old. Lissar goes into premature labor, and in her confusion and pain, the princess hallucinates a vision of her parents, although she does not recognize them. A man who laughs at her fear and shows her "the long curling fiery tongue of a dragon" is her father, while a laughing woman made of fire, with fingernails tipped by phallic flaming serpents hissing, *"At last"* (117) represents her mother. That her father should become a dragon fits with Jungian analysis, wherein the beast symbolizes ego-destroying regression in the unconscious (Jung 120). Typically a male hero defeats the dragon, rescues the beautiful maiden and achieves a balanced persona. Lissar has been healing, but here is a turning point. She must triumph over the dragon to rescue herself. Help will not come from the dead queen, who colludes with the dragon-man and whose fingers encircle the daughter in flames; once trapped by those arms, Lissar feels her father touch her shoulder.

Expecting death, Lissar meets, at last, a revised fairy godmother, an earth goddess the locals call the Moonwoman. The Lady greets her as a daughter, as well she should, since her own legend casts her as a raped princess. The Moonwoman refused to marry, and when one young man assaulted her, her father, blaming the victim, "told her that she deserved no better for rejecting her suitors and running away from her responsibilities" (213). The princess removed herself from all kinship systems that depend on daughter-trading for alliance and fled with her favorite fleethound to the moon, from which she descends occasionally to help children. Lissar survives an even worse version of the Lady's tale, but the goddess does not (or cannot) intervene directly until this desperate moment. The Moonwoman offers Lissar time to heal and gently pushes all of the girl's painful memories deep into her unconscious. Lissar thinks of her old life as a Pandora's box: "I can close it for now, and put it away. I will draw it down later, and open it again; but the Lady has given me time and healing, time for healing. I will be strong again when I open that box; strong enough to open it" (119). After the traumatic setback of miscarrying her father's child, Lissar prepares in earnest for the long, hard work of integrating a mature personality.

She wakes to springtime and new appearances for both her and Ash. The close-cropped hound now has long curling fur. Lissar's scars, patches of numb skin, and wounded limbs are whole. While her black hair has turned pure white, her hazel eyes are the stark black of despair, and a white deerskin dress that resists all stains serves as physical and psychological armor. Deerskin could not be a more fitting material; in Greco-Roman mythology, deer are sacred to Artemis / Diana, protector of young girls and virgin goddess of the moon and childbirth. Artemis also loves the hunt, which she pursues with the help of her dogs. At the same time, a white dress is a far cry from the dirty donkey skin of Perrault's fairy tale or similar stories of threatened incest. D.L. Ashliman notes about such a heroine, "She typically alters her appearance by smearing her face with soot, and attempts to hide herself from the outside world by enveloping herself in a grotesque cloak. Her self-imposed unattractive appearance is a central symbol in most tales." Bettina Knapp agrees that the donkey skin represents "a deep-seated need on her part to descend to the lowliest of social echelons by wearing such an offensive garb" (74). That princess, shamed by the king's sexual advances, punishes herself. By contrast, McKinley's heroine, actually victimized by her father, takes on a virginal appearance guaranteed to inspire curiosity and awe, since she now resembles the Moonwoman. Lissar enters a kingdom where belief in the goddess is widespread, so "other people seemed to leave a little space around her" (165), and most address her as "lady," despite her bare feet. Rather than being noticed for her physical resemblance to her mother, Lissar experiences admiration based on what people think she (or the Lady) can *do*: rescue the innocent. And, although she is not conscious of its significance, the heroine's Moonwoman disguise reveals her true identity as a rape survivor.

After a two months' journey through the mountains, she arrives at the yellow city, home to Cofta, King Goldhouse the Seventeenth, coincidentally the only man with enough sense to drop his suit for the hand of Lissar's mother. His heir, Prince Ossin, sent Ash to the princess, and fittingly, the only person who thought of Lissla Lissar upon the queen's death now gives her work. She ends up caring for newborn fleethound puppies, an "impossible" task that brings purpose to her wandering and also echoes the dirty work given to Donkey Skin. "They'll be sick at both ends" (167), Ossin warns, and he is right, for Lissar spends sleepless weeks sitting in the kennel straw, covered in milk, vomit, diarrhea, and squirming puppies. Yet in her determination that all six orphans live (in contrast to her own stillborn baby), Lissar, calling herself Deerskin, becomes what she never had, a fiercely protective mother, assisted by an equally concerned father in Ossin, who spends every other night with the litter. She experiences a nurturing family unit with two parents mutually absorbed in rearing their dog-children, a much-needed corrective to the neglect of her own early years.

Once Lissar masters the nursing of helpless hounds and grows to love something other than Ash, she must learn a new skill: the Moonwoman's knack for finding what is lost. A frantic mother, convinced that the princess *is* the goddess, begs her to locate her missing son, Aric. In the search Lissar faces the second physical fight of her new existence. The first one wasn't much—back in the mountains she encountered a dragon about the size of her fleethound. With memories of her past locked away, Lissar fails to see the connection between the terrifying dragon-king of her hallucination and the very real beast pursuing her.

At this early stage in her recovery, she launches a small physical assault from the safety of the tree she has climbed. Her single stone strikes this dragon in the eye, distracting it long enough for Lissar and her dog to escape. (She also misses the symbolism of blinding a creature that represents the father whose eyes she sought to avoid.) Later, when she mentions the episode to others, they inform her, in disbelief, that no one outruns a dragon. For the sake of her healing, Lissar needed to elude the dragon / her incestuous father.

Now, confronted by an even larger predatory animal, she hurls a stone into its eye, but it isn't enough. Lissar actually thinks to herself, "It's a pity we cannot simply leave it and run, as we did the dragon" (206), but then her puppies join the attack. Still the fierce mother prepared to defend her children as she was not protected by her own parents, she chooses fight over flight. She grabs the creature around the neck and kills it with three uncertain blows of her knife, previously used only in the nurturing activity of cutting meat for the dogs. Lissar, the incest survivor, learns to face her attackers, to defend herself and those she loves. Like the amorphous monster of the heroine's nightmares, the animal has no specific identity beyond "a creature" and "the thing." The heroine just knows it cannot win. She earns additional knowledge when she butchers the beast and bites into its heart in hopes of gaining some of its fierceness. What she gets instead is certainty about where to find Aric. For perhaps the first time ever, Lissar knows exactly where she is going and why. Valuable lessons abound in this adventure. Some mothers love their children desperately. Lost children can be found if someone searches. Fighting an assailant can lead to clarity.

Lissar is less clear about the state of her heart. Without being aware of it, she has fallen in love with Ossin, who is, in his own words, "the stodgy prince of a rather small, second-class country … rather dullish and brownish" (214). He represents her father's opposite: unattractive, unassuming, and uninterested in impressing others. Marriage is not on Deerskin's mind, but Ossin knows he must settle down and produce an heir. When the prince shows Lissar a room full of portraits of potential brides, she sees a painting of herself, as Princess, or more specifically, as a king's daughter, and she remembers everything, so paralyzed that

> any cry would drive her over the lip of the pit, the pit she had forgotten, though her feet had never left its edge, and now that she had looked, and seen again, she could not look away. There were some things that took life

94

and broke it, not merely into meaninglessness, but with active malice flung the pieces farther, into hell ... even now the memory of that act of violence would shatter her; she could not contain the memory even as her body had not been able to contain the result of its betrayal [222].

As a characterization of the lasting effects of sexual assault, the imagery is sobering. Lissar's memories (the pit) remain because she has repressed the episode, but that is a necessary step in recovery. Christine A. Courtois, perhaps the most respected expert on the treatment of incest survivors, cautions, "When the incest is worked on directly, it is only when the patient has achieved enough stability, skills, and ego strength and mastered enough healing tasks to be able to manage and tolerate the strong emotions likely to be generated without serious regression" (475).

Though she thinks bleakly, "I still cannot bear it" (224), Lissar asks Ossin about the princess she once was. In the sanitized version of her fate circulated by her kingdom's ministers, she tragically died young ... *five years earlier*. The chronology is bewildering. Lissar stayed five months in her isolated mountain hut before her miscarriage and the arrival of the Moonwoman, and she has lived in King Cofta's realm for half a year since she awoke as Deerskin. That slumber lasted far longer than she ever imagined. With mingled disbelief and awe, the princess realizes, "I lay four years on a mountaintop, till the shape of my and my dog's bodies had worn themselves into the mountain itself" (226). The Moonwoman indeed gifted her daughter with enough time to face painful memories. Lissar even feels strong enough to smile at Ossin's jokes, and the narrator offers an honest assessment of the psyche of an incest survivor:

> What happened to her the night she had fled her father's court and kingdom was a part of her, a part of her flesh and of her spirit. It was perhaps better to know than not to know—she was not yet sure—but the knowing did not make the chasm any less real, the grief any less debilitating, it only gave it a name, a definition. But the fact of definition implied that it had limits—that her life went on around it. They were only memories. She had lived. They were now only memories, and where she stood now the sun was shining [226].

These descriptions show young female readers of *Deerskin* how trauma can work. Repressing the memories creates a safe space for Princess Lissla Lissar to rebuild her life, and when she finally confronts the abuse, it does not diminish her pain so much as the truth helps her see beyond what happened. The heroine cannot just "get over" the incest—it permanently changes her. Too often, girls are urged to move on, but "telling people that they are not responsible for the abuse and that they are not damaged is not an adequate substitute for the difficult process of helping the survivor gain new self-understanding" (Haakan and Schlaps 46). McKinley's novel gives sympathetic voice to the process and the time required for an incest victim even to name her trauma.

Lissar feels strong enough to agree to attend Prince Ossin's ball, expected to be the occasion of his marriage proposal to the Princess Trivelda. Even though her own birthday dance held nothing but horror, she can separate the two balls in her mind, and she wants to support her friend. She receives four dresses from Ossin's mother, Queen Clementina, and three mimic the garments in Charles Perrault's "Donkey Skin." Lissar rejects the first, red satin the color of passion and blood, as well as the next two, a pale blue gown the color of an innocent sky and a golden one resplendent as the sun. In the fairy tale, the princess's second demand is a gown the color of the moon, and this is what McKinley's Moonwoman heroine chooses. The silver-gray dress shines with "tiny, twinkling stones, colorless, almost invisible, but radiant as soon as the light touched them" (231). Princess Lissla Lissar's seventeenth-birthday gown "was to have a vast skirt, and to be covered with so many tiny glinting stones as to be blinding to look upon" (47). Whether consciously or not, Lissar chooses a shadow version of the only ball gown she has worn.

At the grand event, Lissar draws attention as one of the most desirable partners. She dances the whole time with many gentlemen, in sharp contrast to when she was seventeen and trapped in her father's arms for hours. Yet, despite all of her psychological progress, she cannot stop memories of a blood-spattered bedroom from springing into her mind when Prince Ossin pulls her onto a moonlit terrace to propose. She flashes back, as the approach of his dark figure reminds her of the king's assault:

> There was a terrible weight against her body, blocking her vision, looming over her, blotting out the stars through the open door, and then a pain, pain pain pain pain
>
> Some things grew no less with time. Some things were absolutes. Some things could not be gotten over, gotten round, forgotten, forgiven, made peace with, released [247].

Convinced of her own unworthiness, Lissar cannot accept Prince Ossin's love, even though she returns it. She has revised most of her past traumas—showing a mother's love to puppies, finding a lost child, killing crazed things that seek to destroy her, attending a ball where she enjoys herself, loving a man—but shame prevents her from saying yes to this second offer of marriage.

Instead, Cinderella-like, she flees again, with Ash and the six fleethounds she raised. The goddess Artemis hunted with seven sisters, who were pursued by the hunter Orion and turned into the star cluster known as the Pleiades, but no one chases Lissar. Ossin, believing she does not love him, lets her be. She spends her days finding lost animals and children, and for months she ventures no farther than the villages that surround Cofta's kingdom. When the snow comes, she feels drawn back to the isolated mountain hut where the Moonwoman rescued her. Helen Pilinovsky notes that "she returns to the forest, to the cycle of healing which had previously been broken by her miscarriage." This time, Lissar tries to keep very different memories at bay: any thoughts of her prince. "Lost him. Run away from him; fled him; threw him away" (269), she reflects in her loneliness.

Something must change. The princess has a third, epic battle with the largest beast she ever has faced, a toro "as tall at the shoulder as Lissar stood; his antlers spread farther than the branches of a well-grown tree" (263). While she hesitates, hoping it will wander off, Ash charges, just as she did when the king burst into the princess's bedchamber years earlier. Once more, the hound suffers severe injury for defending Lissar. The heroine then breaks the toro's leg with a heavy stick and ruthlessly slashes its throat; any shock is pushed away by the need to nurse Ash, who seems resigned to dying of her wounds. The roles have been reversed. Bloody and beaten in her father's castle, Lissar welcomed death, but Ash's frantic licking urged her to fight. Now she pleads with her beloved fleethound to heal.

This all occurs nine months after Lissar started working in the Goldhouse kennels, long enough to give birth to a new, stronger self. Appropriately, then, the Moonwoman appears to the princess again, gently urging her to actually start living: "Your battle was from death to life no less than Ash's is now; would you deny it? But you have not accepted your own gift to yourself, your gift of your own life" (271). Although facing her trauma was a crucial step in recovery, the incest still cripples her, and her feet remain at the edge of that pit. Lissar must move toward a real future, which means relinquishing some self-protective measures. While recovering from her battle wounds, Ash loses her disguise of long, curling fur and again looks like the dog of Princess Lissla Lissar. The heroine dreams, without any terror, of a nightgown she wore as a small girl, and the tiny mountain hut where she recovered from her rape vanishes by morning. It is time to rejoin humanity.

When Lissar hears that a grand wedding is planned in King Cofta's palace, she goes numb, grieving the loss of Ossin but still drawn back to the yellow city. She starts running in earnest when she learns the happy couple is her own father and Ossin's seventeen-year-old sister, almost exactly the same age as Lissar when the king raped her. She cannot bear the thought of an innocent like Camilla being tied in any way to the king. Fittingly for a girl who grew up hearing the boy's fairy-tale quest of prince-saves-damsel, Princess Lissla Lissar plans to rescue the princess. To do this she marches into the throne room, where the marriage ceremony is in progress; confronts her abuser; and announces the incest in front of two hundred gathered dignitaries. No one stands in the princess's way, no one stops her from speaking, and no one, aside from the incestuous king's subjects, doubts her accusations. The locals recognize her as their Moonwoman, who would not lie. "Rescue us and our princess," they whisper (297), but the foreign ministers once again cast the victim as villain and blame Lissar for ruining the expected marriage. They have not changed, and neither has the king. Still mourning the daughter he believes died five years earlier, he has not repented his incestuous actions. "He had mourned her.... He missed her still" (297), but nowhere does it say he ever *loved* her.

While her father is lost in his thoughts, Lissar begins to bleed from the palms of her hands like a martyr, and the blood stains her white hair, restoring both its original mahogany shade and the truth of her assault. She tells the whole court how she carried her own father's child for five months, until it arrived, stillborn. "I often thought that I would choose to die than risk remembering what drove me to madness, for I believed the shame was mine. For you were king, and your will was law, and I was but a girl, or rather a woman, forced into my womanhood" (298), she says thoughtfully, echoing her father's patriarchal reasoning for why he raped her three times. But Lissar places the blame first on both her parents for robbing her of a childhood and then on her father for taking her virginity. She declares that she returns all of the negative, painful emotions that he visited upon her, and immediately "a burst of blood flowed from between her legs … secret female blood, heavy with mystery" (299). With her pent-up anger (and sexuality) released, she flares up in magical fire, covered in her own blood just as she was the night of her rape, and approaches her father.

In that fire, some, but not all, people see two mirror images: Lissar / Deerskin and her mother. If the queen had not made her husband promise to marry her equal in beauty, he might never have cast lustful eyes on his own daughter. So does she intend to rectify the doom unwittingly bestowed on Lissar and to assist her child in reclaiming her life? To prevent any vengeance on her true love? Or, even more menacing, to punish the woman dominating the king's thoughts for five long years? A darker motive seems more plausible, for when her figure appears, the narrator comments, "perhaps it was those who had nightmares to remember who saw the second woman: and they watched fearfully" (299). The terribly beautiful flame-woman, the queen, reaches both hands towards her daughter in an echo of Lissar's stillbirth nightmare where two fiery arms stop her flight from her father's dragon-like figure. Unable to trust this embrace, the daughter stretches forth one hand to defend herself; her other hand feels burnt "as if a rope had been thrown, awkwardly and almost too late, a homely rope" (300). The homely Prince Ossin has extended his own hand to Lissar, creating a metaphysical lifeline. Before, Ash alone anchored the princess to life, but now Ossin saves her from her mother's fire.

The dead queen, aware that her daughter's beauty outshines her own because it inspires rather than terrifies, clearly attempts to destroy the competition. Her husband's oath ought to have been unbreakable, preventing any remarriage, yet like Snow White, Lissar surpasses the woman once thought the most beautiful in seven kingdoms. Rather than pitying her traumatized child or "guiding her daughter to confront and expose her father's crime," as Diana Dominguez argues, the queen's spirit attempts to pull Lissar into fiery anger or hell itself. Even when the mirror-image vanishes, the heroine sees her mother's face *again* and momentarily stops, confused about her purpose. Only when Lissar rejects the queen completely does she remember her purpose in the throne room. At her touch, her strong father withers into a trembling old man, much like her grandfather at the sight of a prince holding an apple of sorrow and a leaf of joy, but he does not die. Typically a fairy-tale villain suffers consequences similar to those visited upon his victim. The king viciously beat and raped his daughter, but the psychological damage endured. Therefore his punishment is recognition of his own evil, the irreversible scars inflicted on Lissar's very soul: "a look of horror, of an understanding beyond the grasp of mortality, and beyond the pro-foundest guesses of the still living about the darkest pits of hell, ran fingers like claws over his face, and left a broken old man where a proud king had once stood" (301).

The flames die down, and as the last vestiges of the Moonwoman's disguise drain from the heroine's eyes, Ossin tries to touch the girl he recognizes as Princess Lissla Lissar. She runs for a third time, but not nearly so far, and the prince chases her in earnest. Ossin offers his love, with full acknowledgment of the emotional and physical scars she carries. Rather than happily accepting the proposal, Lissar gives up, with an exhausted sigh, and allows the prince to embrace her. In his arms, she says to herself that "she would stay there—for now ... she would try to stay there, for as long as the length of their lives.... But I do not know how strong I am, she said. I cannot promise" (308). This dark fairy-tale novel refuses an unrealistic happy-ever-after ending in favor of a tenuous "maybe," acknowledging the fragile nature of recovery for an incest survivor.

One 1994 book review of *Deerskin* concludes, "McKinley has captured the feelings of a brutalized child and, by placing her story in a fairy tale setting, has written a cautionary tale once removed" (Dice and Havens). In truth, readers are so deep inside Lissar's head, feeling her struggles and pain, that the emotions of the tale do not feel very removed. Such empathy is necessary, however, for an adolescent audience. Bruno Bettelheim writes that fairy tales teach preschoolers that "a struggle against severe difficulties in life is unavoidable, is an intrinsic part of human existence ... if one does not shy away, but steadfastly meets unexpected and often unjust hardships, one masters all obstacles and at the end emerges victorious" (8). Such a simplistic worldview may reassure the unconscious of the young child, but the young adult more likely sees life as unfair, parents as unreasonable, and some challenges as insurmountable. *Deerskin* offers a mature fairy tale that honors the darkness experienced in adolescence, especially for readers whose traumas go far beyond sibling rivalry or a nasty stepmother.

Works Cited

Ashliman, D.L. "Incest in Indo-European Folktales." *Folklore and Mythology Electronic Texts*. University of Pittsburgh, 19 Feb. 2013. Web. 22 Feb. 2013.

Bettelheim, Bruno. *The Uses of Enchantment: The Meaning and Importance of Fairy Tales*. New York: Alfred A. Knopf, 1976. Print.

Courtois, Christine A. "Healing the Incest Wound: A Treatment Update with Attention to Recovered-Memory Issues." *American Journal of Psychotherapy* 51.4 (1997): 464–496. Web. 12 Dec. 2012.

Diamond, Diana. "Father-Daughter Incest: Unconscious Fantasy and Social Fact." *Psychoanalytic Psychology* 6.4 (1989): 421–437. *PsycARTICLES*. Web. 5 Nov. 2012.

Dice, Nancy, and Shirley E. Havens. "Word of Mouth." *Library Journal* 119.14 (1994): 244. *EBSCOHost*. Web. 20 Jan. 2013.

Dominguez, Diana. "Slipping into a New Skin: Robin McKinley's *Deerskin* as Reclamation of the Feminine Tradition in Fairy Tales." *Journal of South Texas English Studies* 2.1 (2010): n. pag. Web.

Grand, Sue, and Judith L. Alpert. "The Core Trauma of Incest: An Object Relations View." *Professional Psychology: Research and Practice* 24.3 (1993): 330–334. *PsycARTICLES*. Web. 5 Nov. 2012.

Haaken, Janice, and Astrid Schlaps. "Incest Resolution Therapy and the Objectification of Sexual Abuse." *Psychotherapy: Theory, Research, Practice, Training* 28.1 (1991): 39–47. *PsycARTICLES*. 11 Jan. 2013.

Jung, Carl, and Marie-Louise von Franz. *Man and His Symbols*. Garden City, NY: Doubleday, 1964. Print.

Knapp, Bettina Liebowitz. *French Fairy Tales: A Jungian Approach*. Albany: State University of New York Press, 2003. Print.

Lawrence, Ann. *Tales from Perrault*. Oxford: Oxford University Press, 1988. Print.

Levi-Strauss, Claude. *The Elementary Structures of Kinship*. Trans. James Harle Bell, John Richard Von Sturmer, and Rodney Needham. Boston: Beacon Press, 1969. Print.

McKinley, Robin. *Deerskin*. New York: Berkley, 1993. Print.

Miller, Mark W., et al. "The Prevalence and Latent Structure of Proposed DSM-5 Posttraumatic Stress Disorder Symptoms in U.S. National and Veteran Samples." *Psychological Trauma: Theory, Research, Practice, and Policy*. 3 Sep. 2012. Web. 4 Dec. 2012.

Pilinovsky, Helen. "Donkeyskin, Deerskin, Allerleirauh: The Reality of the Fairy Tale." *The Journal of Mythic Arts*. The Endicott Studio, 2007. Web. 3 Jan. 2013.

Putnam, Frank W., et al. "The Clinical Phenomenology of Multiple Personality Disorder: Review of 100 Recent Cases." *Journal of Clinical Psychiatry* 47 (1986): 285–293. Print.

Rosenbaum, M., and G.M. Weaver. "Dissociated State. Status of a Case After 38 Years." *The Journal of Nervous and Mental Disease* 168.10 (1980): 597–603. Print.

"Transform, and twist, and change"

Deconstructing Coraline

LISA K. PERDIGAO

Neil Gaiman's novel *Coraline* can be read as an allegory of children reading fairy tales. While indebted to Lewis Carroll's *Alice's Adventures in Wonderland, Coraline* does not begin with its protagonist reading (or falling asleep during the reading of) a book; when Coraline begins her adventure, "she'd read all her books" (6). More reflective of the Alice in *Through the Looking-Glass*, Coraline crosses into a mirrored world and there encounters what many critics interpret as the uncanny—the other mother as well as the possibility (or threat) of another Coraline. While a door and a key grant Coraline access to this other world, these objects and the journey itself symbolically represent the act of reading. Coraline, seeking adventure and escape, finds in the other world parents who appear to adore her and a world that seemingly revolves around her. However, Coraline learns of this fantastic world's *other* reality. Rather than being a constant source of enchantment, this world becomes dangerous, and Coraline eventually becomes disenchanted, longing for a return to her real world and real parents.

The lure of the fantastic world behind the door becomes a representation of the enchantment of the fairy tale, of the child's bedtime story. In fact, it is after bedtime, as Coraline wanders through the house, that she finds the "big, carved, brown wooden door at the far corner of the drawing room" (8) slightly open although her mother had shut it. The transformation of the magical and fantastic other world can be interpreted as the transformation of the fairy tale itself. As the landscape of Coraline's world is a pastiche of other stories, Gaiman's novel can be read as the "other" version of those fairy tales. The house and garden that Coraline inhabits and explores recall Alice's as well as Hansel and Gretel's and Goldilocks' adventures. Even a talking cat helps Coraline navigate her world, returning us to Alice's Wonderland. But this journey through the looking glass, to those other familiar sites, reveals not a breaking of the rules of language and logic but the threat of mutilation, erasure, and death. In *Coraline*, fairy tales and children's stories are uncanny, at once familiar and strange. Robin Lydenberg argues that Freud's theory suggests that "What is most intimately known and familiar, then, is always already divided within by something potentially alien and threatening" (1073).[1] In *Coraline*, Gaiman returns to the landscapes of familiar fairy tales and children's literature to expose what was always already lurking beneath the surface. As Gaiman self-consciously explores the tradition of fairy tales—their effects on their audience and their critical reception—his protagonist Coraline straddles the divide between enchantment and disenchantment in the liminal space where fairy tales are re-membered as well as dismembered.

Critical discussions of *Coraline* treat the novel as a case study for Sigmund Freud, Jacques Lacan, and Bruno Bettelheim, highlighting how Coraline's struggles with her identity are central to the novel.[2] Roberta Seelinger Trites identifies how, in "books that younger children read," "much of the action focuses on one child who learns to feel more secure in the confines of her or his immediate environment, usually represented by family and home. Children's literature often affirms the child's sense of Self and her or his personal power" (2–3). Here, Trites' description of children's literature is suggestive of Bettelheim's argument about the "uses of enchantment" specific to fairy tales, the idea that the fairy tale "enriches the child's existence in so many ways" (12). Assessing the field, Karen Coats notes how Bettelheim's and Marie-Louis von Franz's work has linked reading fairy tales to a child's development of identity, describing how fairy tales "provide concrete images of villains and monsters on which to project undirected anxieties and fears ... facilitate psychic integration, and to assure the child of the possibility of happy endings when present trials are overcome" (78). However, *Coraline* complicates the idea of a "happy ending" that results in psychic integration or affirmation of self that critics argue is characteristic of the fairy tale or children's story.

As a result, the novel, like Coraline herself, can be located on the threshold between childhood and adolescence and between children's and young adult literature. In *The Case of Peter Pan*, Jacqueline Rose discusses how the production and dissemination of children's literature indicates a division, writing, "Children's fiction sets up a world in which the adult comes first (author, maker, giver) and the child comes after (reader, product, receiver), but where neither of them enter the space in between" (1–2). Responding to customer reviews of the novel in 2002, and, as Richard Gooding suggests, attempting to guide the reception of the novel, Gaiman notes the disparity between adult and child readers of *Coraline* when he says that adults have thought it was too terrifying for children while children read it as an adventure, even going further to state that children "don't get nightmares, and they don't find it scary" (qtd. in Gooding 391). Gaiman's comment that the novel has a "double audience" (qtd. in Gooding 391) reflects the novel's liminality and suggests a redefinition of Rose's terms. Following Gaiman's assessment, the child reader can be seen as a double to Coraline, crossing boundaries to enter the liminal space that the novel represents.

While the character Coraline is trapped between the two worlds—real and Other—the novel is poised in a similar ambiguous space. The cat, bearing an uncanny resemblance to Alice's Cheshire Cat (or Dinah, or the black cat of *Through the Looking-Glass*), gracefully crosses between worlds while Coraline is, in many instances, caught on either side looking for escape.[3] In Gaiman's novel, Wonderland is made both familiar and strange. As Maria Nikolajeva writes, "While *Alice* may be considered dark, *Coraline* is darker, and while Alice comfortably wakes up from her nightmare, nightmare pursues Coraline into her reality" (259). This "darkness" that Nikolajeva finds in *Coraline* is indicative of the novel's placement within a subset of children's literature that Anna Jackson, Coats, and Roderick McGillis map out in *The Gothic in Children's Literature*. Coats makes the case that the appearance and prevalence of the Gothic in contemporary children's literature results from an attempt to "fill the gap that the loss of the traditional fairy tale has created" (79). With *Coraline*, Gaiman does not merely attempt to fill the gap; he returns to the site to explore what lurks beneath the surface of traditional fairy tales.

Jack Zipes locates the "enchantment" of fairy tales in their "irresistibility and inexplicability" to suggest why contemporary writers return to those sources. He notes that fairy tales' "underlying dramas" are "re-created and redesigned to counter as well as collide with our complex social realities" (Zipes 136). According to Zipes, these literary revisions become productive sites for self-consciously exploring our world, as he says, "Collisions do not have to end in destruction. They are necessary to disrupt and confront clichés and bad habits. They are necessary to shake up the world and sharpen our gaze" (136). Discussing a movement in contemporary visual art, Zipes mentions how collisions with past fairy tale conventions endow the fairy tale with a "more profound meaning through the creation of dystopian, grotesque, macabre, and comic configurations" (136). While Zipes concentrates on the visual arts here, his notion of collision helps to define the landscape for Jackson, Coats, and McGillis' study of Gothic children's literature that is also representative of Gaiman's project in *Coraline*.

In "The Gothic Architecture of Children's Books," Rebecca-Anne C. Do Rozario highlights how intertextuality is central to both Gothic and children's literatures; her analysis suggests *Coraline*'s fit within and between the genres. She writes,

> There is a Gothic architecture of books, both as objects of and within children's literature: books filled with secrets and potentially dangerous passages, the narratives as labyrinthine as any castle interior or ruins, the dust jackets as intimidating as any fortress walls. Entering such a book is, potentially, as perilous to the reader as to the characters within the story [Do Rozario 209].

Here is an application of Zipes' theory of collision. As the Gothic is recontextualized in the space of children's literature, the key for survival for the characters within the stories lies in unlocking the secrets and deciphering texts; the child reader also must attempt to make meaning out of the texts within the texts, forging connections and, by extension, understanding. As children's literature draws on Gothic conventions, its collisions with the genre yield new meanings. Do Rozario notes that intertextual excesses become the "architecture of the Gothic novel through which the secrets of children's literature can be endlessly whispered and through which the distinctions between reader and text can be repeatedly dispelled" (210). Applying Do Rozario's terms to *Coraline*, the child reader of Gaiman's novel becomes like Coraline, unlocking the door to the other world, learning its secrets and deciphering its meaning.

As much as *Coraline* makes use of its intertexts—fairy tales, children's literature, and Gothic narratives—it also self-consciously explores the field of literary criticism. Vanessa Joosen writes, "Contemporary retellings are thus in line with tendencies in criticism of the fairy tales, and could even be argued to be influenced by critical analyses (or vice versa)" (237). Coraline, both character and novel, traces a history of literature and literary criticism as the character navigates the world beyond the other door. When Coraline encounters the cat, a character from Alice's world, she does not merely play Alice's role. Coraline's questions about this other world lead to its "unraveling," explicitly representing the deconstruction of its terms. When Alice leaves Wonderland, she leaves it intact, accessible for the future Alices as well as the sister who remembers her own Wonderland. The end of Coraline's visit to the other world is marked by the deconstruction of that world, its origins, meaning, and sustainability. Returning to Coats' terms, Gaiman does not represent a Wonderland for *other* Coralines to dream of; instead, in deconstructing, even destroying, the other world, he offers the reader a site for critical examination and re-examination.

While drawing upon fairy tale conventions, Gaiman's *Coraline* self-consciously explores the effects of stories—of the other fantastic world—upon children. In this way, *Coraline* is a novel that highlights the collision and fragmentation involved in such retellings as well as critical examinations of the genre, ideas about the uses and misuses of enchantment. While Coraline is initially enchanted by the other world (and other mother especially), her disenchantment with that world and desire to return home is inscribed with ideas about the limitations of such escapism in literature. Joosen writes,

> As the genre of the fairy tale evolves and some stories lose their magical features, the retellings develop an interaction between the traditional texts and a contemporary environment. The fairy tale drops some of its defining characteristics in the process, and the retellings blur the boundaries between fairy tales and novels. The literary experience for reader and writer, however, may benefit from this dialogue between the fairy tale and other literary genres. The strategies that authors have developed to make ambiguous the occurrence of magic show that although the contemporary retellings may lose some of the tales' magic, they gain, however, a new field for literary creativity, a new kind of magic [238].

According to Joosen, the disappearance of magic in contemporary retellings of fairy tales "increase[s] the contact with contemporary reality" and the intertextuality of these stories introduces "a certain degree of (intentional) indeterminacy, open-endedness, humor, and irony"

(237). To survive, Coraline must return to reality, escaping the fantasy that almost (quite literally) consumes her. Yet it is the collision between worlds, and Coraline's navigation of the space between them, that generates meaning.

Reflecting critical debates about the forms and functions of fairy tales, *Coraline* begins with a statement about its own relationship to texts. When Coraline, suffering from boredom in her new house, asks her mother, "What should I do?" her mother responds, "Read a book.... Watch a video. Play with your toys. Go and pester Miss Spink or Miss Forcible, or the crazy old man upstairs" (6). All Coraline wants to do, though, is explore, but the weather keeps her indoors. Reflecting on her mother's suggestions, the narrator states, "Coraline had watched all the videos. She was bored with her toys, and she'd read all her books" (6). *Alice's Adventures in Wonderland* begin with the question "What is the use of a book without pictures or conversations?" (Carroll 51). Also bored with books, Alice escapes into a fantastic world where she is called upon to recite her lessons and defend the purpose of didactic stories, the Victorian model of children's literature. The detail that Neil Gaiman's *Coraline* does not read any books during the course of the narrative or refer to any specific books is significant. Children's literature—myth, fairy tale, folk tale, and fantasy—is the absent presence that haunts Coraline, the character and the novel.[4] Examining the significance of intertextuality in Gothic children's literature, Do Rozario turns to works that emphasize the physical presence of books. For example, in Cornelia Funke's *Ink* trilogy and William Goldman's *The Princess Bride*, stories are revealed to the characters and are the source of meaning for the protagonists' adventures while J. K. Rowling's *Harry Potter* series depicts the wonders to be found in books as well as libraries (Do Rozario 213, 214). In contrast, in Coraline's house and in the novel itself, books remain hidden yet, in their absent presence, make meaning.

In children's literature, fantastic books hold secrets for the protagonist to discover, decipher, and use, and more ordinary books, like a personal diary, often hold the key to their success and survival (Do Rozario 215). In *Coraline*, the key is made literal and performs like the book in both *Harry Potter and the Chamber of Secrets* and John Connolly's *The Book of Lost Things*. For Do Rozario, in Rowling's novel, Tom Riddle's diary reflects an "endless possibility for narrative fragments to resolve between the secret and the exposed, always suggesting, but never completely revealing, the whole from which they originate," for "the origin remains obscured even as the fragmentary textual materialisations multiply" (215). While Tom Riddle manifests from the diary—as the embodied text—he meets his demise through the damage done to that text. The threat of the second book in Rowling's series is contained and destroyed as Harry pierces the diary with the Basilisk tooth, drawing blood through the pages, but the diary is merely a fragment of Voldemort; he persists as what Do Rozario calls a "fragmented ruin" (215) and continues to threaten Harry—and his world—throughout the entire series. Gaiman's novel takes a tradition of fairy tales as its text and embodies that text in the space beyond the door, that other world. Like *The Chamber of Secrets*, *Coraline* offers "endless possibility" in the introduction, navigation, reconfiguration, and deconstruction of that world.

Similar to Rowling's novel, Connolly's *The Book of Lost Things* presents the diary as a key to survival and meaning. The protagonist David is introduced to the power of stories from his mother who teaches him that these books "were both an escape from reality and an alternative reality themselves" (9) and that "sometimes the wall separating the two became so thin and brittle that the two worlds started to blend into each other" (10). The key to David's survival hinges on the discovery of "The Book of Lost Things," a treasure that he learns is a diary that contains "tokens and souvenirs of a life not unlike his own" (258). The discovery and interpretation of the diary help David to navigate the fantasy world and offer him a return home. By the novel's end, the book inspires David's own writing, his very own Book of Lost Things. While Riddle's diary performs as a more literal embodiment of the antagonist, *The Book of Lost Things* similarly represents the power of the text over the child—both the dangers and the possibilities that the texts present. The mastery of the text and discovery of its secrets mark not only the transition between worlds for the child protagonist but also the process of maturation, from childhood to adolescence and adulthood.

In *Coraline*, the doorway symbolically represents the act of crossing into the fictional world of the story using yet another trope in children's literature. Like the Pevensie children who travel through a wardrobe to Narnia and even Alice who falls down the rabbit hole into Wonderland, Coraline is granted access to this other world through a secret passageway. Maria Tatar argues that fairy tales function "as portals to wonder worlds, to sites that combine danger and beauty in ways so alluring that they inspire the desire to wander into new imaginative domains" (56). The first line of the novel is "CORALINE DISCOVERED THE DOOR a little while after they moved into the house" (2). Coraline's entry into this other world self-consciously evokes the trope to explore the sites, their beauty as well as danger.

While Alice's desire to see the garden leads her to a radical experiment in size, Coraline almost immediately finds access to another garden. Gaiman writes,

> The day after they moved in, Coraline went exploring. She explored the garden. It was a big garden: at the very back was an old tennis court, but no one in the house played tennis and the fence around the court had holes in it and the net had mostly rotted away; there was an old rose garden, filled with stunted, flyblown rosebushes.... There was also a well [4–5].

While the Red Queen's rosebushes contain a secret of their own, the rosebushes in Coraline's landscape are stunted, static in their growth. The well, which becomes a key itself by the novel's end, is another entry point for the novel: "Miss Spink and Miss Forcible made a point of telling Coraline how dangerous the well was, and they warned her to be sure she kept away from it" (5). Coraline's reaction, typical of a child, is predictable: "So Coraline set off to explore for it, so that she knew where it was, to keep away from it properly" (5). Here, the well can be read as the stories that are the novel's sources. It—and they—are dangerous but enchanting to Coraline. And while it is originally presented as something dangerous to avoid, Coraline's familiarity with it helps to guarantee her survival by the novel's end.

Returning to the house, Coraline's exploration leads her to the discovery of fourteen doors; of the fourteen, this "other—the big, carved, brown wooden door at the far corner of the drawing room" (8) is initially locked and becomes Coraline's, and the novel's, focus. When Coraline asks, "Where does that door go?" her mother responds, "Nowhere, dear." Coraline's response is that "It has to go somewhere" (8). Again colliding with the Gothic, the novel depicts her mother (and the novel) producing "the oldest, biggest, blackest, rustiest key" (9). When the door swings open to reveal a brick wall, Coraline's mother explains that the brick is the result of the redesign of the house into flats. But Coraline appears to be unconvinced that the door does not lead anywhere and notes that her mother does not relock the door. This speculation marks the beginning of Coraline's fascination with the door, the idea that it might still open up to something.

Reality and the dreamworld intersect and collide after Coraline is introduced to both door and key. After dreaming of "black shapes that slid from place to place, avoiding the light" (11) that night, shapes that sang and "made Coraline feel uncomfortable," Coraline is able to dream of "nothing at all" (12). While her dreams fail to yield anything exciting or dangerous, reality promises something *other*. Embarking on a walk the next day, Miss Forcible tells her, "Don't get lost, now" (15), but Coraline finds that she cannot get lost when she keeps sight of the house: "After about ten minutes of walking she found herself back where she had started" (15). When Coraline returns to the house, she meets up with Mr. Bobo who gives her a message from his mice, "Don't go through the door" (16) and asks her if that means anything to her. When Coraline tells him no, he tells her that they are funny creatures; "they get things wrong. They got your name wrong, you know. They kept saying Coraline. Not Caroline. Not Caroline at all" (16). Ironically, Coraline originally thinks that the mice are the products of Mr. Bobo's imagination and fantasy. Yet they are the ones to correctly refer to her as Coraline, when the other adults repeatedly call her Caroline. Seeking recognition as well as excitement, Coraline finds neither in the real world and longs for what the world of fantasy brings. After hearing the message, and trying to decipher its meaning, Coraline is even more enchanted by the door, and the passage that she thinks it represents. Like the well, the door becomes a place that Coraline, the explorer, must seek out.

Evoking tropes and scenes from texts in both literary traditions—children's as well as the Gothic—Gaiman transforms his landscape into a mist of free-floating signification where the reader, like Coraline, attempts to find meaning in her actions. Still bored, Coraline repeats the question to her mother: "What shall I do?" (17). When her mother suggests that she draw something, Coraline attempts to draw the mist. All she comes up with is a sheet of paper with M I S T written on it. Her mother's response is "Very modern, dear" (17). Critics have highlighted this passage as indicative of Coraline's struggle with her self-identity. In her rendering, the I is located below the rest of the letters. And it is her mother's rejection of her—her boredom, her drawing, her struggles—that leads Coraline back to the door, which she discovers is again locked. Coraline's visit to Miss Spink and Miss Forcible leads to a tea party, signaling another return to Alice, but, rather than ponder time and timelessness, this mad tea party leads to the revelation, through the women's reading of Coraline's tea leaves, that the girl is in danger. She is given a stone that she is told is "good for bad things, sometimes" (21). When Coraline leaves their company, she steps outside into the mist and sees the world as a "ghost-world" (21). Thinking of what it means to be "in danger?" Coraline concludes that it is "exciting," not a "bad thing," "not really" (21). The next day, Coraline's boredom leads her back to the door and to danger.

Tellingly, it is after Coraline flips through a book that "her mother was reading," which seems "particularly pointless to Coraline" (25), that she finds the key that her mother has placed in the cupboard. This time, when Coraline opens the door, it does not reveal a brick wall; a dark hallway appears and Coraline crosses the threshold. As she walks down the hallway "uneasily," she realizes that "there was something very familiar about it" (27). Richard Gooding writes, "The house Coraline discovers on the other side of the drawing room is, for one of Gaiman's posited audiences, a near-literal manifestation of the *unheimlich*: a home that is familiar but unknown…" (394). Coraline is confused by its appearance: "She knew where she was: she was in her own home. She hadn't left" (27). Coraline's terrain in the other world is familiar to readers as well, inscribed with allusions to other stories.

The introduction of the cat in the other world is perhaps the most explicit allusion to *Alice in Wonderland* and it—both the cat and the scene—offers guidance for interpreting how Gaiman's world is making use of its source material. Coraline greets the cat and says, "I saw a cat like you in the garden at home. You must be the other cat" (35). The cat responds by saying, "No … I'm not the other anything. I'm me" (35–36). Unlike people, it says, cats "keep ourselves together" (36). When Coraline asks it how it can talk, and if it is the same cat, it asks, "Cats don't talk at home?" (36). Coraline tells it that they don't and it responds, "Well, you're the expert on these things…. After all, what would I know? I'm only a cat" (36). It starts to walk away, disappearing like that other cat, until Coraline calls it back, apologizing, much like Alice. Although Coraline tries to remain the polite little girl, another Alice, it tells her that it does not have a name, saying, "Now, *you* people have names. That's because you don't know who you are. We know who we are, so we don't need names" (37). When she asks it where they are, its definition, like the Cheshire Cat's, is relative; the cat tells her, "It's here" (37).

Although the other world is initially a magical place that offers the fulfillment of Coraline's wishes for excitement, recognition, and inclusion, it begins to reveal its very real danger to her. When Coraline first enters the other world she finds that, instead of being ignored by her parents and left alone to explore their new surroundings, her other parents pay attention to her and she is fed her favorite foods. Her other mother tells her, "It wasn't the same here without you. But we knew you'd arrive one day, and then we could be a proper family" (29). But when the other mother reveals the buttons, needle, and thread that she will use to sew buttons onto Coraline's eyes, saying, "We only want what's best for you" (45–46), Coraline recognizes that the place is more threatening than she initially imagined. Coraline's adventure begins with the attempt to cure both her boredom and loneliness. This journey through the looking glass reveals another world that threatens to take Coraline's eyes, erase her identity, and transform her into a ghost.

The other world—like Wonderland and even the forest of Hansel and Gretel's and Little Red Riding Hood's worlds—is a place of enchantment. The danger, the other outcome that lurks beneath the surface of Bettelheim's analysis, is that the child can lose his sense of self and even life if he is unable to negotiate its terms. Coraline's survival is contingent upon her ability to see, to recognize the difference between the worlds and outsmart the other mother to regain control over her reality. The masterplot that facilitates her escape is a deconstruction of the site itself.

Coraline's return home reveals how her time in the other world has altered her reality. Coraline notices her parents' absence and starts to worry. Alone, she sits at her father's computer and writes a story, "Coraline's Story," about a girl named Apple who "used to dance a lot" (51). She runs herself a bath, drying herself and the floor "as best she could," and goes to bed (51). After waking in the middle of the night to find herself still alone, Coraline cries and then climbs into her parents' bed to sleep. Here, the child tries to perform the rituals of bedtime but they are distorted, not quite right. And it is when she goes to the mirror, after the cat awakens her, that she figures out what had happened. Back through the looking glass Coraline goes and finds that her real parents are reflected from—and trapped within—another world. Even their message is backward, but still signifying meaning: "HELP US" (53). And yet the mirror is not just a mirror. It is a mirror but only ... something other. Gaiman writes, "The mirror had been, a long time before, the inside of a wardrobe door" (53).

Part C. S. Lewis' *The Lion, the Witch and the Wardrobe*, part *Through the Looking-Glass*, *Coraline* becomes another point of collision, fracture as well as cohesion. Coraline realizes that she must return to the other world, to her other mother, to retrieve—and even save—her parents. Telling the cat a story about her father's bravery when they encountered a wasps' nest, and the lesson that "when you're scared but you still do it anyway, *that's* brave" (59), Coraline suggests the uses of enchantment, what stories can teach. After she is greeted by the other mother, and her offer, "We're here. We're ready to love you and play with you and feed you and make your life interesting" (60), Coraline again turns to the mirror, and returns to Alice's plot:

> Coraline walked down the hallway until she reached the mirror at the end. There was nothing reflected in it but a young girl in her dressing gown and slippers, who looked like she had recently been crying but whose eyes were real eyes, not black buttons, and who was holding tightly to a burned-out candle in a candlestick. She looked at the girl in the mirror and the girl in the mirror looked back at her. *I will be brave*, thought Coraline. *No, I am brave* [61].

In Carroll's text, Alice uses the mirror to read the mirror-text, the "Jabberwocky" poem. In it, a boy becomes the Jabberwocky-slayer. In Gaiman's novel, playing the part of Alice, Coraline uses the mirror and remembers the significance of the text: bravery. She too will have to defeat a monster in order to return home a hero. Unlike Carroll's text, she is the slayer—not some boy. The mirror reveals not a book but the image of Coraline herself. As the other world in *Coraline* can be read as the embodiment of fairy tales, in this scene, Coraline becomes a textualized presence, representative of the novel itself; here, Gaiman illustrates how he revises *Alice* for a new age and a new reader.

The conclusion of *Coraline* offers sites of collision—between Coraline and the other mother as well as the novel and other texts within the tradition. Trying to devise an escape from the other mother's plot, Coraline continues to rely on the guidance of the cat—and Carroll's text—as she asks it what she should do. The cat borrows from another storyline when it responds to Coraline's question about why the other mother wants her here: "She wants something to love, I think.... Something that isn't her. She might want something to eat as well. It's hard to tell with creatures like that" (65). Here, the other mother has also become the witch in the Hansel and Gretel story. Her house, though not quite edible for the trespassing child, produces tempting goods and her masterplot proves to be more sinister than Coraline initially thinks. When Coraline asks the cat for advice about what she should do, it proves more helpful than her mother was and tells her that she should "challenge her"; "There's no guarantee she'll play fair, but her kind of thing loves games and challenges" (65).

When Coraline awakens in her other room the next morning, unable to return to her real world or real parents, she does not know "where she was" and "she was not entirely sure *who* she was" (67). Almost repeating Alice's musings of the difference between Alice and Mabel, of waking up as another, or even the wonder of whose dream it actually is after all, Coraline struggles to define herself:

> Sometimes Coraline would forget who she was while she was daydreaming that she was exploring the Arctic, or the Amazon rain forest, or Darkest Africa, and it was not until someone tapped her on the shoulder or said her name that Coraline would come back from a million miles away with a start, and all in a fraction of a second have to remember who she was, and what her name was, and that she was even there at all [67].

Getting dressed, Coraline wonders, "Was there an other Coraline? No, she realized, there wasn't. There was just her" (69). But accompanying this passage is a drawing of another Coraline, with button eyes and a claw-like hand. While Coraline's illustration of Apple in "Coraline's Story" complemented its meaning, in her act of storytelling here, the image belies the conclusion. The other Coraline haunts this text. And the struggle for control over the story becomes the battleground for the text. As familiar and strange collide, Coraline must unveil what lurks beneath the surface of the other world, navigating her escape once— and only once—she is able to deconstruct the other mother's masterplot.

When Coraline goes looking for the other mother, she finds the other father instead and a startling concept when he tells her that there is "no point" to exploring; he says, "There isn't anywhere but here. This is all she made: the house, the grounds, and the people in the house" (71). As Coraline begins to examine the house, she realizes the difference from her other reality, her real home: "Where Coraline came from, once you were through the patch of trees, you saw nothing but the meadow and the old tennis court. In this place, the woods went on farther, the trees becoming cruder and less treelike the farther you went" (72). As she continues to walk out into this mist, she realizes that "the world she was walking through was a pale nothingness, like a blank sheet of paper or an enormous, empty white room. It had no temperature, no smell, no texture, and no taste" (73). The cat appears, and disappears in the mist, telling her that it is a "bad place ... if you want to call it a place, which I don't" (73). When Coraline repeats what she had said since the novel's beginning, "'I'm exploring,' the cat replies, 'Nothing to find here.... This is just the outside, the part of the place *she* hasn't bothered to create'" (74).

From the novel's beginning, with its allusions to children's stories as well as its uses of Gothic conventions, Coraline exposes its metafictionality, its self-consciousness of its own fiction. Claudia Nelson writes, "children's metafiction contemplates the psychology of reading while simultaneously functioning to define what reading should be" (223). As Coraline attempts to figure out how to navigate this storybook world, this other world, she also begins to examine its foundations. As she attempts to gain control over the world—or text—by a mastery of its design and rules, she illustrates the ways that the reader becomes actively engaged within the text and participates in the process of making meaning. Coraline's control over the world is at odds with the other mother's attempts. Nelson cites Robyn McCallum's comment that metafiction for children involves a "heightened sense of the status of fiction as an elaborate form of play, that is, a game with linguistic and narrative codes and conventions" (226) as she explores how children's metafiction introduces games and features messages about the "pleasures of narrative in general" (226). Nelson writes, "Among their defining traits is a shared emphasis on the delight associated with immersing oneself in story, a delight that the complexity of their construction seeks to replicate for the reader" (226). It is fitting, then, that Coraline take the cat's advice (or the advice from Carroll's texts) and challenge the other mother to a game. She had offered three options for play—"Hopscotch? Happy Families? Monopoly?" (77)— with two as actual children's games and the other as her narrative, her construction of this other world.

The foundations of this other mother's world can be traced to the origins of children's literature. While Carroll's text experiments with the didactic function of children's literature in the Victorian world—with Alice reciting her lessons and, in Wonderland, confusing those terms as well as her own self-definition as "little girl"—the other mother reflects that tradition in her demands for "manners!" (79). After producing a tiny silver-colored key, the other mother tells her, "This is for you, Coraline. For your own good. Because I love you. To teach you manners. Manners makyth man, after all" (79). The other mother locks Coraline on the other side of the mirror when Coraline misbehaves, telling her, "You may come out when you've learned some manners.... And when you're ready to be a loving daughter' (79).

As Coraline is sent through the looking glass, she, like the character before her, is led to examine the meaning of these stories. In this mirrored world, Coraline finds lost children who, like the cat, are unable to produce names for her. "Names, names, names," one says. "The names are the first things to go, after the breath has gone, and the beating of the heart. We keep our memories longer than our names" (83). While Coraline had constantly asserted her identity—Coraline, not Caroline— in the other world, here she faces the obliteration of her self in more dramatic terms. Wiped of their names and corporeal selves, these children "belong to the dark and to the empty places" (87), part of the other mother's world, her creations.

These lost children are manifestations of Coraline's fears about the other mother's masterplot, a plot derived from fairy tales. With corollaries in the stories "Snow White," "Hansel and Gretel," and "Little Red Riding Hood," Coraline suggests the fear of cannibalism, of being consumed by another and disappearing.[5] Encountering and overcoming this fear—and the very real threat that the other mother presents—is the key to Coraline's survival and is representative of the process that Bettelheim identifies at work in fairy tales.[6] Coats argues that Coraline must find "a way to asset her identity apart from her parents, but she must also find a way for them to be part of her without being all of her" (91). And her dreams provide her a glimpse of how to achieve this goal. As Coraline falls asleep, within the mirror world and surrounded by ghost children, she hears a voice tell her to "look through the stone" (87). After she awakens from the dream within the dream world, Coraline introduces her challenge to the other mother. They will play "an exploring game ... a finding things game" (92). If the other mother wins, and Coraline cannot find her parents and the souls of the children, Coraline will stay there forever, playing Happy Families, and let her sew buttons in her eyes. If, as the mother puts it, Coraline does not lose, already weighing the odds, the other mother will have to let Coraline, her real father and mother, and the dead children—everyone she has trapped there—go.

When Coraline plays the game, she decides to do so on her terms, including wearing her own clothes. Her only clothes available in the other world are her pajamas, though, and her clothing suggests the dream or nightmarish quality of this world. Her tool for the game is the stone that Miss Spink and Miss Forcible gave her, for bad things, but it figures as an eye-piece, again highlighting the act of interpretation. Coraline must perform a close reading of this landscape in order to win (or not lose). After Coraline finds two of the souls, the world around her begins to change: "OUTSIDE, THE WORLD HAD become a formless, swirling mist with no shapes or shadows behind it, while the house itself seemed to have twisted and stretch" (105). Gaiman writes, "It seemed to Coraline that it was crouching, and staring down at her, as if it were not really a house but only the idea of a house—and the person who had had the idea, she was certain, was not a good person" (105).

As Coraline attempts to win this "exploring game," she encounters the limits of the other mother's world, and imagination. Gaiman writes,

> There was nothing here that frightened her. These things—even the thing in the cellar—were illusions, things made by the other mother in a ghastly parody of the real people and real things on the other side of the corridor. She could not truly make anything, decided Coraline. She could only twist and copy and distort things that already existed [117–118].

According to Perry Nodelman, "Fairy tales are almost too obvious an example of what Derrida calls 'the effacement of the signifier' (20)—the way our distrust of the words we read causes us to see them as mere containers of something more important, to the point of making the words themselves disappear from our consciousness" (144). Nodelman argues that the critic of fairy tales "assumes that their real significance, the core of their inner truth, is something which in actual fact lies outside of them" (144). Coraline's discovery of the limits of the other world, of the other mother's ability to create, highlights this notion.

Like the word MIST that Coraline tries to write earlier in the story, the world itself begins to lose its concreteness. As Coraline wrestles with the recovery of the last soul in Mr. Bobo's apartment, "Coraline had time to observe that the house itself was continuing to change, becoming less distinct and flattening out, even as she raced down the stairs. It reminded her of a photograph of a house, now, not the thing itself" (121). When Coraline ventures out to the ends of the world that the other mother creates, she learns that there are limits to the other mother's (and, by extension, author's) world; the other mother is the literary revisionist, attempting to re-create the fairy tale world for Coraline. After recovering the last soul, with the help of the cat, Coraline attempts to solve the last part of the challenge. As she contemplates the last piece of the puzzle—the location of her parents—she identifies the key: "The other mother could not create. She could only transform, and twist, and change" (124).

This revelation of the limitations of the other mother's authorship as well as the limits of the fairy tale world marks the "unraveling time," which leads to the deconstruction of the elaborate other world. Here, Gaiman suggests the reflexivity that Joosen notes between contemporary retellings and critical analyses: *Coraline* renegotiates the relationship between the adult (as maker) and child (as receiver/reader). Coraline re-investigates the landscape and find that "the house had flattened out even more. It no longer looked like a photograph—more like a drawing, a crude, charcoal scribble of a house drawn on gray paper" (124). In her introduction to Derrida's *Of Grammatology*, Gayatri Spivak describes "the text coming undone as a structure of concealment, revealing its self-transgression, its undecidability" (qtd. in Waugh 72). Coraline's exploration game is a metafictional one, an investigation of the relationship between the reader and the fictional world. Nodelman writes,

> Deconstruction is not, however, an act of destruction. In seeing the degree to which the worlds constructed by literature are artificial, we can surely develop a deeper appreciation of their artifice. What more of us need to do is to deconstruct our assumption that children themselves should not be given the tools to see the artifice of these works, that it is somehow good for children to be innocent, that is, to believe in the transcendental signified of these clearly limited visions of reality [144].

Following Zipes' interpretation, more profound meaning is located through critical engagement with the texts. Coraline deconstructs the other mother's world as Gaiman depicts the unraveling time as dénouement; the text (at least the other mother's version) comes undone. The "ways in and out of this place" go flat, the cat tells Coraline, and Coraline struggles to return home. After wrestling control of the key and then door away from the other mother, Coraline, with the help of the cat and the wraiths, locks the door on the other mother, ultimately returning to her life, once boring and ordinary and now, comparatively, "so interesting" (137). That night, she falls asleep, a "deep and dreamless sleep" (137), protected from the nightmarish other world.

After she is reunited with her parents, when Coraline returns to sleep with the key around her neck and the gray marbles beneath her pillow, this time, she dreams. The three "ghost" children whom Coraline had rescued join her at a picnic. After they play, she tells them, "I'm just pleased it's all over" (144). One of the girls tells her, "It's over and done with for *us*…. This is our staging post. From here, we three will set out for uncharted lands, and what comes after no one alive can say…" (144). Coraline, frustrated, asks, "But I got you three back … I got Mum and Dad back. I shut the door. I locked it. What more was I meant to do?" (144). They tell her that they can only give her a clue but that she should be careful—and wise, and brave, and tricky (145). When she awakens from her dream, Coraline hears a noise and realizes what it is—"the other mother's right hand" that is searching for the black key (147). Although Miss Spink tries to read Coraline's tea leaves again, she says, "Oh dear. No. I have no idea what that signifies. It looks almost like a hand" (151). Signification is obfuscated for the adults, a constant theme, but Coraline deciphers its meaning.

Coraline's dream of the children provides her with insight into the other mother's plan and time to "plot and plan and ponder" (152). She then takes control of the dénouement by turning to an unlikely source: a children's story. Gathering her dolls for a picnic, the stuff of dreams, Coraline sets off to trap the other mother. Her real mother says, "I didn't think you played with your dolls anymore" (153) and Coraline tells her, "I don't… They're protective coloration" (153). Coraline's plot takes her back to the story's beginning, to the well that, like the door, was revealed to be dangerous yet exciting. Staging a tea party for her dolls, Coraline waits until the hand appears, reaches for the key on the tablecloth poised over the well, and falls down the shaft. Coraline puts the boards back on the well "as carefully as she could" because "she didn't want anything to fall in" and "didn't want anything ever to get out" (159). The story's end leads her back to the beginning, to again speak with her neighbors, learning that the mice say that she is their savior and hugging Miss Spink and Miss Forcible after returning their stone. That night, Coraline anticipates beginning the year at a new school but is not afraid. And less the Alice that runs off for tea and instead more like Alice's nostalgic sister at the end of Carroll's story who contemplates Alice's dream, "Coraline imagined that she was back again in her dream, with the two girls and the boy under the oak tree in the meadow, and she smiled" (162). Coraline falls asleep, about to cross another threshold, for "summer was almost done" (162).

As Coraline faces another school year, she marks the transition from childhood to adolescence and even adulthood. Her collisions—all too literal—with various conventions and tropes of Gothic and children's stories as well as fairy tales lead to her recognition of the uses and misuses of enchantment. The threat has been addressed and removed from Coraline's world; the doors are closed; the key and hand are buried; and the well is covered. That Coraline buries the other mother's hand in the well is significant. It is the hand that can create—or twist or shape—the other world. That it is now buried suggests another reading of the relationship between the two worlds. Coraline has, in effect, effaced the creator but, in burying the hand, she has permanently located it in her world. The covered well remains both dangerous and magical. The effacing signifier and the act of effacing the signifier are at the story's source.

At the end of the novel, Coraline has transitioned from the reader to the writer of the story, and her writing is an act of revision. She recreates a scene from Alice's adventures as well as Gaiman's own reimagining of the tea party in the readings given by Miss Spink and Miss Forcible. The source of her plot is also taken from her dream-world picnic reunion with the lost children. The tea party itself, the stuff of Coraline's own childhood, becomes protective coloration. The novel *Coraline* ultimately survives in a similar way: it takes the fairy tale, children's novel, and Gothic story and adapts them for a contemporary world and audience. By baring the device of Coraline's masterplot, the novel exposes the artifice of the work of fairy tales, children's literature, and Gothic stories and offers a critical examination of the genres. The "new kind of magic" that Joosen describes as literary creativity can be traced throughout Gaiman's novel. *Coraline* blurs the lines between author and reader, child and adult, becoming an experiment in liminality, transforming, twisting, and changing the world of children's fiction.

Notes

1. David Rudd notes that "Gaiman has given us a quite overt fictional representation of the Freudian Uncanny," "'that class of the frightening which leads back to what is known of old and long familiar'" (161), tracing the instances of the uncanny in the representations of the other home and other mother. Even the doll that Coraline finds, Coraline's miniature double, highlights Freudian theory. Yet the uncanniness of and within the novel is more pervasive, traceable to its foundations.

2. Kara Keeling and Scott Pollard write that articles by Karen Coats, Richard Gooding, and David Rudd "use an admixture of Freud, Lacan, and Bettelheim, to assert that through the fantasy world of the other mother, Coraline achieves self-definition and autonomy" (2).

3. Maria Nikolajeva writes that *Coraline* is "in every respect a dialogical response to *Alice in Wonderland*, with every indication of postmodern literature present" (259). According to Nikolajeva, "The cat's elevated position is reminiscent of the Cheshire Cat as well as Humpty Dumpty" (260). Both challenge Alice's sense of self and attempts at self-definition.

4. Henry Selick's 2009 film adaptation notably changes the context for Coraline's adventure and the foundations of the story for the medium. Lindsay Myers writes, "Gaiman's novel deploys, as many scholars have demonstrated, two main frames of reference—the literary fairy tale and the fantasy—both of which can be said to hold a particular affinity for the young. The split mother, the locked room, the deceptive lure, the magical talisman, and the fear of being eaten are all common fairy-tale tropes, while the eccentric cat and the magical wardrobe are indirect allusions to *Alice's Adventures in Wonderland* and *The Lion, the Witch and the Wardrobe*, two iconic children's fantasies, which Gaiman, himself, has admitted exerted a considerable influence over him as a child (Austin). The main influence on Selick's *Coraline,* however, is the Hollywood horror film, a genre, which until recently, was the exclusive domain of adults" (Myers 252). In Gaiman's novel, Coraline does not return to her books; however, she does watch television before becoming bored again. While Myers is critical of Selick's reinterpretation of the story, it too evidences the kinds of collisions that Zipes discusses. In their self-conscious explorations of their genres, both versions of Coraline—the original and that other filmic one—offer models for interpreting the effects of the medium upon its audience.

5. Keeling and Pollard's "The Key Is in the Mouth: Food and Orality in *Coraline*" trace the relationship between the "fairy-tale threat of cannibalism" (3) and the depictions of food within the novel.

6. Coats writes, "And this is the true horror of the other mother—for her, love is a regressive desire to consume Coraline. The ghost children that Coraline finds in the closet are mere husks because they didn't learn the paradoxical lesson that Coraline does, that desire doesn't work by getting everything you want" (88).

Works Cited

Carroll, Lewis. *Alice's Adventures in Wonderland*. Ed. Richard Kelly. Ontario: Broadview, 2000. Print.
Coats, Karen. "Between Horror, Humour, and Hope: Neil Gaiman and the Psychic Work of the Gothic." *The Gothic in Children's Literature: Haunting the Borders*. Ed. Anna Jackson, Karen Coats, and Roderick McGillis. New York: Routledge, 2008. 77–92. Print.

Connolly, John. *The Book of Lost Things*. London: Hodder and Stoughton, 2006. Print.

Do Rozario, Rebecca-Anne C. "Fantastic Books: The Gothic Architecture of Children's Literature." *The Gothic in Children's Literature: Haunting the Borders*. Ed. Anna Jackson, Karen Coats, and Roderick McGillis. New York: Routledge, 2008. 209–225. Print.

Gaiman, Neil. *Coraline*. New York: HarperCollins, 2002. Print.

Gooding, Richard. "Something Very Old and Very Slow": *Coraline*, Uncanniness, and Narrative Form. *Children's Literature Association Quarterly (CLAQ)* 33.4 (2008): 390–407. *Project Muse*. Web. 20 Feb. 2013.

Joosen, Vanessa. "Disenchanting the Fairy Tale: Retellings of 'Snow White' Between Magic and Realism." *Marvels & Tales: Journal of Fairy-Tale Studies* 21.2 (2007): 228–239. *JSTOR*. Web. 12 Feb. 2013.

Keeling, Kara K., and Scott Pollard. "The Key Is in the Mouth: Food and Orality in *Coraline*." *Children's Literature: Annual of The Modern Language Association Division on Children's Literature and The Children's Literature Association* 40 (2012): 1–27. *Project Muse*. Web. 20 Feb. 2013.

Myers, Lindsay. "Whose Fear Is It Anyway? Moral Panics and 'Stranger Danger' in Henry Selick's *Coraline*." *Lion and the Unicorn* 36.3 (2012): 245–257. *Project Muse*. Web. 20 Feb. 2013.

Nelson, Claudia. "Writing the Reader: The Literary Child in and Beyond the Book." *Children's Literature Association Quarterly* 31.3 (2006): 222–236. *Project Muse*. Web. 20 Feb. 2013.

Nikolajeva, Maria. "Devils, Demons, Familiars, Friends: Toward a Semiotics of Literary Cats." *Marvels & Tales* 23.2 (2009): 248–267. *MLA International Bibliography*. Web. 20 Feb. 2013.

Nodelman, Perry. "The Hidden Meaning and the Inner Tale: Deconstruction and the Interpretation of Fairy Tales." *Children's Literature Association Quarterly* 15.3 (1990): 143–148. *Project Muse*. Web. 20 Feb. 2013.

Rose, Jacqueline. *The Case of Peter Pan: Or, the Impossibility of Children's Literature*. Philadelphia: University of Pennsylvania Press, 1993. Print.

Rudd, David. "An Eye for an I: Neil Gaiman's Coraline and Questions of Identity." *Children's Literature in Education* 39 (2008):159–168. *MLA International Bibliography*. Web. 20 Feb. 2013.

Tatar, Maria. "Why Fairy Tales Matter: The Performative and the Transformative." *Western Folklore* 69:1 (2010): 55–64. *MLA International Bibliography*. Web. 20 Feb. 2013.

Trites, Roberta Seelinger. *Disturbing the Universe: Power and Repression in Adolescent Literature*. Iowa City: University of Iowa Press, 2000. Print.

Waugh, Patricia. *Practising Postmodernism/Reading Modernism*. London: Arnold, 1992. Print.

Zipes, Jack. *The Irresistible Fairy Tale: The Cultural and Social History of a Genre*. Princeton: Princeton University Press, 2012. Print.

"Comparatively innocent"
The Terrible Search for Nobility in A Series of Unfortunate Events

Tim Sadenwasser

Psychologist Sheldon Cashdan writes that abandonment is "perhaps the most dreaded fear of childhood" (14), so it is natural that it is also a popular fairy tale motif. By so prominently featuring abandonment, Cashdan argues, fairy tales from "Hansel and Gretel" to "Snow White" help children confront their nightmares of neglect (68) and, by observing a villain's punishment, "destroy the witch" that causes them (74). Simon Grolnick adds that for the very young child, "the tale is experienced as comforting because of the steadying, stabilizing effects of having it read … by a constant, comforting parent" (210). But what of older children who have moved beyond hearing "Cinderella" and "Rumpelstiltskin" at bedtime? Can the fairy tale still help these older readers as they begin to face the world on their own? In Lemony Snicket's *A Series of Unfortunate Events*—thirteen books published from 1999 to 2006—three orphaned children endure fairy tale sufferings while learning to confront adult questions of morality. Fourteen-year-old Violet, twelve-year-old Klaus, and infant Sunny first flee and then pursue the villainous Count Olaf, but lacking adult refuge or guidance, they are in danger of becoming the evil that torments them. The series' juvenile readers likely recognize themselves in the orphans' struggles. Although physical desertion is relatively rare, juveniles can feel abandoned or vulnerable in more mundane ways. Approaching adolescence, they must begin to find their own answers as their parents exert less direct control over their lives. They will also learn that their parents are imperfect but that such flaws are not, to reference the Giuseppe Verdi opera that recurs throughout the series, "*la forza del destino*," or "the force of destiny." Snicket—both the pen name of Daniel Handler and a character in the series—employs a fairy tale structure of desertion and endangerment but uses increasingly adult moral dilemmas to guide both his orphaned protagonists and his young readers into mature independence. At the same time, he demonstrates how children can overcome their parents' flaws and become noble, even when doing so requires ethical compromises.

Fairy tales featuring abandonment and desertion often work to alleviate children's fears that parents will fail to provide a safe haven against predators. Cashdan writes, "Before children can strike out on their own, before they are able to function independently, they need to know there are people in their world on whom they can rely…. [W]ithout human anchors, the world is a frightening and unpredictable place" (49). Fairy tales old and modern are rife with homes that do not provide safety. In versions of "Snow White" and "Cinderella," for example, fathers replace their daughters' nurturing mothers with cruel stepmothers. In rarer cases, the father is the direct source of harm. The vain miller in "Rumpel-stiltskin" mortally endangers his motherless daughter, and a body of tales discussed later depicts fathers' incestuous lust for their daughters. "Hansel and Gretel," however, portrays a case of child endangerment and youthful heroism extreme even for fairy tales. Iona and Peter Opie describe this and related narratives as "a series of tales … in which small children outwit an ogre into whose hands they have fallen" (236). During a severe famine, a mother of two young children—sometimes their biological mother but more often their stepmother—convinces her weak-willed husband to abandon them. Left twice in the forest to die, Hansel and Gretel eventually encounter the witch. The mother and the witch seem to be opposites: while one starves the children, the other satisfies their cravings, first with her house and then with a "meal of milk and pancakes, with sugar, apples, and nuts" (53). But the women actually work in deadly tandem. According to Bettelheim, the mother's actions create the "uncontrolled craving" (160) that makes them easy prey for the gluttonous witch, who kills, cooks, and eats any child she can catch (Tatar 54). The witch, Maria Tatar claims, "represents an intensification of the maternal evil at home" (qtd. in Grimm 57n), an idea emphasized by the description of the children sleeping on "two beautiful beds … made up … with white sheets" (53) while the witch gazes at their "soft red cheeks" (54). The next morning, the witch cages Hansel and forces Gretel to help fatten him for her feast. Although the crone in the forest becomes the tale's unforgettable villain, it is the father's weakness and the mother's cruelty that consign the children to their abominable fate.

In response to their parents' deserting them, the children must transform from passive victims to active heroes: they will overcome their fear, outsmart the witch, and return home. First, Hansel delays his death by tricking the witch into thinking he is staying thin, and then Gretel pushes her into her oven, where she "burn[s] to death in a horrible way" (53). Hansel and Gretel's triumph cleanses their world of danger, for when they return home, they find that their mother has also died. Cashdan writes that the mother's unexplained death is no mystery, for "she and the witch ... are two sides of the same evil coin" (78). What is more, he claims, their deaths symbolically purge the children of the hunger that drove them from home and toward the witch. That they embrace their father despite his failure to protect them also makes sense: with the cause of their suffering destroyed, the children can forgive him as easily as they can renounce their former gluttony. The Grimms end by writing of the family, "Their worries were over, and they lived together in perfect happiness" (54). The family is restored, not through direct magical intervention, but because the children protected one another until they could return safely home.

Like their fairy tale antecedents, the Baudelaire orphans are quickly abandoned in a nightmarish world, and their plight too derives from what seems to be inattentive parenting. In the first chapter of *The Bad Beginning*—subtitled *Orphans!* in the paperback edition—the family banker Mr. Poe informs them that their house has burned and their parents have been killed. Orphans in such circumstances would normally be entrusted to their most suitable relative, but because the Baudelaires' will stipulates their children "be raised in the most convenient way possible" (15), they are instead sent to live with their physically closest relative, Count Olaf, who is "either a third cousin four times removed, or a fourth cousin three times removed" (15). Olaf's proximity is no accident. In book six, *The Ersatz Elevator*, Klaus discovers a tunnel connecting the Baudelaire mansion to the apartment building of Esmé Squalor, Olaf's villainous girlfriend, and in book twelve, *The Penultimate Peril*, the children learn that Olaf's two most feared associates have been tracking the orphans' every movement. The parents perhaps thought they were helping their children by keeping them in familiar settings, but they instead play right into the hands of the ogre who would steal the family's fortune.

Much as the death of Cinderella's mother casts her from economic privilege into servitude, the children's placement with Count Olaf destroys the domestic comfort they had once enjoyed. En route to Olaf's house, they observe a tantalizing image of their former lives:

> The Baudelaire children looked out and saw the prettiest house on the block. The bricks had been cleaned very well, and through the wide and open windows one could see an assortment of well-groomed plants. Standing in the doorway, with her hand on the shiny brass doorknob, was an older woman, smartly dressed, who was smiling at the children [19].

As Violet shakes the woman's hand, she "felt as if her life and the lives of her siblings might turn out well after all" (19), but Justice Strauss, a high court judge, reveals she is not Olaf's wife, and Olaf's house is "the dilapidated one next door":

> The bricks were stained with soot and grime. There were only two small windows, which were closed with the shades drawn even though it was a nice day. Rising above the windows was a tall and dirty tower that tilted slightly to the left. The front door needed to be repainted, and carved in the middle of it was an image of an eye. The entire building sagged to the side, like a crooked tooth [20–21].

The house, a travesty of the witch's tempting home, accords with Olaf's character. Snicket writes that although "first impressions are often entirely wrong," the orphans' initial surmises "that Count Olaf was a horrible person, and his house a depressing pigsty … were absolutely correct" (27–28). He is the unnatural guardian set in contrast with the goodness the orphans perceive in their parents, and his house's appearance shows he will provide none of the comforts to which they are accustomed.

Olaf immediately asserts his plan to exploit the orphans until he can steal the fortune they are to inherit once Violet turns eighteen. As one of his first villainous acts, he creates a version of the impossible task that challenges the orphaned or abandoned hero's competence to succeed independently. The children awake one morning to find a note from Olaf:

> "My theater troupe will be coming for dinner before tonight's performance. Have dinner ready for all ten of them by the time they arrive at seven o'clock. Buy the food, prepare it, set the table, serve dinner, clean up afterwards, and stay out of our way" [30].

Lacking direct parental protection, fairy tale heroes typically overcome such tests through supernatural help, often a dead parent's spiritual assistance. The Grimms' Cinderella, for example, must pick lentils from the cinders, but the "little doves, little turtledoves, and … little birds in the sky" (80) assist her. According to Tatar, such help occurs only after "the hero has proven himself in the preliminary character test"—which Cinderella does by remaining loyal to her late mother and tending her grave—so "the achievements of the helper redound to the hero" (90). The Baudelaires' tasks are not impossible, but for privileged children with no housework experience, they seem so. Violet's first reaction, like Cinderella returning to her mother's grave for help, is to recall her parents: "I wish they were here…. They would never let us stay in this dreadful place" (31–32). But when no supernatural help arrives, she herself assumes the parent's role and orders her siblings "to keep our chin up" (32). Later, Justice Strauss welcomes them into her library where they find a recipe for Puttanesca (39), a simple dish with an adult translation—it means "whore's pasta" in Italian ("Pasta")—and they spend the afternoon roasting garlic and pitting olives and feeling "less miserable than they had since their arrival at Count Olaf's" (44). Their task exceeds what one can realistically expect of children, but Violet proves her character, and with the Justice's assistance, she and her siblings endure.

This domestic idyll ends with the return of the unnatural parent, whose cruelty creates despair. Angered by the orphans' choice of dinner, Olaf asserts his power over them: "I have become your father, and as your father I am not someone to be trifled with. I demand that you serve roast beef to myself and my guests" (46). When Sunny objects, Olaf unleashes "an inhuman roar" and "pick[s] her up in one scraggly hand … so she was staring at him in the eye" (46). She is physically unharmed, but the scene foreshadows the mortal danger to which he will soon subject her. Later, while the children serve dinner, one of Olaf's henchmen tells Violet, "You're a pretty one. … If I were you I would try not to anger Count Olaf, or he might wreck that pretty little face of yours" (49). The threat is filled with sexual violence, which likewise becomes more terrifying as the book progresses. Finally, Olaf's physical threats become immediate when Klaus declares that the Baudelaire fortune is "not to be used until Violet is of age," prompting Olaf to knock him to the floor (53). The chapter ends with "Klaus in the bed, Violet on the floor, Sunny on her little cushion of curtains," all three "crying quietly all night long" (55). Snicket himself often intrudes upon the narrative to weep copiously over the Baudelaires' plight, but Kim Hong Nguyen contrasts such weeping with the orphans' real tears, here claiming that while the author's embellishments create humor, "the children's sadness seems sensible" (275). This distinction between humor and pathos is important, for the young reader's appreciation of the orphans' resilience depends upon their being truly threatened and forsaken. With memories of their recent comfort heightening their misery, the children's crying less resembles Snicket's comic hyperbole than the pitiful plight of the miller's daughter in "Rumpelstiltskin," who, threatened with death if she cannot spin straw into gold, "felt so miserable that she started crying" (180). The Baudelaires' danger is worse, however, because in their world, no magical helper can relieve or even delay their suffering.

Olaf's designs on Violet add an unsettling hint of incest to his violence. After Mr. Poe rebuffs the children's pleas for help, Olaf coerces them to participate in a play, *The Marvelous Marriage* (75), in which Violet will play a beautiful young woman whom Justice Strauss is to marry to Olaf's character. Tison Pugh argues that "the repeated emphasis on Violet's beauty establishes her as an object of male desire" (168), suggested when Olaf "gently" but menacingly touches her chin (78). Violet makes explicit such incestuous overtones when she addresses Olaf as "*Father*" (77; original emphasis) and later queasily imagines "sleeping beside Count Olaf, and waking up each morning to look at this terrible man" (109). The "motif of incestuous desire," Marina Warner writes, can be traced in folk literature back to Giambattista Basile's "L'Orsa" (320–21) and exists within such related tales as Perrault's "Donkeyskin," the Grimms' "Thousandfurs," and Jane Yolen's "Allerleirauh" (Tatar, *Hard* 149; Pilinovsky). To Tatar (and Antti Aarne) this motif represents the converse of the evil stepmother (*Hard* 149–50): in one, the father is overshadowed to the point of absence; in the other, the mother's absence heightens his aggressiveness. But while these folk narratives hinge upon a widower's lust for his beautiful daughter, incest in *ASoUE* never goes beyond suggestion, for although Olaf admits that he "may be a terrible man," his ultimate goal is not to ravish Violet but "to concoct a foolproof way of getting [her] fortune" (110). By emphasizing greed, Snicket softens the incestuous suggestions, much as later iterations of "Little Red Riding Hood" downplay disturbing sexual implications, but doing so hardly negates

Olaf's threat. As Violet recognizes in dismay, "He wasn't merely an unsavory drunken brute, but an unsavory, clever drunken brute" (108).

Olaf's plan to marry Violet establishes a central conflict of the series' first half, that between the orphans' growing self-sufficiency and the ineffective, even pernicious parenting to which they are subject. By transforming himself from guardian to father-husband, Olaf will make official his power over the orphans, formally replacing the dead parents while quashing Violet's emerging leadership. Olaf actually exploits Violet's feelings of duty to motivate her to marry him: he stuffs her youngest sibling inside a birdcage and dangles her outside "the forbidden tower" of his home (105). This image of entrapment—which recalls both Hansel's imprisonment as he waits to be eaten and Rapunzel's isolation in the witch's tower—emphasizes not just Sunny's predicament but the hopelessness all three children feel. Their abandonment to Olaf appears complete: their parents are dead, Justice Strauss unwittingly helps Olaf triumph, and Mr. Poe sanctions Olaf's every cruel deed by citing his privilege to act "in loco parentis," a Latin legal phrase he translates as "acting in the role of parent" (65–66). To save Sunny, Klaus and Violet must therefore themselves act "in loco parentis." Klaus goes first, using his research skills to study nuptial and inheritance law, but it is Violet— recalling her parents' admonition that "as the eldest, it will always be your responsibility to look after your younger siblings" (117)—who most assumes the parental burden. She builds a grappling hook and climbs the tower but is captured and forced on stage under the threat of Sunny being dropped to her death. Both Violet and Klaus have failed: Violet cannot spring her sister from the cage, and Klaus cannot extricate Violet from the wedding. Nonetheless, they display the courage required to overcome evil, and their persistence is rewarded. While the play wedding is underway, Violet signs the marriage contract with her left hand, subverting the rule Klaus discovered that parties must sign in their own hand. This technicality, the judge rules, voids the contract: instead of becoming "a miserable contessa," Violet remains "a miserable orphan" (153), but one who is free to raise her siblings.

Were this a traditional fairy tale, the social systems created to protect the helpless would step in to provide the orphans a loving home, reassuring the reader that the world is a good place that rewards virtuous and ingenious children. But Snicket reminds us that happy endings have no place in his stories:

> If you like, you may shut the book this instant and not read the unhappy ending that is to follow. You may spend the rest of your life believing that the Baudelaires triumphed over Count Olaf and lived the rest of their lives in the house and library of Justice Strauss, but that is not how the story goes [137].

The children's misery must continue precisely because they are wards of a system that cannot effectively act "in loco parentis." Discussing the series' conclusion, Nguyen claims that *ASoUE* subverts the basis of happy endings by confronting "the definition of family, [and] the social and political role of guardianship" (269), but Snicket is already questioning here these protective structures. Mr. Poe and Justice Strauss—banker and judge—represent respectable institutions that should intervene to protect the orphans. Mr. Poe, however, is so preoccupied with economic interests that he fails to notice Olaf's villainy, and even when it is revealed, he declares it only to be "financially dreadful" (149). Likewise, a high court judge surely should be trusted to act "in loco parentis," but the legal system embodies—in all the wrong ways—the adage "Justice is blind." When Justice Strauss tearfully declares, "I would never do anything to harm you children," Olaf correctly responds, "You *were* easily tricked" (148). What is worse, these institutions ignore the children's desires and instead subject them to new dangers. The orphans hope they might live with the judge, who, despite her deficiencies, does care for them, but, Mr. Poe tells them, "your parents' will is very specific. You must be adopted by a relative" (160). Deprived of a chance for a home, a kitchen, and a library, they are instead entrusted to impersonal social bodies that care more for money and legalities than their wellbeing.

Few of the guardians to whom Mr. Poe will subject the children are as vicious as Olaf, but whether they are kind or cruel, Olaf's machinations will deceive them and force the children to protect themselves. Beginning with book two, *The Reptile Room*, and continuing into book eight, *The Hostile Hospital*, Olaf uses disguises to approach and imperil the orphans and their guardians. In *The Wide Window*, for example, he becomes Captain Julio Sham, a renter of sailboats. Over the children's protests, Aunt Josephine—really their "second cousin's sister-in-law" (5)—accepts Olaf's false identity. Snicket describes her gullibility while explaining "an expression … appropriate for this part of the story":

The expression is "falling for something hook, line, and sinker," and it comes from the world of fishing. The hook, the line, and the sinker are all parts of a fishing rod, and they work together to lure fish out of the ocean to their doom. If somebody is falling for something hook, line, and sinker, they are believing a bunch of lies and may find themselves doomed as a result. Aunt Josephine was falling for Captain Sham's lies hook, line, and sinker, but it was Violet, Klaus, and Sunny who were feeling doomed [52].

The mechanics of endangerment in this and other early books closely follow Vladimir Propp's classic fairy tale morphology. According to Propp, the villain's first direct action against the hero is usually "reconnaissance" (ε), in which he "find[s] out the location of children, or sometimes of precious objects" (28). Olaf's ability to locate the children no matter where Mr. Poe places them represents the "delivery" (ζ; 28–29), but it is not sufficient to gain him their fortune. He therefore resorts to "trickery" (η), which frequently combines disguise with persuasion (29). Although such deception fails on the orphans, it works on their flawed protectors, resulting in their inadvertent "complicity" (θ; 30). Once Olaf has fooled these guardians, he removes them by committing what Propp labels "villainy" (A; 30). The act of villainy—often murder, as when Olaf kills Uncle Monty in *The Reptile Room*—typically concludes the narrative's *"preparatory part"* (31; original emphasis) because it forces the hero to react either out of self-preservation or to satisfy some lack and thereby creates "the actual movement of the tale" (30). In the series' first half, the Baudelaires, as victim heroes, must overcome their guardians' incompetence simply to preserve themselves from the disguised villain; only later, as they come to understand that adults cannot help them, will they actively seek and investigate the evil that torments them.

Olaf's predations in *The Wide Window* upset traditional parent-child relationships, forcing the children to act "in loco parentis" to protect their aunt as well as themselves. Josephine is hardly an ideal guardian. Despite her house clinging to a cliff above Lake Lachrymose, she avoids even the slightest risks, which include using the oven, the radiator, the telephone, and the welcome mat, "which … could cause someone to trip and break their neck" (16). Despite her mania for safety, she, like Justice Strauss, fails to discern Olaf's threat until too late and even then lacks the courage to oppose him. She instead flees him and abandons her charges, creating a role reversal that requires the children to rescue her. After performing detective work that foreshadows their later becoming active heroes, they confront her for her cowardice. When she corrects their grammar instead of explaining her actions, Snicket writes,

> The Baudelaires ... understood that she was so wrapped up in her own fears that she had not given a thought to what might have happened to them. They understood that Aunt Josephine had been a terrible guardian, in leaving the children all by themselves in great danger. They understood and they wished more than ever that their parents, who never would have run away and left them alone, had not been killed in that terrible fire which had begun all the misfortune in the Baudelaire lives [158].

The children's idealization of their parents throws Aunt Josephine's paralyzing fear into harsh relief, but unfortunately, her cowardice is not her worst trait; that trait is her disloyalty. While they cross the lake in a sailboat Violet and Klaus stole from Olaf, Josephine and the children are attacked by the Lachrymose Leeches, and Olaf appears just as they are to capsize. The orphans threaten to reveal his disguise to Mr. Poe, but Olaf accurately assesses the situation—"Why should he believe three runaway pipsqueaks who go around stealing boats?" (186)—and moves to kill Josephine. In response, she offers to trade the children's lives for hers: "You can have the fortune! You can have the children! Just don't throw me to the leeches!" (188). Although Klaus will later refer to Aunt Josephine as "kind and sweet" (206), Snicket makes clear that, like the miller in "Rumpelstiltskin," she is an inept guardian who selfishly endangers her charges. Her fearfulness forces the children to take unnecessary risks, and her disloyalty almost places them in the villain's hands.

The Wide Window ends with the orphans surviving to expose their pursuer's identity, but Olaf again outsmarts the adults and eludes justice. As the children wait despondently to be sent elsewhere, Snicket contrasts the book's events to fairy tale endings:

> In most stories, as you know, the villain would be defeated, there would be a happy ending, and everybody would go home knowing the moral of the story. But in the case of the Baudelaires everything was wrong. Count Olaf, the villain, had not succeeded with his evil plan, but he certainly hadn't been defeated, either. You certainly couldn't say that there was a happy ending. And the Baudelaires could not go home knowing the moral of the story, for the simple reason that they could not go home at all [211–12].

Unlike how "Goldilocks" instructs children to "Never break into someone else's house" or "Snow White" carries the moral "Never eat apples" (212), the orphans' suffering brings no justice and teaches no lessons.

From their parents' death through their time debarking logs in book four, *The Miserable Mill*, the children have been sentenced to live as adults, to cook and work and parent and care for weak guardians. While this suffering strengthens them for active heroism, their having to endure without adult guidance fuels their feelings of vulnerability and anger that will later jeopardize their morality. Cashdan writes that a psychologically rich aspect of parents and children experiencing fairy tales together is that parents can help explore questions of evil and allow children to "resolv[e] struggles between positive and negative forces in the self" (15). Such movement to resolution reflects the hero's journey, which begins with both external and internal deficiency and ends by satisfying both. Unlike Hansel and Gretel, however, the orphans cannot return to what psychologist Margaret Mahler calls a "safe-base" (qtd. in Cashdan 49), for that base has been burned and their caretakers killed; indeed, the dynamism of their characters means they would be returning so differently that any sense of homecoming would, as Joseph Campbell suggests, feel illusory and unreal (218). Instead, they forge ever deeper into the world, accumulating its impurities. Only the knowledge they can always rely upon one another consoles them, and "to have each other in the midst of their unfortunate lives felt like having a sailboat in the middle of a hurricane" (*WW* 214). Their sibling loyalty, a trait they share with Hansel and Gretel, must sustain them until they can act against Olaf and his confederates and find or create their own home.

After performing so many adult duties, the Baudelaires return to the child's world in book five, *The Austere Academy*, only to find it a place that methodically deals out cruelty. Administrators and educators at boarding schools are charged to act "in loco parentis," but Prufrock Academy's despotic Vice-Principal Nero and teachers Mrs. Bass and Mr. Remora confirm children's suspicions that school exists only to bore and torment them. Mr. Remora's teaching comprises eating bananas while telling purposeless anecdotes: "One afternoon a man named Edward got into a green truck and drove to a farm. The farm had geese and cows. The end" (57). Ms. Remora is obsessed with the metric system and forces the children to measure objects and record their lengths. Nero, however, is the worst offender, his every action betraying childish malice. Like his namesake, he is a violinist, and he subjects his captive audience to nightly concerts; should students miss one of his six-hour recitals, they must buy him a bag of candy and watch him eat it. He also mocks the Baudelaires by employing one of the child's most irritating behaviors: repeating somebody's words in a high-pitched voice. Worst, however, is his marking the orphans for ostracism. Just as her stepmother isolates the noble-born Cinderella by forcing her to work and sleep among the ashes, Nero singles out the once-privileged Baudelaires when he sentences them to live in "the Orphans Shack."

Besides introducing the children to new varieties of torment, *The Austere Academy* marks a turning point in the series: instead of repeatedly eluding Olaf, the Baudelaires will now begin to investigate what caused the feud between him and their parents. The children have made their first lasting allies in Isadora and Duncan, two of the three Quagmire triplets and heirs to the family sapphire fortune. The Quagmires are as studious as Violet and Klaus—supporting their missing brother Quigley's theory that "well-read people are less likely to be evil" (*SS* 95)—and they use their intelligence to guard their new friends from Olaf. They fail, however, and all they can do is yell "V.F.D.!" as Olaf's henchmen kidnap them. The Baudelaires will soon learn that V.F.D. is a secret organization to which belonged both Olaf and their parents. V.F.D., which denotes, among other things, "Volunteer Fire Department," once put out both literal and figurative fires, but a schism erupted, with "Villains" starting fires to kill "Volunteers." This generations-long rupture, Violet surmises, touches their entire lives: "Maybe all our guardians have been members of V.F.D., on one side or the other of the schism" (*SS* 209). By not sharing their knowledge of the schism, the Baudelaire parents have again endangered their children, for the orphans cannot protect themselves in a conflict they do not understand. Their awareness of this organization, however, gives purpose to their suffering: to understand the forces that have shaped their lives, they will discover the identity of V.F.D. and their family's relationship to it.

As the orphans' actions move beyond pure self-preservation, the early books' episodic repetition of endangerment and survival yields in books 5–8 to a more dramatic, overarching narrative in which they progress toward what Propp calls the "departure," designated   (39). In the early books, Olaf's "villainy" has removed their parents (A), and the passive heroes are taken from their home ("mediation," B), but instead of accepting their victimhood, the orphans now undertake a "beginning counteraction" (C) against the villain. The "complication" represented by the ABC sequence compels action, which ultimately takes the form of their departing from their ineffective guardian (↑). This departure will demonstrate Snicket's assertion that "there are times to stay put, and what you want will come to you, and there are times to go out into the world and find such a thing for yourself" (*CC* 204). The orphans' departure will also break their cycle of victimization, and until they can reunite with the Volunteers, they will put out fires while testing their goodness in ways that parented children need not.

As the orphans become firefighters, they confront a world of moral complexity that extends into their own family. They begin to understand the breadth of the conspiracy, which includes even Lemony Snicket, in book seven, *The Vile Village*. Taking literally the adage "It takes a village to raise a child," Mr. Poe has placed the orphans under the collective parentage of the Village of Fowl Devotees, where they become immersed in their first V.F.D. plot. Esmé Squalor, disguised as Officer Luciana, claims to have apprehended Olaf, but before the village can execute the imprisoned man, who is actually the author's brother Jacques, the real Olaf murders him. The village's lack of responsible adult leadership forces the Baudelaires to become detectives, first investigating Jacques' murder and then renouncing Mr. Poe's guardianship so they can delve further into the V.F.D. conspiracy. What they find in the late books (9–13) is that evil can arise in the safest of bases. In book eight, *The Hostile Hospital*, the children wish they were home with their parents, but by book eleven, *The Grim Grotto*, they will recall times their parents were unfair or unkind—such as when they yelled at them for ruining an atlas (147–48)—and "admit that their parents were sometimes difficult" (149). Finally, in *The End*, Snicket alludes to the elder Baudelaires' complicity in the murder of Olaf's parents:

> The children had recently learned another mysterious fact about their parents and their shadowy past—a rumor concerning their parents and a box of poison darts. Violet, Klaus, and Sunny, like all children, had always wanted to believe the best about their parents, but as time went on they were less and less sure [17].

Morality, their research teaches them, is malleable and complex; one can start good but become evil, and one person can include both good and evil. Could constantly fighting fires have corrupted their parents' nobility? And could investigating V.F.D. now turn themselves evil? In book ten, *The Slippery Slope*, Klaus recalls Nietzsche: "I was remembering something I read in a book by a famous philosopher. He said,

'Whoever fights monsters should see to it that in the process he does not become a monster[']" (273). Their parents' devotion to a cause perhaps drove them to commit monstrous acts, so to stay noble, says Laurie Langbauer, the orphans must "remain responsible to others while avoiding the mistaken certainties of their guardians" (507). While disillusioning, seeing the bad in their parents will in the end help them achieve the sophistication necessary to develop their own morality.

The orphans' progress toward maturity, however, comes with great difficulty, for the more they investigate the V.F.D. schism, the more they learn that the adult world demands moral compromise. Snicket, himself a firefighter, exemplifies this principle when he laments the "necessary thing" he had performed on V.F.D.'s behalf: "*Was it absolutely necessary to steal that sugar bowl from Esmé Squalor?*" (*HH* 90–91; original emphasis). The Baudelaires face a similar dilemma in book eight when they must steal keys from a kind hospital worker. This theft creates a slippery slope, and they will soon become accessories to arson, kidnapping, and murder. In *The Carnivorous Carnival*, the orphans must decide whether to help kill a phony clairvoyant and continue their investigations or be left behind. Esmé asks them, "If you don't choose the wicked thing, what in the world will you do?" (200). "[T]he wicked thing" is the practical thing, but Olaf graphically illustrates how expediency compromises morality: "Sometimes a few people need to die in fires or get eaten by lions, if it's all for the greater good" (*SS* 58). To survive in this corrupt world, the orphans begin to absorb and reflect the villains' pragmatism. After Sunny is kidnapped by the villains, her siblings plan to trap Esmé in a pit to force a hostage exchange, a scheme Klaus describes with the familiar phrase, "We'll fight fire with fire" (252). Quigley Quagmire, however, refutes such rationalization: "Throwing people into pits isn't the greater good! … It's villainous treachery!" (277). But ultimately it is the youngest Baudelaire who exemplifies the orphans' moral descent. In *The Penultimate Peril*, the authorities corner the orphans and Olaf, who threatens to use a sample of Medusoid Mycelium—a poisonous mushroom the Volunteers had created as a biological weapon—to kill everyone in the hotel. To escape without such wholesale slaughter, Sunny proposes a marginally better solution: "Burn down hotel" (317). The orphans have become fire starters, but as Snicket writes, "it is very difficult to make one's way in this world without being wicked at one time or another, when the world's way is so wicked to begin with" (316). To

Quigley, good ends never justify evil means, but the Baudelaires learn that moral relativism—even when it means sacrificing volunteers and villains alike—is sometimes the "necessary thing." Unfortunately, yielding to such pressures means that the villainy that destroyed V.F.D. and corrupted their parents has taken root in them. Lacking adult protection and guidance, the children have too early and too often had to fight fire with fire and have consequently descended the moral slippery slope.

But would Quigley oppose pushing old women into ovens? The Baudelaires' actions resemble the steps fairy tale heroes routinely perform to survive, but the consequent moral struggles are theirs alone. Hansel and Gretel must of course fight fire with fire: the witch intends to cook them in her oven, so Gretel pushes her in instead. The children afterwards exhibit no guilt; their own survival outweighs the witch's life, and the punishment for her villainy is in fact legally and ethically fitting. Gerhard Mueller, drawing upon the work of German prosecutor Eric Wulffen, notes that the villain's crime of "witchcraft and attempted cannibalism" (220) was especially heinous but uncovered by medieval law. Death by fire, "the principal punishment for witchcraft" (222), is therefore the most fitting sentence. Similarly, the stepsisters in the Grimms' "Cinderella" suffer gruesome injuries to their feet and eyes as retribution for their scheming against the heroine. Because their penalties are fitting—"they were punished for their wickedness and malice with blindness" (85)—Cinderella need feel no guilt and the reader no remorse. The defined lines between good and evil relieve the innocent heroes of moral qualms; indeed, quibbling about the hero's actions or the villains' sufferings would blunt the tales' therapeutic value for children. The Baudelaires, however, cannot share these heroes' confidence in their own goodness. In *The Penultimate Peril*, the orphans accidentally kill Dewey Denouement with a harpoon in Olaf's possession, and all are tried for the crime. When ordered to enter a plea, Olaf declares himself "unspeakably innocent," but the orphans struggle with the dilemma until Klaus, echoing Dewey's earlier assessment of them as "noble enough" (188), describes them as "comparatively innocent" (279). Unlike fairy tale heroes, the orphans can find no refuge from the worlds' evils, and in the course of investigating the cause of their miseries have become so like their persecutors they can no longer see themselves as good.

The physical setting of *The End*, the series' final book, creates an illusion of escape from the schisms that plague humanity. The orphans and Olaf flee the burning hotel together—literally all in the same boat—and eventually beach upon a coastal shelf that is home to an island civilization. Ishmael, who envisions himself as "the island's parent," believes he must keep his children safe from "the world's terrible secrets" (227–28). Because "everyone's story has an unfortunate event or two—a schism or a death, a fire or a mutiny, the loss of a home or the destruction of a tea set," he claims that one should "stay as far away from the world as possible and lead a safe, simple life" (222). He even institutes a safe, bland diet forbids them from eating from the apple tree in the arboretum. In so secluding the island, Ishmael forges a prelapsarian Eden, "a colony safe from the world's treachery" (57).

Despite Ishmael's precautions, the world intrudes, for, as Klaus tells him, "you can't live far from the treachery of the world, because eventually the treachery will wash up on your shores" (292). As at the hotel, such treachery involves both schism and the poisonous Mycelium. The Baudelaires learn that their parents had once lived on the island but fled when the residents succumbed to schism. History repeats itself when Olaf encourages a faction to rebel against Ishmael's rule, prompting the orphans to ponder man's turbulent nature: "[They] could imagine what the other schisms must have been like, from the schism that split V.F.D., to the schism that drove their parents away from the very same island, to all the other schisms in the world's sad history" (248). Olaf carries out his plans by donning one last disguise, dressing as a woman so he can feign pregnancy and hold the Mycelium in a diving helmet under his dress, but Ishmael harpoons his stomach, causing him figuratively to birth a plague. Schism has ruined the orphans' lives, and now it threatens to end them.

It is at this late point in the series that Snicket reveals the rescuing power of the elder Baudelaires, who have made mistakes grievous enough to endanger their children's lives but have also left behind the literary means to save them. The children discover their parents had contributed to the island's history, also titled *A Series of Unfortunate Events*, and they turn to this book to find where their parents had stored the only known antidote to Mycelium: horseradish. While the orphans search for information, Snicket writes, "they caught glimpses of other secrets their parents had kept" (275), before learning that the horseradish is infused into the apple tree. Too weak to return to the arboretum, they are saved by a serpent, the gentle and misnamed Incredibly Deadly Viper, who brings them an apple. In this reversal of Eden, knowledge brings life, and it is the parents who supply both. They have grown the antidote and, communicating through their own *Series of Unfortunate Events*— a book that acts "in loco parentis"—have revealed it to their children. Like the godmother in Perrault's "Cinderella" or the enchanted birds in the Grimms' version, the book is the conduit for the parents' spiritual help, but the children must actively decode, not just receive, their parents' assistance. Perhaps a fairy tale cannot save Snicket's readers, but, as Klaus repeatedly shows, active reading can bring life-saving knowledge: without his and his sisters' research skills, they all would have joined the islanders as the Mycelium's victim.

The children are rescued, but the ethical question remains: given humanity's tendency to violent self-destruction, how can a "noble enough" person avoid becoming evil? The easy answer lies in a poem Olaf recites to Kit Snicket, the author's sister. Kit, who has also washed ashore, had been romantically involved with Olaf before they took opposite sides in the schism. Now pregnant with Dewey Denouement's child, she is dying from the spores but cannot take the antidote for fear of harming her baby. Olaf, also having inhaled the spores, recites to her the end of Philip Larkin's "This Be the Verse":

> "Man hands on misery to man…. It deepens like a coastal shelf. Get out as early as you can—" Here he coughed, a ghastly sound, and his hands clutched his chest. "And don't have any kids yourself," he finished, and uttered a short, sharp laugh. Then the villain's story came to an end [318].

The one certain way to escape misery and prevent more in the future is to stop living and never procreate. Kit does the former but only so she can save her daughter and allow her to begin "her series of unfortunate events" (321). To live in a fallen society, Snicket shows, is to encounter the dissension and betrayal that will jeopardize one's goodness, but the only alternative is to die or hide. Rather than stay forever on the island, the Baudelaires return with Kit's child to confront the world's strife, knowing that doing so will test the infant's innocence and their own relative nobility. Rather than assure the reader that the children grow to be happy and good, Snicket ends the series with an image of the sea with a "?"—the sign of "The Great Unknown" (304)—on its turbulent surface. Their nobility cannot be assured as long as they mix with the world.

The young reader's experience of traditional story structure makes this ambiguous conclusion feel disorienting. From his first mention of V.F.D. through all the clues about fires, schisms, and sugar bowls, Snicket has repeatedly stated how thoroughly he has researched the Baudelaire family history. Such diligence should create resolution, but as Kendra Magnusson writes, while the series' "ceaseless inquisitiveness ... strengthens as it reaches its conclusion," the books resolve very little (92). Why does Snicket so defy narrative convention? The answer lies in part in his description of the difference between an "end" and a "denouement":

> "Denouement" comes from the French, who use the word to describe the act of untying a knot, and it refers to the unraveling of a confusing or mysterious story. ... The denouement is the moment when all of the knots of a story are untied, and all the threads are unraveled, and everything is laid out clearly for the world to see. But the denouement should not be confused with the end of a story [PP 176].

To illustrate his claim, Snicket describes how most fairy tales conclude with images of unalloyed happiness that obscure their true and less pleasant endings:

> The denouement of "Snow White" ... occurs at the moment when Ms. White wakes up from her enchanted sleep, and decides to leave the dwarves behind and marry the handsome prince, and the mysterious old woman who gave her an apple has been exposed as the treacherous queen, but the end of "Snow White" occurs many years later, when a horseback riding accident plunges Ms. White into a fever from which she never recovers. The denouement of "Goldilocks and the Three Bears" occurs at the moment when the bears return home to find Goldilocks napping on their private property, and either chase her away from the premises, or eat her, depending on which version you have in your library, but the end of "Goldilocks and the Three Bears" occurs when a troop of young scouts neglect to extinguish their campfire and even the efforts of a volunteer fire department cannot save most of the wildlife from certain death [176–77].

True to Snicket's description of an ending, *The End* complicates, not resolves. Instead of providing definite answers—revealing what was in the sugar bowl or what instigated the schism or who killed whom—he teaches his young readers that their lived events will not adhere to the neat contours that mark the fairy tale. Children's tales can end with their narrative threads unraveled, but real lives continue, usually messily, sometimes tragically.

The series' conclusion is also disorienting because of how Snicket the author weaves himself into the narrative. Snicket begins as a shadowy chronicler about whom the reader knows just two apparently unrelated facts: first, he is inconsolably devoted to the lost Beatrice, to whom he dedicates each book; second, he feels compelled to record the Baudelaires' sad history. Slowly, however, the reader realizes that Snicket's entire history is entangled with both the schism and the Baudelaires themselves. Like the orphans, he too has lost loved ones to the schism—first Jacques and finally Kit—but he shares his most traumatic loss with the children, for Beatrice is eventually revealed as their mother. His ongoing relationship with V.F.D. and the orphans explains why he cannot provide a definitive ending: the story, which includes him, will continue as long as Beatrice's children and his own niece endure. Snicket claims in "Chapter Fourteen"—a coda to *The End*—"my investigation is over" (12) and therefore "the story is over" (13), but he more accurately states in the previous chapter, "no matter how much one reads, the whole story can never be told" (323). He can stop investigating and writing, but the grief he and the orphans share will never end, any more than Snow White's domestic life stops at her tale's denouement. What is more, if the Baudelaires' continuing influence on both their children and Snicket is any indication, even death does not end the story. The words and actions of Villain and Volunteer alike ripple outward to touch generations of the living. In sending the children into The Great Unknown, Snicket imitates not just life's uncertainty, but its boundlessness. *The End* is not the end; for Lemony Snicket's niece—another Beatrice—it is just the beginning.

While he denies his young readers the narrative resolution associated with the fairy tale, Snicket also guides them into adult content. Throughout the series he creates what Pugh calls "a chain of signifiers in literary history" (172). Many juveniles already know some of these works, such as fairy tales and the *Alice* books, while others are allusions they will soon understand, such as Olaf's guise as Detective Dupin, the children's wealthy guardians Jerome and Esmé Squalor in *The Ersatz Elevator*, and the main characters' names, which point to Decadent poets (not to mention the notorious von Bülow marriage and trial). Still others, however, are more challenging, even disturbing. Snicket references Thomas Pynchon when Olaf and Esmé kidnap the Quagmires in a red herring statue being auctioned as "Lot #48"; a riddle the orphans must solve references Tiresias foretelling the clerk's seduction of the typist in *The Waste Land*; and their travails in the Village of Fowl Devotees echo the grisly sufferings of Candide and his companions. Pugh argues these "allusions are so diverse, so wide-ranging ... that they subvert the very literary canon from whence they arise" (175), but perhaps Snicket is preparing his precocious readers for the uncomfortable, unresolved regions of literature they will soon explore. Nowhere does he do so more explicitly than in his use of "This Be the Verse." Snicket's frequent challenges to parenthood and guardianship reach their apex in his invocation of a poem that begins "They fuck you up, your mum and dad." At his most—indeed only—sympathetic moment, Olaf tells young readers that parents need not be abusive or neglectful to create problems. They might nurture and care for and maybe save you in the end, but even the best ones "fill you with the faults they had / And add some extra, just for you." The poem reminds the orphans that their parents indeed were flawed, perhaps murderous, and that they too, as soon-to-be parents, will damage their young charge. Far from comforting his readers about their future or—as in the case of "Hansel and Gretel"—whitewashing parental flaws, the ending sends the children into adulthood with greater cognizance of its pains and difficulties.

After reading *ASoUE*'s first six entries, critic Bruce Butt deplored their "predictability" and argued that nothing would change because "repetition has been at the centre of the series' success" (282). But change they did—for the worse. The opening books offer repetition as a source of melancholy comfort: the Baudelaires will suffer but endure, and their adventures will reset at the start of the next book. When their parents' world intrudes in the form of V.F.D., however, the children must prematurely negotiate the moral complexities of the adult world. Leaving the island to sail into the "strange, unreadable shape of some great unknown" (322), the Baudelaire orphans carry their young readers into a new literary world that will expose them to similar complexities. Snicket repeatedly admonishes his readers to drop his books and enjoy others that lack the misery he must describe, and two of his flawed parent figures echo him: Captain Widdershins tells his daughter, "There are secrets in this world too terrible for young people to know, even as those secrets get closer and closer" (*GG* 88), and Ishmael warns the orphans, "No sensible parent would let their child read even the title of this dreadful, sad chronicle" (*TE* 230). But children can no more avoid corruption than they can avoid adulthood, so they must prepare and fortify themselves for both. Snicket and two generations of Baudelaires prove in their own ways that reading and writing provide the means of confronting, explaining, and even thwarting the evils all readers will encounter as they become adults. And just as the island version of *A Series of Unfortunate Events* allows the orphans to assume adult responsibilities, so too can the complex and emotional experience of reading Snicket's version help its young readers feel prepared to do the same.

Works Cited

Bettelheim, Bruno. *The Uses of Enchantment: The Meaning and Importance of Fairy Tales.* New York: Knopf, 1976. Print.

Bottigheimer, Ruth H., ed. *Fairy Tales and Society.* Philadelphia: University of Pennsylvania Press, 1986. Print.

Butt, Bruce. "'He's Behind You!' Reflections of Repetition and Predictability in Lemony Snicket's *A Series of Unfortunate Events.*" *Children's Literature in Education* 34.4 (2003): 277–86. *EbscoHost.* 25 May 2012.

Campbell, Joseph. *The Hero with a Thousand Faces,* 2d ed. Princeton: Princeton University Press, 1973. Print.

Cashdan, Sheldon. *The Witch Must Die: How Fairy Tales Shape Our Lives.* New York: Basic Books, 1999. Print.

"Cinderella." In Tatar, *The Grimm Reader,* 77–85. Print.

Grolnick, Simon A. "Fairy Tales and Psychotherapy." In Bottigheimer, 203–15. Print.

"Hansel and Gretel." In Tatar, *The Grimm Reader,* 46–54. Print.

Langbauer, Laurie. "The Ethics and Practice of Lemony Snicket: Adolescence and Generation X." *PMLA* 122.2 (2007): 502–21. *JSTOR.* 31 Jan. 2013.

Larkin, Phillip. "This Be the Verse." *Collected Poems.* New York: Farrar, Straus and Giroux, 1989. 180. Print.

Magnusson, Kendra. "Lemony Snicket's *A Series of Unfortunate Events*: Daniel Handler and Marketing the Author." *Children's Literature Association Quarterly* 37.1 (2012): 86–107. *EbscoHost.* 11 Jan. 2013.

Mueller, Gerhard O. "The Criminological Significance of the Grimms' Fairy Tales." In Bottigheimer, 217–27. Print.

Nguyen, Kim Hong. "Mourning *A Series of Unfortunate Events.*" *Children's Literature Association Quarterly* 37.3 (2012): 266–84. *Project Muse.* 28 Feb. 2013.

Opie, Iona, and Peter Opie, eds. *The Classic Fairy Tales.* New York: Oxford University Press, 1974. Print.

"Pasta Puttanesca." *Mediterrasian.* Mediterrasian.com, 2013. Web. 1 May 2013.

Pilinovsky, Helen. "Donkeyskin, Deerskin, Allerleirauh: The Reality of the Fairy Tale." *The Journal of Mythic Arts.* The Endicott Studio, Spring 2007. Web. 30 Dec. 2012.

Propp, Vladimir. *Morphology of the Folktale.* 2d ed. Trans. Laurence Scott. Austin: University of Texas Press, 1968. Print.

Pugh, Tison. "What, Then, Does Beatrice Mean?: Hermaphroditic Gender, Predatory Sexuality, and Promiscuous Allusion in Daniel Handler/Lemony Snicket's *A Series of Unfortunate Events.*" *Children's Literature* 36 (2008): 162–184. *EbscoHost.* 11 Jan. 2013.

"Rumpelstiltskin." In Tatar, *The Grimm Reader,* 179–82. Print.

Snicket, Lemony [Daniel Handler]. *The Austere Academy*. New York: HarperCollins, 2000. Print.

_____. *The Bad Beginning*. New York: HarperCollins, 1999. Print.

_____. *The Carnivorous Carnival*. New York: HarperCollins, 2002. Print.

_____. *The End*. New York: HarperCollins, 2006. Print.

_____. *The Ersatz Elevator*. New York: HarperCollins, 2001. Print.

_____. *The Grim Grotto*. New York: HarperCollins, 2004. Print.

_____. *The Hostile Hospital*. New York: HarperCollins, 2001. Print.

_____. *The Miserable Mill*. New York: HarperCollins, 2000. Print.

_____. *The Penultimate Peril*. New York: HarperCollins, 2005. Print.

_____. *The Reptile Room*. New York: HarperCollins, 1999. Print.

_____. *The Slippery Slope*. New York: HarperCollins, 2003. Print.

_____. *The Vile Village*. New York: HarperCollins, 2001. Print.

_____. *The Wide Window*. New York: HarperCollins, 2000. Print.

Tatar, Maria. *The Hard Facts of the Grimms' Fairy Tales*. Princeton: Princeton University Press, 1987. Print.

Warner, Marina. *From the Beast to the Blonde: On Fairy Tales and Their Tellers*. New York: Farrar, Straus and Giroux, 1995. Print.

Earning the Right
to Wear Midnight
Terry Pratchett's Tiffany Aching

EILEEN DONALDSON

In the last few decades the study of fairy tale motifs in literature for children and young adults has become widespread, particularly as these motifs are used to different effect by various authors. In general, however, as Bruno Bettelheim, Marie-Louise von Franz, Jack Zipes and other fairy tale scholars have suggested, the fairy tale—when read in an archetypal, psychoanalytical manner—is uniquely poised to serve as an evocation of the transition from childhood to adulthood and the psychological fears and anxieties that mark this period. Fairy tales are therefore a rich source of "ready-made" meaning on which authors of children's literature may draw in order to explore these fears because most young readers should be conversant with at least some fairy tale tropes. This chapter considers the significance for the child reader of selected dark fairy tale motifs in Terry Pratchett's *Tiffany Aching Series*.

Tiffany says that when she is "old" she "will wear midnight," a statement replete with the implications of growing up. Like many other fantasy books written for children, Pratchett's *Tiffany* series (*The Wee Free Men* [2003], *A Hat Full of Sky* [2004], *The Wintersmith* [2006] and *I Shall Wear Midnight* [2010]), traces the protagonist's journey from childhood into adolescence and maturity and in this context, "midnight" takes on various meanings. Firstly, wearing midnight, the color favored by witches, signifies the acquisition of agency for Tiffany who wants to be a witch. It also foregrounds Pratchett's feminist subversion of the bad woman/witch stereotype so that Tiffany's wearing midnight empowers his readers to question the conventional gender roles available to them. Secondly, midnight suggests the witching hour, a time when monsters

145

roam free and when Tiffany overcomes her fears she earns the right to "wear midnight" like a trophy of battle. And lastly, at midnight enchanted things traditionally revert to their natural forms: Pratchett cautions against being seduced or terrified by appearances and so, when Tiffany learns to see clearly, she thus achieves the maturity of "midnight." This essay suggests that Pratchett explores the fears of the "knowing child"—the fears of death, responsibility, separation, and desire—in this series, using the subversion of dark fairy tale motifs to equip his readers with cognitive strategies against fear that they can transfer into their own worlds.

The fact that popular, contemporary authors such as Terry Pratchett acknowledge and examine childhood anxiety and fear is essential because, as Peter Appleton writes, "anxiety disorders are one of the commonest forms of psychological disorder in children and adolescents" (40, 45). Findings also suggest that if childhood anxieties and fears are not dealt with, "it is likely that (they) may be the seeds for more pervasive and severe anxiety symptoms or disorders" in adulthood (Muris and Field 76). Fortunately, however, contemporary psychological studies identify a key to developing preventative strategies. As Peter Muris and Andy Field suggest, "fear and anxiety originate from threat, and threat has to be conceptualized. Conceptualization, in turn, critically depends on cognitive abilities" (81). Theorists therefore propose that cognitive "resilience processes" may protect children from pervasive childhood anxiety. Appleton writes, "resilience ... is not a trait, or a specific feature of an individual ... but rather refers to processes during development which open up opportunities and lead to success" (9) and children can be taught these processes in order to better cope with anxiety and fear. The encouragement of resilience may also be more useful than pointed 'interventions' because "long-term evidence ... suggests that gains (from such interventions) are inconsistent ... and may not maintain over the long term" (Appleton 359). The model proposed by Weisz, Sandler, Durlak and Anton in 2005 (in Appleton 362) is now considered the most useful for long-term alleviation of anxiety: they propose creating a culture aimed at children that acknowledges their fears and responds by modeling appropriate resilience strategies in media that appeal to them. Such a culture of resilience may help youth develop cognitive strategies that equip them to deal with the ambiguities and complexities of a world in which almost everything can be perceived as a threat to the self.

The role that children's literature may play in creating such a culture of resilience is significant. Scholarly writing has long advocated that children's literature may provide a "safe" space in which to explore childhood fears because the distance between child reader and fictional catalyst offers a protection against the dissolution that fear threatens. Literature of the fantastic particularly serves this need because, as Ursula Le Guin claims, "it [is] to ... the unknown depths in [the child], that the story [speaks]; and it [is] the depths which [respond] to it and, nonverbally, irrationally, [understand] it, and [learn] from it" (51). Her claim is that literature of the fantastic encourages children to resolve the issues contained in the Shadow, the angry, frightened, dark part of the psyche identified by Jung, because of the symbolic language in which the fantastic speaks (53). Bettelheim, von Franz, and others have also acknowledged that fairy tales in particular, may meet this need to explore the Shadow. Bettelheim writes that "more can be learned from [fairy tales] about the inner problems of human beings, and of the right solutions to their predicaments in any society, than from any other type of story within a child's comprehension" (Bettelheim 5). And Von Franz supposes that "[fairy tales] have the great advantage of being naive (not 'literary') and of having been worked out in collective groups, with the result that they contain purely archetypal material unobscured by personal problems" and that today we have rediscovered "their immense psychological value" (von Franz 1). And so "fairy tales have always been 'stories to think with'" (de la Rochere ii, Warner 1995 xiv), suited to consumption by both children and adults.

Fairy tale monsters specifically encourage this kind of engagement with the text because from the very beginning, "etymologically speaking, the monster is something ... that demonstrates (Latin *monstrare*: to demonstrate) and [warns] (Latin *monere*: to warn)" (Punter and Byron 263). Monsters thus challenge the reader's expectations and assumptions, asking us to learn from the truths they demonstrate. The monsters and dark fairy tale tropes that recur throughout the *Tiffany Aching Series* reflect Tiffany's (and Pratchett's readers') anxieties to do with the transition from childhood to early adolescence: the struggle to define oneself, the fear of responsibility (and its counterpart, the fear of separation), the fear of desire and the fear of death. They also enable Tiffany to model resilience strategies that equip the child reader to survive his or her fear just as she does.

Very briefly, the broad outline of each of the books is as follows: In *The Wee Free Men* (2003; references are from the 2004 Corgi Edition) Granny Aching has died. Because she was the "hag of the hills" her death leaves the edges of the world unguarded and the Fairy Queen invades Tiffany's home; as the new "hag," Tiffany must defend the Chalk hills. In the second book, *A Hat Full of Sky* (2004; references are from the 2005 Corgi Edition), Tiffany trains to be a witch and her growing magical awareness awakens a hiver, a spirit that possesses her for her power. Her task is to expel the hiver and take back her body. In *The Wintersmith* (2006; references are from the 2007 Corgi Edition), Tiffany watches the dance of the seasons and steps into Summer's place, and the Wintersmith falls in love with her, with disastrous consequences. In *I Shall Wear Midnight* (2010; references are from the 2011 Corgi Edition), the Cunning Man, a dead witch-hunter, is woken and spreads prejudice against witches throughout the Discworld; it is Tiffany's task to defeat him.

As the books progress, Pratchett explores various childhood anxieties to do with growing up but he also purposely foregrounds the difficulties girls face when they are limited by the gender-roles available to women. He therefore focuses attention not only on Tiffany's need to overcome the powerlessness associated with being a child but specifically a *girl* child so that she can achieve agency. The first fairy tale "monsters" that Pratchett examines in these books are, therefore, "monstrous gender expectations" that may con girls into believing that the only roles available to them are those of the passive princess or the female monster, both of which disadvantage them and suggest that they are unfit for active participation in masculinist society.

Throughout the series, Tiffany often reflects on the fact that her plain brown eyes and hair mean she cannot be a princess because they only have blonde hair (or red hair, at a push) and blue eyes. She says, "stories create our destinies" (38) and because "she couldn't be the prince and she'd never be a princess, and she didn't want to be a woodcutter ... she'd be the witch and *know* things, just like Granny Aching" (38). Pratchett almost seems to be echoing Joanna Russ's dry rhetoric when she asks, "What can a heroine do? What myths, what plots, what actions are available to a female protagonist? Very few.... Women in ... literature seem pretty much limited to either Devourer/Bitches or Maiden/Victims" (Russ 7). It is dispiriting that Pratchett feels the need to address this same issue when feminists such as Russ raised it in the 1970s but, as Jack Zipes offers,

> despite the advances made by the feminist movement, the toy industry, television, Hollywood, and advertising have remained almost immune to pressures by activist groups that seek to change the negative images conveyed by all sorts of cultural objects that influence social roles and relationships [Zipes, *Relentless Progress*, 15].

In these books, Tiffany is aware that she is at a disadvantage because she does not fit the "princess profile" that illustrates "successful femininity" and so she adopts the only role left to her—that of a female monster: the witch. However, the fact that she wants to be a witch challenges young readers to re-evaluate their assumptions about this female monster, who is "invariably represented as an old, ugly crone … capable of monstrous acts [such as] cannibalism, murder, castration of male victims, and the advent of natural disasters" (Creed 2). Pratchett subverts this stereotype beginning with Tiffany's first encounter with the "wicked witch" in "The Goode Childe's Book of Faerie Tales." Her immediate reaction upon her introduction to the character is to ask for proof (37). The two reasons Tiffany gives for becoming a witch also challenge the stereotype. First, she wants to be like Granny Aching and "know things" (38). In this way, Pratchett links the witch positively with wisdom and knowledge. Second, when the villagers murder an old lady accused of witchcraft, Tiffany reasons that if she becomes a witch, she can protect the weak and "speak up for those who don't have voices" (43). As a child and a girl, Tiffany can relate to Mrs. Snapperly's powerlessness and she wants to be able to defend herself and others. These qualities move the stereotyped witch from the category of monster to that of "hero" in Pratchett's world.

Rather than being monsters, Pratchett's witches are therefore helpful figures in this series and Tiffany often receives guidance and support from them. At the beginning of the first novel, *The Wee Free Men*, she meets Miss Tick, a witch who teaches her two important strategies for dealing with fear: first sight and second thoughts. First sight is the discipline to see what is really there, not what you think you should be seeing. And second thoughts (and eventually third and fourth thoughts) help you to think beyond the surface of a situation. Although these skills are described as "magical," they are ordinary and therefore within the reader's grasp as well as Tiffany's. These "magical" strategies are supported by the findings of child psychologists Liat Sayfan and Kristen Hansen Laguttuta. They argue that "with increasing age children evidence ... more sophisticated knowledge that fear reactions are mediated by the person's mind" (1769). If children know that they can mediate their fears and anxieties with their thoughts, then the cognitive strategies of first sight and second thoughts modeled by Pratchett are of immediate practical use to his young readers; as the narrator tells us, "It's amazing what a child who is quiet and observant can learn, and this includes things people don't think she's old enough to know" (163).

Because the witch lives on the fringes, she is also an appropriate monstrous double for Tiffany who is between childhood and adulthood. Like traditional witches, Pratchett's are associated with life's bloody moments of transition: birth, menarche, sex and death. Because they preside over birth and they deal with corpses, because they are both monster and hero, I propose that his witches embody Kristeva's abject which both fascinates and revolts, and of which she writes: "abjection is above all ambiguity ... it does not radically cut off the subject from what threatens it—on the contrary, abjection acknowledges it to be in perpetual danger" (Kristeva 2). That borderland of the abject, which "disturbs identity, system, order" (2) is an apt descriptor of the ambiguity associated with growing up, which means power, but also danger, sex and death; the young self is abject, and therefore young readers are fascinated by the abject inherent in most dark fairy tale motifs. Pratchett invites his readers to feel out this frightening border-space in which they find themselves, but he does not cast them into it without support because there are older witches to help them: Granny Weatherwax, a powerful witch, tells Tiffany that witches "'look to the edges.... There're a lot of edges, more than people know. Between life and death, this world and the next, night and day, right and wrong ... an' they need watching. We watch 'em'" (304).

The significance of Pratchett's witches is thus twofold. First, as abject figures at home on the border, they help young readers accept a "postmodern vision of childhood, crossing borders [that have limited Western childhood] and subverting the modernist view of children as docile" (Chappel 284), thus undermining the anxieties associated with change and growing up. Secondly, Pratchett's witches empower child-readers to defy convention because, as masters of first sight and second thoughts, they challenge stereotypes and unfounded prejudices, defying the symbolic order that defines them as "wicked" (Creed 76). Pratchett's witches encourage child-readers to question what is right and wrong, what is wicked and what is good, what is true and what is illusion.

However, although Tiffany wants to be a witch and is proud of the skills and independence such a role allows her, she is still "other" because she has taken up this role. Throughout the series Pratchett continually foregrounds the prejudices of "ordinary folk" against witches and so the reader remains constantly aware that, while Tiffany may have made the best of a bad situation, the witch is still a fairy tale monster fraught with ambiguity. This comes to the fore in the fourth novel, *I Shall Wear Midnight*. In this book Tiffany expresses insecurity about her sexual/romantic destiny because she is a witch and witches are "*apart* ... among people but not the *same* as them" (9; italics in the original). At the scouring fair, where all the teenagers on the Chalk pair off, we are told, "[she] hadn't had a kiss, but after all, she was the witch. Who knew what they might get turned into?" (5); and two curious young girls ask if she has any "passionate parts" at all (14). The fact that she is a witch dehumanizes her for the villagers to the extent that her body is no longer female or capable of reproduction. Once again, she is disadvantaged because she does not fit "the fairy tale princess" stereotype expected of girls.

The irony is that the character who is billed "the princess" in *I Shall Wear Midnight* is just as frustrated by the stereotype that limits her. Letitia, who comes to the Chalk hills to marry Roland, the baron, is described as pretty, blonde, delicate and feminine. Although Tiffany envies her, we find out later that she envies Tiffany when she retorts, "Hah! I wanted to be a witch when I was little. But just my luck, I had long blonde hair and a pale complexion and a very rich father. What good was that? Girls like that can't be witches!" (285). Neither girl understands that stereotypes limit them both (until the end of the novel when Tiffany finds love and a married Letitia begins training as a witch). Pratchett criticizes the limitations that these stereotypes enforce, suggesting that the resulting frustrations are not only damaging for the girls but dangerous for society: Letitia, who cannot channel her unused energy into anything constructive, unleashes her fears and jealousy in a spell against "the witch" which wreaks havoc across the Discworld.

Significantly, the competition between the two girls is a traditional element of fairy tales. Usually, however, the witch is an older woman whose position is threatened by a younger, nubile female and because both of them depend on a single male to survive, their competition is often to the death (Warner, *From the Beast to the Blonde*, 226). One has only to consider the "wicked stepmothers" who play the witch in stories such as "Snow White," "Cinderella," "Vasalisa the Wise" and so on to understand the damaging psychological angst perpetuated by this competition. Pratchett reflects the senselessness of this situation and finally proposes that both girls defy the fairy tale stereotypes of witch and princess. It is significant that he not only subverts the negativity associated with the witch but that he problematizes the pervasive glamor associated with the princess, suggesting that this traditional fairy tale protagonist is monstrous if one considers the gendered implications for girls who cannot meet its demands. Through his examination and criticism of these stereotypes, Pratchett exposes the anxieties girls might feel during this period of transition: as they begin to fashion their adult identities, the masculinist metanarratives (of female passivity and powerlessness) that story perpetuates affects the choices girls have and may leave them feeling that there is no "fit" for them in public society. In subverting these stereotypes, Pratchett encourages his female readers to question these metanarratives and attempt to create more authentic personal destinies.

While Pratchett directly challenges the powerlessness of girls in these novels, he also defies the passivity of "the child' in fairy tales in which children are often victims, their "innocence" and "purity" a lure for adults and monsters that want to devour or destroy them. From the first time we meet her, Pratchett characterizes Tiffany as capable and he enables her to learn the skills of first sight and second thoughts, equipping her to see clearly and identify real dangers as opposed to fairy tale trickery. As she gains confidence in herself, she models resilience processes that empower Pratchett's readers, enabling him to strip away the disabling illusion of childhood passivity perpetuated by adult society and the fairy tale. As Drew Chappel suggests, "Adults conceive childhood not in terms of living children, but an assumed 'the child,' onto which they ascribe whatever markers are useful to work out their hopes, fears, ideologies" (283). The adult construction of the defenseless child not only discourages most children from attempting agency, it enforces a social hierarchy that ensures adult superiority over children.

For Pratchett, the adult tendency to keep information from children in order to "protect" them also maintains a damaging adult hegemony and his perspective correlates with Appleton's studies on childhood anxiety: children are more anxious if they do not have enough information about a given situation or object to make a sound decision regarding their response. Giving them correct information encourages a greater feeling of control and the promise of a positive outcome (Hadwin et al. in Appleton 117). Michel Foucault tells us, "power and knowledge directly imply one another … there is no power relation without the correlative constitution of a field of knowledge, nor any knowledge that does not presuppose and constitute at the same time power relations" (129). That children are disadvantaged because they are not given correct information is reflected in the fact that all of Tiffany's knowledge about fairyland comes from the very obviously sanctioned-by-adults "The Goode Childe's Book of Faerie Tales." The title itself suggests that "good" (as defined by adults) children will enjoy (and subscribe to) the tenets set down by adults in these tales. The misinformation spread by the book is dangerous. When Tiffany enters fairyland to do battle with the Queen she thinks she is in the wrong place, exclaiming, "'*Fairyland*? No, it's not! I've seen pictures! Fairyland is … is all trees and flowers and sunshine and, and tinklyness!'" (179). Because adults have "protected" her from the truth her expectations of fairyland are incorrect and she is vulnerable to the Fairy Queen's attack.

Pratchett also deals with the condescending attitude of (most) adults to children, suggesting that this too perpetuates helplessness in children and encourages childhood anxiety. Miss Tick, who identifies Tiffany as a prospective witch, exclaims: "At that age? Impossible!" (15); although she can sense Tiffany's potential, even she cannot believe that a child has what it takes to be a witch. And when Tiffany needs to know how to defeat monsters she cannot ask the adults around her because they will think she's "telling stories" (14). When she finally asks a teacher, he replies:

> "Zoology, eh? That's a big word, isn't it?"
> "No, actually it isn't," said Tiffany. "Patronising is a big word. Zoology is quite short."
> The teacher's eyes narrowed further. Children like Tiffany were bad news [29].

These attitudes could dissuade Tiffany from attempting any independent action but instead she refuses to believe the adult assessment of her "childish" capabilities. From the beginning, she is suspicious of what they tell her and the narrator reveals that she "never really liked ('The Goode Childe's Book of Faerie Tales') [because it] seemed to her that it tried to tell her what to do and what to think" (62). Although there are some helpful adults in the series, notably the witches and Granny Aching, most of the "ordinary" adults find it impossible to believe that children are capable of anything. In exposing these attitudes Pratchett encourages his child readers to re-evaluate what adult society tells them, and Tiffany's heroism empowers them to challenge the vulnerability that still influences western metanarratives of childhood.

Apart from Tiffany's acquisition of agency and the anxieties that mark this process, Pratchett also explores other childhood fears in each of the four books. Although the fears of death and loss weave their way through this series, they are marked in the first novel, *The Wee Free Men,* in which they are connected with Tiffany's response to Granny Aching's death. Significantly, one of the recurring motifs in fairy tales is the abandoned female protagonist; her caregiver—most often her birth mother—dies, leaving the young girl alone and at the mercy of a suddenly dangerous world. This motif echoes stories such as "Snow White," "Cinderella," "Donkeyskin," "Little Two Eyes" and Andersen's "The Little Matchstick Girl." Although temporary independence is a salient feature of children's literature, in fairy tales this independence is seldom chosen by the female protagonist and it always comes at a great cost: she goes from being loved to being outcast or orphaned and from being wealthy to being poverty-stricken. When Granny Aching dies, the narrator tells us that "[Tiffany] was seven and the world had ended" (151) and "in the years since then, everything had gone wrong" (132). Her world ends because the one person to whom she is special is gone. And Granny Aching's death also results in a change of Tiffany's physical fortunes because the monstrous Fairy Queen can now begin her assault on the Discworld.

However, fairy tale has a built-in defense mechanism against death: the fairy godmother who may or may not be the spirit of the dead caregiver. Yet, as the Opies write, "the power of godmothers is limited. Sometimes all they are able to offer is advice" (16). Granny Aching fills the role of the fairy godmother in this way in that Tiffany's memories of her help her at crucial moments in the story. The most important thing Granny Aching does is remind Tiffany of who she is so that when the Fairy Queen tries to overwhelm her with thoughts of abandonment and worthlessness, Granny rises in her memory and connects her with the Chalk—which is, after all, made up of the bones of long-dead things that live again in the "hag o' the hills"—and the narrator tells us:

> [Tiffany] could feel the thousands of little lives all around her, smell the scents on the breeze and see all the shades of the night.... She knew exactly where she was, and who she was, and what she was....
>
> "I never cried for Granny because there was no need to," she said. "She has never left me!" [290–291].

Tiffany is not destroyed by her loss because Granny connects her to her history and the Chalk, teaching her to become the new hag of the hills. Tiffany's resilience is reflected in her seeing "all the shades of the night" rather than the featureless black usually associated with night, pain, and death: midnight is living because death is not what she expected it to be. And so Pratchett suggests a kind of resolution to the fear of death and loss because, like Tiffany, his readers can draw strength from the memories of their loved ones. The magic of the fairy godmother is that she buffers the protagonist, and the child reader, against the emptiness that death and loss bring.

Pratchett's monsters also encourage his readers to re-evaluate their fears and anxieties. The first of these is the Fairy Queen. Her beauty is an illusion that she uses to seduce children away from reality, preventing them from growing up and proscribing their behavior (they must "skip and play" because "that's what children do" [226–227]); as such, she may also be an embodiment of adult condescension. Pratchett's Fairy Queen is reminiscent of Andersen's Snow Queen because she steals young boys away to a kingdom of ice and will be the "death" of the Discworld. The threat these Queens represent is that of stasis and while it may be tempting to follow someone who allows you to "eat sweeties" for all time, being frozen in childhood would not always remain the comforting thing it may at first seem. And so Tiffany fights the Fairy Queen, an archetypal "monstrous mother" who wants to keep children from growing up.

Using the skills of first sight and second thoughts, Tiffany sees through the illusions spun by the Fairy Queen and she realizes that "the secret is not to dream.... The secret is to wake up.... I have woken up and I am real.... You cannot fool me anymore" (291). Such reality affirmation strategies are advocated by psychologists (Sayfan and Lagattuta 1758) and as Pratchett models ways of using them he encourages his readers to see through the things that frighten them, promising that they are stronger and more resilient than they have been taught to believe. Pratchett's criticism of illusory fairy tale glamor culminates in the revelation of the small, monkey-like appearance of the once glorious Fairy Queen at the end of the novel. Although her power creates the seductive illusion of beauty, it only masks her bitterness and smallness and in the end she is pitiful. Finally, Tiffany defeats the Fairy Queen and rescues the Baron's son, Roland, subverting the stereotypical fairy tale pattern of prince rescuing princess and offering readers the resilience needed to defy the western metanarratives of the powerless child and girl.

The second group of "monsters" Tiffany meets in this book are the Wee Free Men themselves, the Nac Mac Feegle. Pratchett satirizes our expectations of fairy-folk (wings, flowers and "tinklyness") through the Feegles who curse, drink, fight, steal, cause chaos and are feared by everyone. However, they become Tiffany's stalwart companions through the series, suggesting a natural sympathy between the two. This subverts the usual fear young children associate with fairy tale monsters (Sayfan and Lagattuta) and encourages an exploration of "monstrous doubles" (Stephens and McCallum 108). Recent postmodern studies of the monster have identified a shift, resulting in "monsters (becoming) children's best friends, alter-egos, inner selves" (Warner, *No Go the Bogeyman*, 15); as the child's "double," the monster allows the experience of uninhibited desires and raucous behaviors that are punishable in the real world. Tiffany and the Feegles are also natural allies according to Jeana Jorgensen who suggests that monsters are "caught between subject and object positions" (288), the position that children (and girl children in particular) have traditionally occupied in Western society and the fairy tale.

The sympathy between Tiffany and the Feegles resonates in the Feegles' defiance of authority; their motto is "Nae King! Nae Quin! Nae laird! Nae master! We willna' be fooled again!" (91). The Feegles also indirectly subvert the fear of death because they insist they are already dead and this world is heaven. The Feegles are indomitable, undisciplined and a constant source of humor, which is in itself a strategy against fear. As Boodman tells us, "according to 'relief' theories of laughter ... humor can serve to release excess emotion and/or nervous energy" (in Cross 59). Like the skills of first sight and second thoughts, Pratchett's use of humor engages his readers' cognitive skills. Julie Cross writes that "much of the humor in some comic Gothic texts for younger readers ... relies on a sophisticated understanding of irony, parody, genre convention, and 'higher' order cognitive forms that offer opportunities for 'sophisticated reader understanding'" (Cross 57). The value of this sophisticated reading is that it challenges the cognitive functions of readers, pushing them to new understandings of society and, in Pratchett's writing, increasing their capability to deal with fear and anxiety; as Tiffany observes in *I Shall Wear Midnight*: "Laughter helps things slide into the thinking" (402).

In *A Hat Full of Sky*, the dark fairy tale motif that Pratchett employs seems similar to that used in stories such as "Beauty and the Beast." In this case, the protagonist is under a spell in which the "bestial" part of their nature takes them over and they revert to their original form only when the lesson of their "humanity" has been learned. Here, Tiffany is taken over by a hiver, which is:

> a sluggish thing indeed, tumbling gently through the endless night between the worlds.... Yet a hiver does have the ability to fear and to crave. We cannot guess what frightens a hiver, but they seem to take refuge in bodies that have power of some sort—great strength, great intellect, great prowess with magic [94].

When hivers possess someone, they amplify their powers or gifts until the host body is destroyed by the stupidity brought on by excessive pride and ego. Like the Beast in the classical fairy tale, who is transformed because he shows no kindness to the old woman, Tiffany's weaknesses allow the hiver to possess her and her least exemplary qualities come to the fore, transforming her into a nasty, prideful creature.

The anxiety Pratchett seems to address here is described in the Fear Survey Schedule for Children (the FSSC-R) as "fear of failure and criticism," which advances when children go to school and have to compete with their peers for the first time (Muris and Field 77–78). The hiver may represent the strategies used by a child to overcome their insecurities, overcompensating with arrogance in order to "fit in" and be "safe" from criticism, and, as Pratchett suggests, losing themselves in the process.

During her training under Miss Level, a research witch, Tiffany questions her abilities and feels that she can't get "real magic" right. She also compares herself unfavorably with the other witches her own age. Annagramma, the snooty leader of the group criticizes Tiffany because she hasn't "dressed the part" (136); the girls all wear black and so much occult jewelry it trips them up, while Tiffany wears blue or green and scruffy boots. It is significant that Tiffany is judged according to how well she performs the role of "the witch" and that the markers, at least for Annagramma, are traditionally feminine ones—clothes and jewelry. Pratchett again foregrounds the gender-expectations that complicate Tiffany's transition into adulthood.

Annagramma is playing at magic; although she revels in the trappings and jargon of the stereotypical "new age" witch, she cannot cast an actual spell or use the "magical skills" of first sight and second thoughts but because Tiffany lacks the confidence to see through Annagramma, her self-doubt allows the hiver to possess her. When it takes her over, it expresses the part of Tiffany that wants to be like Annagramma: she suddenly feels that "looking good [is] important" (184) and that people "should be made to fear witches" (185). The narrator reveals that the hiver gives people what they want (296) and what Tiffany wants is the protective shield of power and respect that children crave, and part of achieving this is "fitting in" through adopting socio-cultural norms, like appropriate gender (and in this case witchy) behaviors. However, there is a part of Tiffany that knows she is possessed and that this isn't who she wants to be; she and the Feegles exorcize the hiver using objects associated with Granny Aching to jolt her memory and remind her of who she is.

In this episode, Pratchett continues to warn his readers against being seduced by illusion; as Granny Weatherwax says, "all that glittery stuff is just toys, and toys can lead you astray" (341). He suggests that ego and pride arise from fear, and they can possess one like an evil spirit, especially if one measures one's worth according to society's expectations. When Tiffany's connection to Granny Aching and the Chalk grounds her, she no longer feels self-doubt and can defeat the hiver and reclaim her humanity. Again, the ordinary is affirmed and Pratchett dispels the illusory "glamors" of society that leech children of self-worth.

The third and fourth books, *The Wintersmith* and *I Shall Wear Midnight,* both explore anxieties to do with sexual awakening and the responsibilities of adulthood. In *The Wintersmith,* Tiffany is thirteen and Miss Treason, the new witch with whom she is training, takes her to watch the dance of the seasons. Tiffany is swept up in the rhythm and steps into the dance, displacing Summer and causing the Wintersmith to fall in love with her.

This story reaches back to myth in its exploration of female coming of age: Tiffany becomes Summer, who represents life and fertility, and she is courted by her first besotted suitor, the Wintersmith, who represents the other end of life—old age and death. Although Pratchett describes the rhythm of the dance as natural and so part of Tiffany's journey into womanhood, Tiffany resents having the role of Summer thrust upon her and her reluctance to step into the role means that winter may continue until her world dies. Because her first romance is with the winter (with its implications of old age and death) and it may result in the death of her world, her sexual awakening resounds with Laura Hubner's assertion that, "despite multiple retellings and re-workings of fairy tales, the fears of burgeoning female sexuality and the ambiguities of the female body, and female desire, remain a controversial talking point that is never finally resolved" (57). Certainly, Pratchett's description of Tiffany's sexual awakening is uncomfortably ambiguous, suggestive as it is of death and dying. This motif resounds in fairy tale, appearing in many stories such as "Donkeyskin," "Sleeping Beauty," "Snow White," "Bluebeard" and "Beauty and the Beast." In each case, a female protagonist, who is uneasy about joining the adult economies of desire and reproduction, either seeks to avoid the transition or experiences it is as a trauma akin to death.

However, the other event that dominates *The Wintersmith* is Miss Treason's death and the way in which Pratchett deals with it helps put the "dying" associated with growing up in perspective. In the Discworld, witches know when they're going to die, so Miss Treason is able to attend her funeral/going-away party which is "just for witches, of course. Other people tend to get a bit nervous" (120). Because the witches treat death as an everyday occurrence, it becomes exactly that. The pragmatism of the witches makes Tiffany puzzle over the fear death evokes in people and she decides that "the start and finish of things [is] always dangerous, lives most of all" (156). What she has yet to learn is that the start of her life as an adult is similarly dangerous, and similarly ordinary. Although the role of Summer is thrust upon her, she has no choice; the continuation of life on the Discworld depends on her accepting this natural part of being human.

Although Pratchett appears to offer his readers only the cold comfort of pragmatism, this too encourages agency. Before she dies, Miss Treason's advice to Tiffany is "I made mistakes. But I didn't make excuses" (110). Her lesson is that a witch deals with things; she does not shirk her duties or avoid the problem before her and in the end Tiffany models this practical courage for Pratchett's readers. When the people of the Chalk send a delegation to ask her to save them, although her immediate response is "I'm only thirteen.... And I can't" (16), she steps out into the snow and says: "This I choose to do. If there is a price, I choose to pay. If it is my death, then I choose to die. Where this takes me, there I choose to go" (18–19). Because she chooses to act, she claims her right to agency. She accepts the burden of adulthood, becomes Summer and her first kiss melts the Wintersmith. Because one cannot avoid growing up, the act of choosing to move forward, rather than being harried along, offers a kind of resilience against the anxieties of aging.

In *I Shall Wear Midnight*, Pratchett again foregrounds the dangerous prejudices that fairy tale stereotypes can encourage. The murder of Mrs. Snapperly in the first novel, *The Wee Free Men*, introduces a theme that comes to a head in this last book: for Pratchett, people are the real monsters, not the fairy tale creatures children have been taught to fear. In these books, people are violent because, unlike Tiffany (and his readers), they do not use first sight and second thoughts to see what is really there and so they react unthinkingly and destructively, like monsters. Pratchett equates maturity with using one's cognitive skills to see through story's illusions because, although "the stories *weren't real* ... Mrs Snapperly had died because of stories" (63). He thus urges his readers to challenge stereotypes and decide the truth for themselves.

At the beginning of this novel, Letitia casts a spell against "the witch" (meaning to cause Tiffany trouble) and it wakes the Cunning Man, a dead witch-hunter. He rises and spreads hatred like a contamination, causing attacks against witches to occur across the Discworld. The narrator reveals that the Cunning Man's power comes from fanning "old stories, old rumours and old picture books [that] have their own hold on the memory of the world" (12) into active hatred and fear. Significantly, the Cunning Man has no eyes, which means he cannot use "first sight" to see clearly because he does not "see" at all. This suggests that when people allow prejudice to frighten them, it is because they have surrendered their ability to see—choosing to see the things they fear as monsters instead of seeing them clearly and objectively. Again,

Pratchett advocates the use of first sight and second thoughts to dispel groundless fears that perpetuate prejudice. The point he makes is that, while the Cunning Man may encourage hatred in this novel, he only has power because

> poison goes where poison's welcome. And there's always an excuse, isn't there, to throw a stone at the old lady who looks funny. It's always easier to blame somebody. And once you've called someone a witch, then you'd be amazed how many things you can blame her for [164].

Like Tiffany's possession by the hiver, people have to allow the Cunning Man to possess them but once they do, their prejudice and hatred turns them into Beasts. Pratchett instead advocates a pragmatic study of the object causing fear, encouraging in younger readers a healthy skepticism about the "monsters" they have been taught to fear and, hopefully, an understanding that fear and hatred are often more dangerous than the monsters.

As Tiffany prepares for her final battle with the Cunning Man she repeatedly has visions of an old Tiffany accompanied by a hare, signifying sexual maturity and fertility (Neumann 141). The implication is that young Tiffany must embrace all aspects of herself because allowing herself to be sexual as well as a witch defies the stereotype that gives the Cunning Man his power. Significantly, the manner in which she defeats him coincides with an action used in an ancient Discworld marriage rite and so, as he "dies," Letitia and Roland are married by Tiffany. At that moment of transformation and new beginnings, she recognizes that the magic inherent in marriage and sexuality is a force of nature that goes beyond the "romantic pattern" of fairy tale and belongs to everyone, not just "princesses." She observes to Letitia that "maybe it's wrong to base one's future on a book of fairy stories" (296) and her newfound capacity to live beyond the stereotype expected of her is the note on which the series ends. Pratchett suggests that fairy tale stereotypes, like "the witch" and "the princess," encourage anxieties that operate on multiple levels and their power must be refuted, refused or transformed for childhood anxieties to be resolved.

Throughout the series, Pratchett therefore uses dark fairy tale motifs to explore the anxiety associated with various borders: between childhood and adulthood; between life and death; between genders; between self and other. And, although it is impossible to finally resolve the open-endedness and threat associated with such spaces, he asks his readers to delve into them using the cognitive strategies he describes to undermine their anxieties and create meaning for themselves. Doing so, they develop the resilience necessary to navigate the postmodern world they inhabit in which nothing is stable and everything is perpetually on the border between beginnings and endings. He asks his readers to welcome the liberating possibilities of such a reality, rather than being afraid of them, because they control what this space signifies. As Granny Weatherwax claims:

> I can tell you in truth that at such times the universe gets a little closer to us. They are strange times, times of beginnings and endings. Dangerous and powerful. And we feel it even if we don't know what it is. These times are not necessarily good, and not necessarily bad. In fact, what they are depends on what *we* are [370; italics in the original].

As Tiffany models the cognitive resilience strategies Pratchett advocates, his readers are invited to learn with her. When the series draws to a close she has mastered the skills of first sight and second thoughts. She has faced her fears and developed the resilience necessary to enter the adult world. And because she has woven an identity that is not limited by societal expectations, she is finally able to say, "I shall wear midnight, and I will be good at it" (412).

Works Cited

Appleton, Peter, ed. *Children's Anxiety: A Contextual Approach.* East Sussex: Routledge, 2008. Print.

Bettelheim, Bruno. *The Uses of Enchantment: The Meaning and Importance of Fairy Tales.* New York: Vintage, 1989. Print.

Chappel, Drew. "Sneaking Out After Dark: Resistance, Agency and the Postmodern Child in J.K. Rowling's Harry Potter Series." *Children's Literature in Education* 39 (2008): 281–293. Print.

Creed, Barbara. *The Monstrous Feminine: Film, Feminism, Psychoanalysis.* London: Routledge, 1993. Print.

Cross, Julie. "Frightening and Funny: Humour in Children's Gothic Fiction." *The Gothic in Children's Literature: Haunting the Borders.* Eds. Anna Jackson, Karen Coats and Roderick McGillis. London: Routledge, 2008. 57–76. Print.

Dutheil de la Rochere, Martine H. Foreword. *Postmodern Reinterpretations of Fairy Tales: How Applying New Methods Generates New Meanings.* Ed. Anna Kerchy. New York: Edwin Mellen, 2011. i–iii. Print.

Foucault, Michel. "From 'Discipline and Punish.'" *Performance Analysis: An Introductory Coursebook.* Eds. Colin Counsell and Laurie Wolf. London: Routledge, 2011. Print.

Hall, Granville S. "A Study of Fears." *American Journal of Psychology* 8 (1897): 147–249. Print.

Hubner, Laura. "Pan's Labyrinth, Fear and the Fairy Tale." *Fear Itself: Reasoning the Unreasonable*. Eds. Stephen Hessel and Michele Huppert. New York: Rodopi, 2009. 45–62. Print.

Jackson, Anna, Karen Coats, and Roderick McGillis. *The Gothic in Children's Literature*. London: Routledge, 2008. Print.

Jorgensen, Jeana. "Monstrous Skins and Hybrid Identities in Catherynne M. Valente's *The Orphan's Tales*." *Postmodern Reinterpretations of Fairy Tales: How Applying New Methods Generates New Meanings*. Ed. Anna Kerchy. New York: Edwin Mellen, 2011. 276–295. Print.

Kristeva, Julia. *Powers of Horror: An Essay on Abjection*. Trans. Leon S. Roudiez. New York: Columbia University Press, 1982. Print.

Le Guin, Ursula K. "The Child and the Shadow." 1974. *The Language of the Night: Essays on Fantasy and Science Fiction*. London: The Women's Press, 1989. Print.

Locke, John. *Some Thoughts Concerning Education*. Eds. John W. Yolton and J.S. Yolton. Oxford: Clarendon, 1989. Print.

Muris, Peter, Harald Merckelbach, Bjorn Gadet and Veronique Moulaert. "Fears, Worries and Scary Dreams in 4–12 Year-old Children: Their Content, Developmental Pattern, and Origins." *Journal of Clinical Child Psychology* 29 (2000): 43–52. Print.

_____, and Andy P. Field. "The Normal Development of Fear." *Anxiety Disorders in Children and Adolescents*, 2d ed. Eds. Wendy K. Silverman and Andy P. Field. Cambridge: Cambridge University Press, 2011. 76–89. Print.

Neumann, Erich. *The Great Mother: An Analysis of the Archetype*. Princeton: Princeton University Press, 1974. Print.

Opie, Iona and Peter Opie. *The Classic Fairy Tales*. New York: Oxford University Press, 1974. Print.

Pratchett, Terry. *I Shall Wear Midnight*. London: Corgi Press, 2011. Print.

_____. *A Hat Full of Sky*. London: Corgi Press, 2005. Print.

_____. *The Wee Free Men*. London: Corgi Press, 2004. Print.

_____. *The Wintersmith*. London: Corgi Press, 2007. Print.

Punter, David and Glennis Byron. *The Gothic*. London: Blackwell, 2004. Print.

Russ, Joanna. "What Can A Heroine Do? Or Why Women Can't Write." *Images of Women in Fiction: Feminist Perspectives*. Ed. Susan Koppelman Cornillon. Bowling Green: Bowling Green University Popular Press, 1972. 3–20. Print.

Sayfan, Liat, and Kristen H. Lagattuta. "Scaring the Monster Away: What Children Know about Managing Fears of Real and Imaginary Creatures." *Child Development* 80.6 (2009): 1756–1774. Print.

Silverman, Wendy K., and Andy P. Field, eds. *Anxiety Disorders in Children and Adolescents*, 2d ed. Cambridge: Cambridge University Press, 2011. Print.

Stephens, John, and Robyn McCallum. *Retelling Stories, Framing Culture: Traditional Story and Metanarratives in Children's Literature*. London: Garland, 1998. Print.

Sully, James. *Studies of Childhood*. London: Longmans, Green, 1895. Print.

Townshend, Dale. "The Haunted Nursery: 1764–1830." *The Gothic in Children's Literature: Haunting the Borders*. Eds. Anna Jackson, Karen Coats and Roderick McGillis. London: Routledge, 2008. 15–38. Print.

Von Franz, Marie-Louise. *The Feminine in Fairy Tales*, rev. ed. London: Shambhala, 1993. Print.

Warner, Marina. *From the Beast to the Blonde: On Fairy Tales and Their Tellers*. London: Vintage, 1995. Print.

Warner, Marina. *No Go the Bogeyman: Scaring, Lulling and Making Mock*. London: Vintage, 2000. Print.

Zipes, Jack. *Fairy Tales and the Art of Subversion: The Classical Genre for Children and the Process of Civilisation*. London: Routledge, 2006. Print.

_____. 2009. *Relentless Progress: The Reconfiguration of Children's Literature, Fairy Tales and Story Telling*. New York: Routledge, 2009. Print.

"Monstrosity will be called for"

Holly Black's and Melissa Marr's Urban Gothic Fairy Tale Heroines

RHONDA NICOL

The two young adult[1] series fiction collections I will be examining in this essay, Holly Black's *Modern Tales of Faerie* series[2] and Melissa Marr's *Wicked Lovely* series,[3] are arguably contemporary fairy tales that, like their folkloric forbearers, are resistant to classification or categorization. Although the fairy tale is difficult to define, we tend to know a fairy tale—or a text that takes it cues from fairy tale patterns—when we see one. Jack Zipes acknowledges that although "the intricate relationship and evolution of folk and fairy tales are difficult to comprehend and define," the fairy tale is, at least in part, a recounting of an individual's personal and social growth, which is facilitated via some manner of fantastical intervention: "[T]he focus of fairy tales, whether oral, written, or cinematic, has always been on finding magical instruments, extraordinary technologies, or powerful people and animals that will enable protagonists to transform themselves [...]" (3; 2).

Cristina Bacchilega argues that even contemporary readers who have perhaps not been exposed to fairy[4] tales beyond Disney retellings "nevertheless respond to stereotyped and institutionalized fragments of [fairy tale] narratives" (2), and for writers of contemporary feminist fiction, they have provided a fruitful starting point for intertextual exploration (see the works of Angela Carter, Margaret Atwood, Emma Donoghue, etc.). Kevin Paul Smith, drawing from Gérard Genette's theories of hypertextuality,[5] suggests that there are a number of "identifiable ways in which the fairytale can operate as an intertext within mass-produced fictions" (10), and it is this element of self-transformation via

165

contact with the extraordinary that renders the fairy tale masterplot legible to readers of Black's and Marr's series, allowing the series to function as fairy tales despite their lack of overt allusion[6] and generic hybridity.

Holly Black's *Modern Tales of Faerie* series is a set of three loosely interconnected novels that adhere to a common chronology. In the first (*Tithe*) and third (*Ironside*), the heroine is Kaye, a teenager who discovers that she is a changeling, left to be raised by the human whose own child had been snatched away and taken to the Seelie Court. Kaye learns further that she is in fact a pixie (complete with green skin and wings), which is considered one of the lesser fey. In the course of her journey of self-discovery, she meets and falls in love with Roiben, a Seelie Court exile who eventually becomes a king. In the second novel (*Valiant*), the heroine is Val, a human teenager who flees a traumatic home life for New York City, falling in with a group of homeless teenagers who are aware of and interact with New York's fairy denizens. Val becomes infatuated with Ravus, a troll living in self-imposed exile from the Seelie Court, and successfully rescues him from the machinations of other exiled fey.

Melissa Marr's *Wicked Lovely* series examines the political inter- and intra-maneuverings of the five extant fairy courts (Summer, Winter, High/Seelie, Dark/Unseelie, and Shadow)[7] via individual stories of growth and development focalized through a multitude of limited third-person perspectives (the focalizer shifts from chapter to chapter and book to book). In this chapter, I will focus primarily upon three significant female characters in the series: Donia, Ani, and Leslie. Like Black's Kaye, two of the three lose their humanity (either because, like Kaye, they weren't fully human in the first place or because they were transformed from human to fey by a force outside themselves), becoming fully fey and eventually ascending to power as regents of their respective courts. The first, Donia, is a former human contender for Summer Queen who becomes first a Winter Court fey and then the Winter Queen. Ani, the half-human, half–Hound daughter of the leader of the Dark Court's Wild Hunt, becomes a fully fey queen of the Shadow Court. Of the three, only Leslie does not ultimately change species; although she is still tied emotionally and metaphysically to both the current and former kings of the Dark Court, she remains biologically human, although forever changed by her intimate association with the fey.

The Modern Tales of Faerie and the Wicked Lovely novels are

inevitably in dialogue with not only the literary fairy tale tradition but also by the discourses of the literary fairy tale as produced and reproduced by and through popular culture. Specifically, the novels are implicitly responding to the Disneyfication of traditional fairy tales by bringing back the darker, more threatening elements of classic fairy tales largely absent in pop culture retellings of fairy tales, particularly those packaged for children. As one *io9* contributor observes: "For the purposes of Hollywood and for mainstream pop culture, Walt Disney is the source material for most fairytale reimaginings, not so much the original texts, which might as well be written in Sanskrit" (Anders), and Marr and Black are responding as much to this sterilization of the fairy tale as they are to the fairy tale tradition itself. Their fairies are figures of genuine menace, and the dangers of interaction with fairy are quite real. Marr's and Black's hearkening back to the darker Gothic elements of fairy tales.

As with the fairy tale tradition, Black's and Marr's texts are in dialogue with not only the literary Gothic tradition but also with the discourses of Gothicism filtered through popular culture. In this sense, the books might be best understood as influenced by both the Gothic and Goth. Catherine Spooner defines "Goth" as a youth sub-culture defined by its affectation of a stylized performance of Gothicism that "embrac[es] beauty in decay" (350). However, Spooner notes that "Goth, and its representations, are always historically situated and resonate both with a subcultural history and a literary tradition" (358); therefore, Gothic and Goth are not separate traditions but interrelated ones, the former textual and the latter performative (255). These series, then, can be read as artifacts of contemporary Goth culture as well as inheritors of a Gothic literary tradition. The Modern Tales of Faerie and the Wicked Lovely novels are Gothic aesthetically (the texts are replete with verbal images of ruin, decay, entropy, etc.) as well as topically and thematically, particular with regard to the figure of the monster and its signifying potential.

Roderick McGillis notes that "[p]opulating the Gothic are various monsters; the genre is something of a teratology, examining freakishness, otherness, abnormality, and deviance" (228). The Modern Tales of Faerie and Wicked Lovely series have in common with their Gothic progenitors a proclivity for exploring the plight of a protagonist who is young, female, and disempowered, and both series manifest the same preoccupation with monsters and monstrousness, ultimately positioning the monster as a counter-hegemonic figure of empowerment for women. Jeffrey Jerome Cohen posits that we can "[read] cultures from the monsters they engender" (3), and the journeys into monstrousness of the protagonists under discussion critique a real-world contemporary American culture that still tends to implicitly equate powerful women with monstrousness in a pejorative sense, a configuration both series seek to countermand by celebrating young women who actively resist gender stereotypes. In the two series, monstrousness is equated with power and agency, especially for women. To be a monster is to be one who steps outside the social order, and by making the journey from human to monster (sometimes literally; three of the five protagonists examined in this chapter change species from human to fairy) an affirmation of female agency, both Black and Marr implicitly argue that inhabiting the subject position of "monster" can be empowering. The protagonists' transformations demonstrate the potentially liberatory powers of becoming a monster; all five young women come to wield personal, cultural, and social power as a result of their embrace of monstrousness.

In the Modern Tales of Faerie and the Wicked Lovely series, questions of monstrousness and negotiations with discourses of power are also tied to issues of embodiment; power comes at least in part from understanding the gendered body as the site of both potential power and powerlessness. Both series' female protagonists' anxieties about the forces to which the body is subject are manifested in a persistent desire to control the body, to subjugate it to one's will and not be subject to its whims. In the two series, this anxiety of embodiment is heightened due to the age of the protagonists; all of the female protagonists under discussion are teenagers.[8] McGillis refers to the state of adolescence itself as a kind of haunting:

> Their bodies as well as their social milieu are in flux, changing as they—both body and social group—morph (or should I say grow?) into maturity. The pressures both within and without on the early adolescent bring trepidation and confusion. [...] Peer pressure and biological urgency haunt the growing person, even in the light of common day [231].

For adolescents, particularly female adolescents struggling with culturally endemic body-image issues, controlling one's own body as well as resisting and/or co-opting the social forces that seek to control it can be a means of self-assertion, and the protagonists' embrace of their own monstrousness offers something of a reprieve from the haunting to which McGillis refers. In Black's and Marr's respective series, becoming a monster necessitates a transformation that is not only psychological and interior but also embodied and externally manifested, and the process of claiming the potential for agency offered by the subject position of "monster" necessitates embracing the emancipatory pleasures of physical transformation. As Cohen points out that "the monster exists only to be read" (4), and for Kaye, Donia, Ani, Val, and Leslie, their monstrousness is inscribed on their bodies, making their transformed natures readable to themselves and to others.

In *Tithe*, Kaye discovers that she is not, and has never been, human. When Kaye looks at her unglamored self for the first time, she must reconcile her sense of self with this literally alien reflection: "[S]he saw that her skin was shadowed with the lush dark green of moss. Not a stain, but a tint, as though a veil of green lay over her. Her ear was longer, sticking up through her hair to the top of her head. Her cheek, sunken and sharp, and her eye, slanted and black, all shiny black, with a pinpoint of white pupil. Like a bird eye or a single bead" (Black, *Tithe* 108). Although she is unsettled to see her true form, she perceives a skin color as "[n]ot a stain," suggesting that although she's wary of the revelation of her true appearance, she's perhaps subconsciously experiencing an uncanny moment of recognition with the reflection that is both self and Other. Kaye comes to accept her glamored human self as an illusion, a kind of chrysalis that housed the pixie form that was hers by right.

However, Kaye is less certain that Ellen, her mother (or the woman she thinks of as her mother), won't reject her when Kaye finally reveals the truth. When Kaye finally confesses her changeling status to Ellen and Ellen reacts with shock and disgust, Kaye wonders if she had always been alien to her mother: "A mother is supposed to know every inch of her baby, her sweet flesh smell, every hangnail on her fingers, the number of cowlicks in her hair. Had Ellen been repulsed and ashamed of her repulsion?" (Black, *Ironside* 109). During the tense confrontation with her mother wherein she reveals her authentic form, Kaye develops a fit of inappropriate giggling, which makes her seem truly monstrous in the pejorative sense of the word, not only to her mother but, for the first time, to herself:

> The nervous giggling wouldn't stop. It was like the absurdity and horror needed to escape somehow and the only way out was through Kaye's mouth.
> Ellen slapped her. For a moment Kaye went completely silent, and then

she howled with laughter. It spilled out of her like shrieks, like the last of her human self burning away [Black, *Ironside* 109].

Ellen's reactions reads as an exaggerated version of any parent forced to confront her child's transition into an adolescent, a time when a child often becomes Other to her parents as well as to herself due to changes both physical and cognitive. Once Kaye accepts her non-humanity, she retrieves the original Kaye (rechristened Kate) from the Seelie Court and she and her mother reconcile. Ellen resumes her role as mother to both Kaye and Kate, assuring Kaye, "You'll always be my baby, Baby" (Black, *Ironside* 310). Despite the reconciliation, though, Kaye's relationship with her mother is permanently altered, and Kaye wonders "if every memory [of her childhood] would snag, like wool on a thorn, making her wonder if it was a symptom of her strangeness" (Black, *Ironside* 310). Ellen's baby is gone, but Ellen, unlike most human mothers, must acknowledge that not only has her baby girl become a young woman but that the baby girl she thought she nurtured had never really existed in the first place. For both Ellen and Kaye, their memories are rewritten just as Kaye's body has been.

Kaye's loss of status as her mother's one and only beloved child sounds a melancholy note in an otherwise triumphant character arc; at the end of the Modern Tales of Faerie series, Kaye has determined that her place in the world is at the nexus of two worlds: human and fairy. Kaye's journey of self-knowledge has shown her that she "didn't want to be fixed in place. She didn't want to pretend to be mortal when she wasn't, nor did she want to have to leave the mortal world. She didn't want to belong to one place or be one kind of thing" (Black, *Ironside* 320). Roiben compares her to Persephone, but unlike Persephone (or Roiben himself, who must split his time between the Seelie and Unseelie courts, since he is now ruler of both), she's choosing the terms of her existence, even though her choice is seen as transgressive to both the human and the fairy worlds.

Donia, too, makes the journey from human to fairy, eventually finding power and satisfaction in her changed state. For love of Keenan, the Summer King, Donia takes up the Winter Staff in an attempt to become the Summer Queen. She is indeed transformed, but not as Keenan's bride, which was her hope. Her punishment for failing to be the destined Summer Queen is to be tied to Keenan and yet forever separated from him; as the new Winter Girl, she's magically bound to watch Keenan seduce girl after girl. After suffering for nearly a century due to her ill-advised attempt to become Summer Queen, Donia eventually regains control of her body and her future by undergoing a semi-voluntary transformation. During the climactic final confrontation with Beira, the Winter Queen and *Wicked Lovely*'s villain, Beira tries to kill Donia with winter's kiss. Donia survives, which marks her as strong enough to be Winter Queen herself, and she chooses to complete the transformation and take up the mantle of the Winter Court once Beira has been defeated. Although Keenan begs her to find a way to reverse the transformation, Donia "wasn't upset. She'd expected to die today. Ruling was far from a bad trade-off" (Marr, *Wicked Lovely* 317). Later, she revels in finally being Keenan's equal in magical power, initially believing that her new status in the fairy hierarchy will make them equals emotionally as well: "[H]aving power over Keenan—that was a dangerous thing. She wanted him to sway to her wishes as she'd done so long to his" (Marr, *Wicked Lovely* 324). However, the dynamic between them stays essentially the same despite her new elevation in status; he still sees her as less than his equal in power and prestige.

As Donia grows into her role as Winter Queen, she becomes more resistant to Keenan's manipulations, at one point warning him, "Don't keep trying to use my love to manipulate me" (Marr, *Fragile Eternity* 35). When Aislinn (Ash), the Summer Queen, also attempts to dictate to Donia, Donia, frustrated with what she perceives as yet another attempt to undermine her authority, stabs her and sends her away as a warning to Keenan, whom she blames for Ash's actions (Marr, *Fragile Eternity* 162). When Keenan confronts her afterward, she tells him, "I don't regret stabbing her. If your court continues to disregard my dominion, she will only be the first of many I'll strike" (Marr, *Fragile Eternity* 195). Her statement serves as a warning to Keenan: if he won't see her as truly changed, she will mark the bodies of his subjects to affirm her own changed state.

Donia eventually tires of the repeated cycle of Keenan declaring his undying love then manipulating and/or betraying her. When he returns after months away and declares his love yet again, Donia contemptuously dismisses him. Despite her continued romantic interest in him, she chooses power over love. In an effort to win her back, Keenan renounces his throne and gives his mantle of Summer to Ash, thus reducing him in status and power to a mere unaffiliated fairy, powerful but far less so than Donia herself. Keenan reiterates his willingness to be Donia's subject, both in the sense of belonging to her court and in the sense of being the less powerful partner in their personal relationship. In a nice reversal of fairy tale tropes, Keenan's body becomes the passive one; she is the one in control. Donia takes Keenan back, but assures him, "If you fail me, I'll kill you. I swear it, Keenan. If you fail me, I'll rip your heart out with my own hands" (Marr, *Darkest Mercy* 222). Their story ends when Keenan proposes marriage, but the marriage proposal here serves as a device to disavow the classic marriage plot so frequently enacted in both the fairy tale and the Gothic novel, one wherein "a happy ending [...] reintegrates the female protagonist into a wider community through marriage "(Brabon and Genz 5). Rather than restoring hegemonic social order in the sense of using marriage as a means of subordinating Donia, Keenan's and Donia's marriage will affirm the unequal power dynamic between them, one that favors Donia. Keenan assures her, "Faery vows are unbreakable. If I phrased it right, you'd *know* that I belong to you. Only you. Always" (Marr, *Darkest Mercy* 244). This particular resolution does not require Donia to relinquish power to get love; in fact, she would not have love without power. It is only when she fully embraces her transformation into the Winter Queen and chooses that subject position over that of endlessly self-sacrificing and accommodating female that she gets her "happily ever after."

Unlike Kaye and Donia, Ani's character arc does not involve her struggling to accept her monstrousness and to integrate it into "an affirmative discourse of identity" (Trites 51). Accepting her own monstrousness is not a problem for Ani—in fact, she revels in it. As Ani sees it, her problem is that she's not monstrous enough to fit in with the Dark Court, where she longs to be accepted. As a half-human, half–Hound, she is pleased when her power grows to the point where she's no longer human enough to live among humans; at the beginning of *Radiant Shadows*, she leaves her beloved siblings, Rabbit and Tish, to live among the Dark Court. However, she is the least among the fairies of the Dark Court in terms of physical power. When their father, Gabriel, leader of the Wild Hunt, tells her she is "too much mine not to be with the Hunt" but too mortal to be fully a part of it, Ani thinks, "Something feral inside her understood that this was why she couldn't live with Rabbit: her brother wasn't as fierce as her father was. Tish wasn't. Ani desperately wanted to be" (Marr, *Radiant Shadows* 18). Ani has the will to be a full member of the Wild Hunt, but not the physical stamina. She's essentially stuck between human and fey: her physical strength doesn't match her ferocity, which leaves her vulnerable in the Dark Court, where regular physical altercations are the norm. Dark Court fairies routinely brawl just for fun, and Ani is barred from participating because her father fears she will be gravely injured or even killed outright. Because of her physical limitations, Ani is prohibited from fully taking what she believes to be her rightful place in the Wild Hunt.

Ani is also constrained by her court because she possesses the ability, unique among the denizens of the Dark Court, to feed off of the emotions of both fey and humans. Ani's ability means that she needs to feed on both the touch of flesh and emotion in order to thrive, and her father wants her to remain abstinent until they understand the full extent of her powers, a condition under which she chafes. She tells Irial, the former Dark Court king and a surrogate father figure to her and her siblings, "'I'm trying to follow the rules.' She ticked them off on her fingers. 'No taking both emotion and touch from mortals. Or faeries. No sex until I'm sure I won't kill them. No fighting with Hounds so they don't kill me. No. No. No. What am I supposed to do?'" (Marr, *Radiant Shadows* 90). Her quandary likely resonates with an audience of adolescent females who live in a real world where women's control over their own bodies is a subject for debate and women, especially young women, are often discouraged or even outright prohibited from acting upon their own physical desires due to fear of objectification and/or victimization. In Ani's case, because she has no safe outlet for satisfying her needs, she exists in a state of literal near-starvation.

When Ani meets Devlin, a High Court fairy, she is drawn to him because he affirms her sense of self; he is a mirror that reflects back at her her vision of herself as capable and worthy of respect. Additionally, he is strong enough that he can shield himself from being fully drained by her, yet still provide her with sustenance. She and Devlin eventually join in a blood binding that gives nourishment to them both, and with their combined strength they bring into being the Shadow Court, a separate court within fairy lands. Perhaps more than any of the other characters in the Wicked Lovely series, Ani has a strong—nearly unshakeable, in fact—sense of self, and Ani's journey is not one of taming one's monstrousness to fit into society but figuring out how to shape society to recognize and accept her monstrousness. With the help of

Devlin and Rae, Devlin's spirit friend, Ani quite literally makes a world in which she can belong without diluting what she sees as her essential nature, discarding her humanity and becoming fully Other along the way. At the novel's conclusion, she has become a powerful agent in the world of fairy; she is a ruler of the Shadow Court and leader of its Wild Hunt.

Ani's newfound status and power also finally makes her an equal in the eyes of her father, from whom she has always sought respect. However well-intentioned, Gabriel's protectiveness had always shamed her and affirmed for all the Dark Court her status as the least among the Wild Hunt, and when he, in accordance with Dark Court tradition, attempts to thrash Devlin for dallying with his daughter without his permission, Ani thwarts the misogynistic display of power by challenging her father herself:

> Gabriel reached out like he'd move her aside, and without thinking, Ani caught his hand in hers—and stopped it.
> His eyes widened, and he grinned. Before she could react, he pulled back his other arm like he was going to punch her.
> "I don't think so." She ducked and swung, and—for the first time in her life—saw her father actually moved by her punch.
> Reflexively, he punched back—not the insulting love taps he'd thrown before, but a true punch from a Hound striking out at an equal.
> "You tried to hit me," she murmured. "You actually tried to *hit* me!"
> "I did"—he touched his face—and you *did* hit me."
> She leaned against him. "Finally" [Marr, *Radiant Shadows* 285].

Like Kaye's mother Ellen, Gabriel must confront the fact that his child is no longer a child. Unlike Ellen, however, Gabriel does not initially reject her, perhaps because he is monstrous himself; for him, Ani's transformation confirms her as like rather than Other. Although he may be motivated in part by narcissism , Gabriel, like Devlin, ultimately validates Ani's sense of self. Ani and her father reach a new level of rapprochement; by becoming wholly monstrous, she becomes a fully actualized and autonomous individual and achieves her quest for agency.

Kaye, Donia, and Ani experience the emancipator power of monstrosity by becoming literally non-human, but as Val (Modern Tales of Faerie) and Leslie (Wicked Lovely) demonstrate, one does not need to undergo a complete physical transformation from human to non-human in order to become a monster. Both Val from the Modern Tales of Faerie series and Leslie from the Wicked Lovely series are human and stay human throughout their respective journeys, but their experiments with body modification function as explorations of monstrousness. By modifying their bodies, Val and Leslie create "secondary bodies" (Cohen 18), effecting their own monstrousness in order to further their understanding of embodiment and its relationship to subjectivity.

Val, the protagonist of *Valiant*, finds empowerment by taking direct action to transform how her body will be read socially, actively rejecting hegemonic beauty standards for women in the process. At the beginning of the novel, Val, angry because she has just discovered her mother and her boyfriend *in flagrante delicto*, takes the train from suburban New Jersey to New York City. At one point in the journey, she looks in the mirror and sees in her reflection traces of her mother, a former beauty queen (Black, *Valiant* 18). Disgusted, Val shaves her head in the train bathroom. Such an act can be read as self-mutilation; indeed, Val's act is motivated in part by a blinding rage: "She was surprised by the force of her own anger. It overwhelmed her, making her afraid she might start screaming at the conductor, at every passenger on the train" (Black, *Valiant* 19). However, the act isn't entirely out of character—Val has "always been a little contemptuous of beauty, as though it was something you had to trade away some other vital thing for" (Black, *Valiant* 158)—and Val's act is not only fueled by righteous anger but also by rejection of the hyperfeminized gender performance her mother embodies.

Once Val has shaved her head, she moves into a more androgynous subjectivity: "The mirror caught her eye again as she straightened. This time, a young man looked back at her, his features so delicate she didn't think he could defend himself" (Black, *Valiant* 20). This liminal space ultimately becomes a powerful one for Val. In a clever performance of the novel's playful reversals of cultural gender scripts (and one that hearkens back to the novel's fairy tale intertext), a newly-shorn Val is called upon to play Prince Charming:

> A drag queen with a beehive wig hanging at a lopsided angle chased a cab, one Lucite shoe in her hand. As the cabbie sped away, she threw it hard enough that it banged into his rear window. "Fucking fucker!" she screamed as she limped toward her shoe.
> Val darted out into the street, picked It up, and returned it to its owner.
> "Thanks, lambchop."
> Up close, Val could see her fake eyelashes were threaded with silver, and glitter sparkled along her cheekbone.

175

"You make a darling prince. Nice hair. Why don't we pretend I'm Cinderella and you can put that shoe right on my foot?"

"Um, okay," Val said, squatting down and buckling the plastic strap, while the drag queen tried not to hop as she swayed to keep her balance.

"Perfect, doll." She righted her wig [Black, *Valiant* 34–35].

The scene is both humorous and pointedly transgressive; the interplay between Val and "Cinderella" underscores the provisional nature of gender as social construct. It can hardly be coincidence that Val interacts with a drag performer in this scene, given drag's associations with an interrogation of gender norms. Judith Butler notes, "Drag is subversive to the extent that it reflects on the imitative structure by which hegemonic gender is itself produced" (125), and the exchange between Val and Cinderella certainly calls our attention to gender as a set of practices enacted by and through bodies. The scene is, in effect, meta-drag; Val and the drag queen are interrogating gender performance not only through their individual gender displays but also through the script that they enact. The story of Cinderella[9] is one of the most common fairy tale intertexts subverted in order "to contest the idealized outcomes of fairy tales and their representations of gender and female identity" (Hasse 20), and her transformation to rescuing Prince in this scene facilitates her hero's journey and presages her role in relation to Ravus's "damsel in distress," a Snow White/Sleeping Beauty–type figure who must wait passively to be rescued.[10] At the novel's climax, Val duels the villainous Mabry for Ravus's heart (literally—like Snow White's wicked stepmother, Mabry has had it plucked out) in order to bring Ravus back to life, which she does by returning his heart to his chest and bestowing upon him a restorative kiss.

Like Val, Leslie, *Ink Exchange*'s main female protagonist, wants to alter her body, to provide a visible sign of her commitment to self-reinvention. When the novel begins, she is struggling with the aftermath of having been a victim of a gang rape, which was arranged by her own brother in order to pay off a debt to his drug dealer. The action is driven by Leslie's obsession with "marking her body, reclaiming it as her own"; she sees getting a tattoo as "a step she needed to take to make herself whole again" (Marr, *Ink Exchange* 6). She thinks,

Getting ink felt right, like it would help her put her life in order, to move forward. It was *her body*, despite the things that'd been done to it, and she wanted to claim it, to own it, to *prove* that to herself. She knew it wasn't

176

magic, but the idea of writing her own identity felt like the closest she could get to reclaiming her life. Sometimes there's power in the act; sometimes there's strength in words. She wanted to find an image that represented those things she was feeling, to etch it on her skin as tangible proof of her decision to change [Marr, *Ink Exchange* 20].

The tattoo is the mark that is readable to others, the outward signifier of her altered body, but the act of being tattooed, the experience of a physically painful act she chooses for herself, is a necessary part of the transformation as well. Leslie feels that her body has been marked by act of sexual assault, and tattooing process is an act of both enunciation and erasure of the "fallen women" subject position to which she has been relegated; to bear the pain of the tattoo is a way not only to reaffirm ownership of her own flesh but to repudiate the rape act that constructed her body as a passive sexual object, something to be used by others without her volition:

If she thought Rabbit would let her, she'd ask to hold the tattoo machine, ask to wrap her hand around the primitive-looking coils and angled bits of metal. [...] She shivered. It looked like a crude hand-held sewing machine, and with it he'd stitch beauty onto her body. There was something primal about the process that resonated for her, some sense that after this she'd be irrevocably different, and that's what she needed [Marr, *Ink Exchange* 45].

As with Val, Leslie's body modification is an assertion of agency. In Leslie's imagining, the tattoo gun in her hands is a "primitive-looking" kind of cyborg phallus that becomes in Rabbit's hands as a "crude hand-held sewing machine," which associates it with women's work. This passage underscores the extent to which the act of tattooing, of being penetrated in this particular way, is meant to serve as a repudiation of the rape act, and her desire to hold the tattoo machine underscores her desire to rewrite her rape. Although Rabbit is the one actually guiding the tattoo gun, she sees him as an extension of her own will. Hers is the hand that wields the phallus that inscribes, even if by proxy. The first tattoo session becomes a transcendent moment, an experience of the sublime, the "ink in her skin" producing a "euphoric zinging that made her feel a confidence she'd not known in far too long" (Marr, *Ink Exchange* 49).

Unfortunately, the tattoo Leslie finds so liberating proves to be another kind of penetration without consent; the magical properties of the tattoo tie her metaphysically to Irial, the seductive, Byronic king of the Dark Court. By the end of the novel, she has finally regained control of her body; at her request, Niall uses magic from the Summer and Winter courts to burn the metaphysical connection with Irial out of her tattoo, rendering it magically inert and blunting her emotional connection to Irial. This physical act, like the tattooing itself, is another kind of reenactment of the rape—when Niall forces the fairy magic into her human flesh, Leslie "screamed, though she tore at her lip to keep that sound inside. She screamed as she'd done only once before" (Marr, *Ink Exchange* 308). The scream is clearly meant to invoke the violation of her rape once again, but, as with the tattooing process, in order to repudiate it; Leslie herself is ultimately in control of the penetration of her body. This scene is another moment of the transcendent sublime; Leslie frees herself from emotional and psychological pain by mastering physical pain. Leslie comes to understand that it is not the mark but the act of *choosing* to mark herself, to reinscribe her body, that is truly powerful. The tattoo remains, present but impotent, drained of color both literally and figuratively, a permanent reminder of her altered flesh and of her connection to Irial, to whom she is still attracted, although she rejects becoming his consort.

Donna Heiland argues, "To inhabit a woman's body is to be a Gothic heroine. End of story. Unless [...] we change the story" (158). Heiland also suggests that the Gothic as a genre explores "the structures that trap women—their bodies, their homes, social convention, the stories that model their lives" (157), and her observation seems particularly applicable to Gothic fairy tales, which Marr and Black have reenvisioned in order to resist inscription of hegemonic gender/genre roles. The Modern Tales of Faerie series and the Wicked Lovely use the tropes and conventions of their generic forbearers, Gothic fairy tales, to produce transgressive and transformative narratives that do successfully change the story, proving their heroines with new and different happy endings.

Notes

1. Although their designation as YA fiction Is not irrelevant to this analysis, a thorough examination of YA as a distinct genre category is beyond the scope of this essay. For a comprehensive examination of the topic, see Roberta Seelinger Trites's *Disturbing the Universe: Power and Repression in Adolescent Literature*.

2. The books in Black's series (in order): *Tithe: A Modern Faerie Tale*; *Valiant: A Modern Tale of Faerie*; *Ironside: A Modern Faery's Tale*. The subtitles of each book

in the series suggest an architectural/chronotopic relationship to the literary fairy tale.

3. The books in Marr's series (in order): Wicked Lovely; Ink Exchange; Fragile Eternity; Radiant Shadows; Darkest Mercy.

4. Because there is no consistent spelling of certain key terms among the critical and literary texts I will be referencing, I will use the terms "fairy," "fairy tale," and "fey" throughout this essay unless I am directly quoting a primary or secondary source.

5. Genette's argument regarding "the palimpsestic nature of texts" postulates that "[a]ny text is a hypertext, grafting itself onto a hypotext, an earlier text that it imitates or transforms; any writing is rewriting; and literature is always in the second degree" (Prince viiii).

6. Margaret Atwood's "Bluebeard's Egg "and Angela Carter's "The Company of Wolves" serve as contrasting examples; both contemporary feminist re-imaginings are overtly allusive.

7. The Shadow Court is not formed until *Radiant Shadows*, the fourth book in the series.

8. Although Donia's chronological age is never specified, her recollection of a night out with Keenan when she was still mortal suggests that she was a teenager sometime during the Jazz Age (Marr, *Wicked Lovely* 94–95). However, her transition from human to fey apparently stopped her from maturing both physically and emotionally, keeping her a perpetual teenager.

9. Although there is no single, definitive Cinderella story, I'm assuming that a twenty-first century audience is most familiar with the story as filtered through Charles Perrault and, much later, Walt Disney Studios.

10. Ravus is not just sleeping; Val actually turns him to stone by exposing him to daylight in order to keep him from dying from his grievous injuries.

Works Cited

Anders, Charlie Jane. "Why Can't Hollywood Make a Decent Fairy Tale Movie?" *io9*. Gawker Media. 28 March 2013. Web. 29 March 2013.

Ashley, Mike. "Fairy Tale." *The Encyclopedia of Fantasy*. Eds. John Clute and John Grant. New York: St. Martin's, 1999. 330–333. Print.

Bacchilega, Cristina. *Postmodern Fairy Tales: Gender and Narrative Strategies*. Philadelphia: University of Pennsylvania, 1997. Print.

Black, Holly. *Ironside*. New York: McElderry Books, 2007. Print.

_____. *Tithe*. New York: Simon Pulse, 2002. Print.

_____. *Valiant*. New York: Simon Pulse, 2005. Print.

Brabon, Benjamin A., and Stéphanie Genz. "Introduction: Postefeminist Gothic." *Postfeminist Gothic: Critical Interventions in Contemporary Culture*. Eds. Benjamin A. Brabon and Stéphanie Genz. New York: Palgrave Macmillan, 2007. 1–15. Print.

Butler, Judith. *Bodies That Matter: On the Discursive Limits of "Sex."* New York: Routledge, 1993. Print.

Cohen, Jeffrey Jerome. "Monster Culture (Seven Theses)." *Monster Theory: Reading Culture*. Ed. Jeffrey Jerome Cohen. Minneapolis: University of Minnesota Press, 1996. 3–25. Print.

Haase, Donald. "Feminist Fairy-Tale Scholarship." *Fairy Tales and Feminism: New Approaches*. Ed. Donald Haase. Detroit: Wayne State University Press, 2004. 1–36. Print.

Heiland, Donna. *Gothic and Gender: An Introduction*. Malden, MA: Blackwell, 2004. Print.

Marr, Melissa. *Darkest Mercy*. New York: Harper-HarperCollins, 2011. Print.

_____. *Fragile Eternity*. New York: Bowen-HarperCollins, 2009. Print.

_____. *Ink Exchange*. New York: Bowen-HarperCollins, 2008. Print.

_____. *Radiant Shadows*. New York: Harper-HarperCollins, 2010. Print.

_____. *Wicked Lovely*. New York: HarperTeen-HarperCollins, 2007. Print.

McGillis, Roderick. "The Night Side of Nature: Gothic Spaces, Fearful Times." *The Gothic in Children's Literature: Haunting the Borders*. Eds. Anna Jackson, Karen Coats, and Roderick McGillis. New York: Routledge, 2008. 227–241. Print.

Prince, Gerald. Foreword. *Palimpsests: Literature in the Second Degree*. Gérard Genette. Trans. Channa Newman and Claude Doubinsky. Lincoln: University of Nebraska Press, 2007. viiii–xi. Print.

Smith, Kevin Paul. *The Postmodern Fairytale: Folkloric Intertexts in Contemporary Fiction*. New York: Palgrave Macmillan, 2007. Print.

Spooner, Catherine. "Goth Culture." *A New Companion to the Gothic*. Ed. David Punter. Malden, MA: Wiley-Blackwell, 2012. 350–365. Print.

Trites, Roberta Seelinger. *Disturbing the Universe: Power and Repression in Adolescent Literature*. Iowa City: University of Iowa Press, 2000. Print.

Zipes, Jack. *The Irresistible Fairy Tale: The Cultural and Social History of a Genre*. Princeton: Princeton University Press, 2012. Print.

Reading in the Dark

Narrative Reframing in the Unheimlich *Underworld of Merrie Haskell's* The Princess Curse

CARISSA TURNER SMITH

"...I wonder what sort of a tale we've fallen into?"
"I wonder," said Frodo. "But I don't know. And that's the way of a real tale. Take any one that you're fond of. You may know, or guess, what kind of a tale it is, happy-ending or sad-ending, but the people in it don't know. And you don't want them to" [Tolkien 379].

J. R. R. Tolkien, through a now oft-repeated conversation between the hobbits Sam and Frodo in *The Lord of the Rings*, posits the idea that a tale is most satisfactory to a reader or listener if the characters within know very little about the shape of their own story. However, in much recent fairy tale and fairy-tale-revision criticism, scholars—especially those writing from a feminist perspective—have censured stories in which a protagonist has little awareness of or agency in her own narrative. In this view, a text's metafictional references, especially in which a character reflects upon her own storied nature, should reinforce the personal empowerment or liberation of the main character. Though the passivity of female characters in some fairy tales and retellings warrants critique, contemporary fairy tale writing and criticism often gravitates toward a monotonously spunky, action-driven, self-aware version of empowerment. How many of us, whatever our gender, could claim to have control at all times over our own narrative? And how desirable would such a life be, even were it possible? As the hobbit Sam Gamgee claims about the most meaningful tales, "Folk seem to have been just landed in them, usually—their paths were laid that way, as you put it" (Tolkien 378). Being landed in a story, however, does not deprive one of the power to act ethically, as Sam makes clear: "But I expect they had lots of chances, like us, of turning back, only they didn't" (Tolkien 378).

Among recent fairy-tale retellings, Merrie Haskell's 2011 novel *The Princess Curse* provides a refreshing break from the entirely self-determining heroines of much recent middle-grade and young adult fiction. While aimed at a middle-grade audience, *The Princess Curse* actually introduces readers to darker existential dilemmas than many young adult novels, even touching on the myth of the rape of Persephone. Haskell has stated in an interview that she wrote *The Princess Curse* in order to get over her fear of the Underworld in its many forms ("The Big Idea").[1] Haskell's novel begins as a retelling of "The Twelve Dancing Princesses"(a tale in which the Underworld is a curse to be escaped) but segues unexpectedly into a retelling of "Beauty and the Beast" combined with the myth of Hades and Persephone. The two latter tales differ significantly in the main character's agency, but Haskell makes her protagonist Reveka's reign in the Underworld a willing choice—at least in part. The change of narrative frames is accompanied by a shift in setting to the Underworld, and the simultaneity of these transitions underscores the connection that Freud, Heidegger, and others have drawn between the *unheimlich*—the uncanny or unhome-like—and the fear that the world lacks a coherent narrative frame over which one can exercise control. While many contemporary fairy tale retellings use metafiction[2] to emphasize a female protagonist's ability to frame her own story, *The Princess Curse*'s metafictional references accentuate Reveka's *lack* of knowledge of the story to which she belongs (and while readers think they possess this knowledge, Haskell shakes that certainty by switching tales halfway through). The protagonist's lack of metafictional awareness helps readers to come to terms with uncertainty about the shape of their lives, and to find moral action possible in the face of such uncertainty. Reveka's choices are morally significant not because they give her power over framing her own story, but rather because she makes them without any knowledge of the story in which she finds herself. The externally determined switch from one fairy tale frame to another thus forces Reveka and readers to confront both the more superficial fear of the Underworld and the deeper, underlying fear of not knowing our own story.

Reading Princesses: Fairy Tale Revisions, Intertextuality and Agency

While all fairy tale retellings are necessarily intertextual, postmodern fairy tale revisions often turn the relationship between texts (including, but not limited to, the "original" tale and its rewritten form) into a metafictional reflection about the nature of story itself. In *Marvelous Geometry: Narrative and Metafiction in Modern Fairy Tale*, Jessica Tiffin argues that the highly structured nature of fairy tales themselves makes them the perfect vehicle for postmodern themes:

> More than the simple shape of a text, narrative structure becomes a powerful tradition, a set of codes which is continually invoked, rediscovered, and recreated with the telling of every new version, and thus relies on a self-consciousness about textuality which moves the narrative into the realm of the postmodern narrative technique of metafiction.... Above all, what fairy tale thus offers as a generic tradition is a level of self-awareness, a deliberate and conscious construction of itself within a set of codes recognized by both writer and reader [3].

While fairy tales depends on the writer and reader recognizing codes such as "once upon a time" and repetition by threes, in postmodern retellings the *characters* are often invited to share in the knowledge of these patterns. Metafictionally aware characters reflect the roles of both reader and writer, recognizing and interpreting patterns as well as taking action to construct narrative.

For this reason, previous scholarship focusing on intertextuality and metanarrative in fairy tale retellings has usually focused on the protagonist's awareness or lack of awareness of the narrative frame around her. An aware protagonist is usually celebrated for exercising the freedom to resist or revise her story; a female protagonist lacking this awareness is often seen as trapped by patriarchal narratives inscribing her into certain roles. Amie A. Doughty's "'I Think You Are Not Telling Me All of This Story': Storytelling, Fate, and Self-Determination in Robin McKinley's Folktale Revisions" traces what Doughty sees as a development from McKinley's first retelling of "Beauty and the Beast," *Beauty* (1978), to her later treatment of the same tale, *Rose Daughter* (1999). Doughty argues, "Though all of McKinley's work contains references to storytelling, it is only in her later works that her characters become aware of their place in stories and of their ability to shape their stories as they see fit" (123). Intertextuality runs through all of McKinley's work, but "it is only her later works that have a significant metatextual element that challenges the authority of the texts upon which they are based. The intertext of the novels lays out the readers' expectations of the novels while the metatext allows for the breaking of these expectations" (Doughty 123). Somewhat troublingly, Doughty's argument depends upon critiquing a heroine for not reading in a certain way. Doughty equates Beauty's reading with powerlessness: "Mythology, particularly Greek, has a strong influence on Beauty's life, and these intertextual elements of the novel dominate McKinley's revision of 'Beauty and the Beast,'" but "[f]or someone who is highly intelligent and who loves to read, Beauty is oblivious to her place in the creation of her story" (Doughty 124). While the resisting reader is often a helpful and valuable role model, especially for young women, other types of reading protagonists merit praise: the scholar caught up in wonder, for example, as Beauty is in the Beast's library. Critique is not the sole liberating posture for a reader. In fact, presenting resistance—and full self-determination—as the only model for a reader can encourage irresponsible reading that traps readers inside another role. If the trope of the protagonist who deliberately resists and rewrites her story becomes a dominant cultural narrative, it becomes a restrictive frame itself in need of revision. After all, one primary theme of fairy tales is transformation, and allowing oneself to be transformed by a text can confer rewards not necessarily lesser than actively transforming a text.

While McKinley's work makes few overt metafictional gestures, A. S. Byatt's contemporary fairy tales, especially "The Story of the Eldest Princess," consciously deploy metafiction and intertextuality. Though "The Story of the Eldest Princess" does not retell a specific familiar tale, it makes use of a structural motif—a quest undertaken by successive siblings, the two eldest of whom will inevitably fail—recognized easily by readers, as well as by the heroine, the eldest princess herself. Feeling that the familiar narrative sets her up inevitably for failure, the princess laments, "I am in a pattern I know, and I suspect I have no power to break it, and I am going to meet a test and fail it, and spend seven years as a stone" (Byatt 16). The princess recognizes the story pattern because she is a reader—a role which, Byatt is quick to clarify, does not make her passive: "She was by nature a reading, not a travelling, princess. This meant both that she enjoyed her new striding solitude in the fresh air, and that she had read a great many stories in her spare time, including several stories about princes and princesses who set out on quests" (15). What is less clear, however, is that the princess's fate is actually different from how it would have been had she not recognized and sought to avoid the typical sibling quest narrative. At several key points, she decides to delay her official quest in order to assist wounded creatures, and at the end of the story, she elects to remain with the old healer in the cottage, rather than continuing on her original mission. Some readers interpret the story's ending as unambiguous: while Jeffrey K. Gibson does acknowledge that "the Princess's fate is, nevertheless, always already plotted by A. S. Byatt" (95), he ultimately declares, "'The Story of the Eldest Princess' offers an inspiring resolution by providing readers with a model heroine who consciously and competently resists the stereotypical trappings of this storytelling tradition" (96). Jessica Tiffin offers a slightly more nuanced interpretation of the relationship between fate and metanarrative in Byatt's work: "paradoxically ... narrative both encloses and empowers; its patterns entrap at the same time they offer the potential for release. Above all, narrative empowers when careful choice is employed: while containing, enclosing, and defining through its inherent structure and nature, it also offers, through that structure and nature, the potential for release, freedom, and choice" ("Ice, Glass, Snow"). Tiffin here acknowledges that the princess needs narrative in order to know the various patterns from which she can choose. However, what both Gibson and Tiffin ignore is the fact that, even though the princess has "chosen" a different path from the quest laid out for her, she ends up conforming to the story she seeks to avoid, at least from the perspective of those back at home: she fails in the quest, leaving her younger siblings to save the kingdom. She may have found satisfaction through believing that she is rejecting the terms of the narrative—and as long as she is the tale's teller, she retains the right to this interpretation. From another perspective, though, she appears to have fulfilled the predestined narrative even in her attempt to evade it. Narrative empowerment is seldom as clear-cut an issue as it seems.

Merrie Haskell's *The Princess Curse* may have a plucky heroine, but it's hard to argue that she displays the same narrative self-determination that Gibson and Tiffin see in Byatt's eldest princess. Yet Haskell's Reveka deals with the darker reality of being unsure of her own narrative frame. When we first meet Reveka, she is unaware that she is part of the tale of "The Twelve Dancing Princesses." As an herbalist's apprentice working at Castle Sylvian (Haskell has set the novel in a Romanian kingdom), her role within the traditional tale is also opaque to readers, since no female characters other than the princesses appear in the original. Unlike Byatt's eldest princess, Reveka seems ignorant of any tale resembling the narrative in which she initially appears, allowing her to comment upon the main element of the plot—the curse afflicting the princesses—with something like the potential reaction of a contemporary reader. She exclaims to her father, "It's the stupidest curse in existence! It's a curse of *shoes and naps!*" (Haskell, *Princess* 13). *The Princess Curse* establishes a metafictional level early on, though, by repeatedly noting Reveka's interaction with a tapestry in the castle, a tapestry depicting a dragon kidnapping a maiden. The dragon is a *zmeu*, a legendary Romanian creature that is especially monstrous because it can appear in human form. The tapestry thus foreshadows Reveka's later dealings with the *zmeu* whose curse ensnares the twelve princesses and ultimately Reveka herself. And yet Haskell suggests that Reveka is no mere pawn: as she stands near the tapestry, her father accuses her of lying—of being a story-teller. Yet, as she literally picks at the thread on the tapestry, he snaps at her, "You'll unravel the whole thing, and you have no skill to put it back together" (Haskell, *Princess* 3). Reveka is simultaneously scolded for having too much and too little control over narrative, mirroring her difficult position as a young girl who wants to escape the role of wife and mother and become an herbalist in a convent.

The dragon-and-maiden tapestry resurfaces several chapters later, now "repaired by expert fingers" (Haskell, *Princess* 88). As Reveka stares at the mended pattern, she reflects to herself, "I wondered how she [the maiden in the tapestry] hadn't figured out that he was a *zmeu* before, maybe at their wedding ceremony. In the stories, you always know who the *zmeu* is; the storytellers always say he's charming and friendly and looks like an ordinary man, but they also drop hints so broad that you can't help but think the girl is stupid for not knowing" (88). Readers at this point are well-prepared to appreciate the irony in Reveka's reaction, for she has recently met a charming and friendly, yet mysterious, man in the forest. Even though Reveka serves as the first-person narrator of her tale, Haskell, through juxtaposition, has managed to drop a few hints about "Frumos's" true identity. Reveka, at this point, doesn't seem to realize that the reader and narrator of a tale always have access to information—or at least the perspective from which to recognize a pattern—unavailable to the protagonist. From Reveka's own experience, readers of *The Princess Curse* can see that one of the factors preventing a character from recognizing a *zmeu* is not that she is unaware of narrative in general, but that she thinks she is involved in a very different sort of story. When Reveka asks the name of the mysterious stranger in the woods, he responds, "Call me Frumos" (Haskell, *Princess* 48). Reveka reflects, "'Handsome,' the name meant; Frumos was also the hero of all the great tales, and further, Prince Frumos was the one who fought the *zmeu*," and she concludes that "this fellow certainly thought a lot of himself!" (Haskell, *Princess* 48). "Frumos's" supposed name leads Reveka to interpret the rest of their conversation, albeit playfully, in light of the tales about Prince Frumos, at one point asking "Frumos" for the opinion of his Marvelous Horse, since "Prince Frumos in the stories was always taking counsel from his horse" (48). "Frumos" replies, "My horse tells me that you're like the old woman on the road who offers Prince Frumos two impossible choices" (48), thus giving Reveka herself a place within the Frumos tales. Reveka resists being placed in this role, though, and in some ways her words echo the narrative self-determination attributed to Byatt's eldest princess:

> I don't think it's an apt comparison. The old women who meet Prince Frumos say things like, "If you turn right, you'll walk through sorrow; if you turn left, you'll walk through sorrow as well." I don't think that's offering impossible choices, anyway. I think that Frumos was a fool for accepting those as the only two choices. What if he went backward? What if he went straight? Maybe saying that left-right thing was the old woman's way of saying, "Don't turn!" [Haskell, *Princess* 49].

Once again, Reveka critiques the apparent blindness of the protagonist in a story to options that seem clear to her as a critic outside the story; her insistence comes across as admirable but slightly naive, especially when she finds herself in situations in which choices are more difficult.

Reveka's blindness parallels that of the princess in the tapestry, since, even when she observes that "Frumos" wears a clasp identical to that worn by Lord Dragos (the *zmeu* responsible for the curse on the princesses), she fails to connect the two, still caught up in the narrative suggested by the *zmeu*'s false name. "Perhaps this really was Prince Frumos, hero, slayer of *zmei*. How else did you get a *zmeu*-spike cloak clasp?" she asks herself when she first notices the similarity (Haskell,

Princess 168). Reveka puts the pieces together only after Lord Dragos has captured her father, by which point her narrative frame has segued once more, transitioning from "The Twelve Dancing Princesses"—in which the princesses are always rescued by a male hero venturing into the Underworld—to "Beauty and the Beast," in which a daughter's sacrifice saves a father—and, in the case of *The Princess Curse*, the princesses and several kingdoms as well. Reveka, without having any knowledge of "Beauty and the Beast," still possesses certainty and conviction about the right course of action to take in the moment of her epiphany: "suddenly sure of myself, suddenly certain of what I had to do then, to save us all" (Haskell, *Princess* 183), she volunteers to marry Lord Dragos and stay in his underground kingdom of Thonos if he will let her father and all his other prisoners return to the above world.

With this single, sacrificial decision, Reveka transforms herself from a minor character (one who doesn't even have a place in the original story) within the frame of "The Twelve Dancing Princesses" to the protagonist of "Beauty and the Beast"—at least in the readers' eyes. Reveka herself remains unaware of this shift and, in fact, is most disturbed after her decision by the realization that she will now be unable to fulfill the narrative she thought she belonged to: finding a cure that will wake the curse-afflicted sleepers in the world above. Interestingly, author Merrie Haskell has stated that she did not intend for "Beauty and the Beast" to be part of *The Princess Curse* at all:

> To me, the whole book from start to finish is "Twelve Dancing Princesses" carried to a logical conclusion, and with a great deal of reference to Hades and Persephone—but is not meant to be a retelling of Hades and Persephone at all, but an exploration of how their story affects the world, archetypally-speaking. I think my only conscious nod to "Beauty and the Beast" is the question the zmeu asks of the princesses each night: "Will you marry me or will you dance?" [Haskell, "The Writing Process"].

However, Haskell is also an unabashed fan of Robin McKinley's *Beauty*, and the influence of that work looms large in *The Princess Curse* (though this is not to say that it is derivative—or at least not beyond the level of intertextuality characterizing most contemporary fairy tale retellings). In a tribute to *Beauty* published in the *Los Angeles Review of Books*, Haskell notes that, in McKinley's work, Beauty's ability to see, in the Beast's library, books that have not yet been written, "is an early sign that she will be able to see beyond the surfaces around her, and break the curse on the castle and its inhabitants" ("A Timeless Romance"). In Haskell's interpretation, unlike Doughty's, Beauty's status as a reader symbolizes her insight, which is what ultimately enables her to act positively to change the world around her. Though Haskell's narrative frame resembles the "Beauty and the Beast" tale, she departs from McKinley's treatment in highlighting her protagonist's lack of insight and her misreading of her circumstances. Yet, as Reveka's time in the Underworld shows, she nevertheless possesses the ability to break curses and transform her surroundings—with decisions made in the dark.

The Unheimlich, *the Underworld, and Narrative Uncertainty*

In the same essay in which she discusses Beauty's insight, Haskell also identifies a theme in *Beauty* that is equally significant in *The Princess Curse*: Beauty must choose whether to "return to the comforts and security of home, or to forge into the unseen beyond" ("A Timeless Romance"). Haskell's statement of this theme echoes Marina Warner's comments about "Beauty and the Beast" and other female-centric transformation narratives:

> Fairy tale as a form deals with limits, and limits often set by fear: one of its fundamental themes treats of a protagonist who sets out to discover the unknown and overcomes its terrors. When women tell fairy stories, they also undertake this central narrative concern of the genre—they contest fear; they turn their eye on the phantasm of the male Other and recognize it, either rendering it transparent and safe, the self reflected as good, or ridding themselves of it (him) by destruction or transformation [Warner 276].

For these fairy tale heroines, the *unheimlich* must become home-like, and only the protagonist herself has the inner resources to accomplish this transformation. Beauty, unlike Reveka, has a stable home and family to which she longs to return; Reveka has lived in Castle Sylvian for only three weeks, and before that has dwelt in various convents while her father, with whom she has a distant relationship, travels as a soldier. However, dwelling in the dark Underworld threatens all that Reveka values from her previous life: the ability to grow plants. Still, for Reveka as for Beauty, the threatening unknown becomes more familiar and home-like than "home" had been. In another interview, Haskell admits

189

her own terror of the Underworld, and that writing *The Princess Curse* became a way to deal with that fear. For Reveka, then, "being scared of the Underworld is the only way to fail" (Haskell, "The Big Idea"). Thus, Reveka's narrative re-framing of the Underworld and its lord becomes a way to succeed, even when the options seem less than ideal.

Haskell is extremely careful to depict Reveka's ultimate acceptance of her role as Queen of the Underworld in such a way that it bears little resemblance to the "rape" of Persephone. Even after her initial sacrificial substitution of herself for her father and her promise to marry Lord Dragos, Reveka cannot be bound forever in the Underworld—nor can she heal it as its Queen—unless she eats of its food or drinks repeatedly from the waters of Lethe. The choice is truly hers, even if it is a somewhat circumscribed choice. She might be helped in her decision by knowledge of the Hades and Persephone myth, one with which she and the other characters in *The Princess Curse* are familiar, but she does not apply it broadly to her situation. Rather, she calls upon the myth to challenge Dragos's claim that drinking only once of the waters of Lethe will not trap her in the Underworld. Dragos's explanation that that consequence applies only to eidolon souls and not to mortals leads Reveka to wonder if all she knows from the myth is false, since obviously Hades himself is no longer lord of the Underworld. This is the first time we have seen Reveka question knowledge gained from her reading. In her pre–Underworld life, she trusts written herb lore as infallible and at one point even declares, "If it was in a book, it must be true" (Haskell, *Princess* 106). Dragos, through Reveka's reference to Hades and Persephone, learns that she is fairly well-read, and, as a result, brings her several codices. Readers attuned to intertextual references might suspect that these texts will be significant, but Reveka barely even scans them, perhaps symbolizing her growing awareness that other narratives may not help her navigate the difficult decisions that she faces in the Underworld.

Other characters, however, are eager to connect Reveka to outside narratives, especially that of Hades and Persephone. When Reveka explains that she is in the Underworld because of her offer to save her father, the nymph of the river Alethe queries, "Your father? What does your father have to do with anything? Where was your mother?" (Haskell, *Princess* 229). Upon learning that Reveka's mother died when Reveka was small, the nymph hastily replies, "No matter. All paths don't have to run the same to be worth walking. Of course, it would be better if you had a mother, but a queen is a queen" (Haskell, *Princess* 229). The nymph also notes approvingly that Reveka is an herbalist's apprentice, and her interest in Reveka's association with plants and in her mother suggests that the nymph hopes that Reveka's role will parallel that of Persephone. However, she does not make this connection explicitly; it is available to readers but does not overly determine Reveka's course of action. The importance of Reveka's lack of awareness of her own parallels to Persephone's story becomes even clearer with the extra-textual knowledge (supplied by Haskell in response to an email query) that the nymph of the river Alethe is, indeed, supposed to be Persephone herself, a widow now and a diminished queen ("Re: Untold stories"). Given that Persephone is not only an intertextual influence but also a character within the internal world of *The Princess Curse*, her potential to turn Reveka into a mere *Doppelgänger* of herself would be quite sinister if she actively pursued it.

Reveka's resistance, whether conscious or unconscious, to merely repeating the narrative of Persephone—or of the maiden in the tapestry, for that matter—is reminiscent of Freud's connection of the *Doppelgänger* to the uncanny, or *unheimlich*. According to Susan Bernstein's interpretation of Freud, the fear that one is merely repeating a pattern connects to anxieties about reading and narrative control: "the fear of mimetic contamination: the fear that 'I,' this subject, am nothing but a copy of one that came before me, that my reading and thinking are compelled to repeat something before, and beyond, me and my control. The fear that I am a double, a copy, an imitation, and not a self-originating essence" (1126). While Freud sees uncanny doubling as robbing the reader of individuality and self-narrating power, Heidegger sees the uncanny as the one force that can free "being" (*Dasein*) from the narratives in which it is trapped. According to Heidegger, the anxiety accompanying an encounter with the uncanny jolts *Dasein* from its "tranquilized self-assurance—'Being-at-home,' with all its obviousness" (233). *Dasein*, through having fallen into everyday complacence, has been alienated from its original, "primordial" state of "not-at-homeness" (Heidegger 236). The uncanny, exerting what Heidegger calls the "call of conscience," returns *Dasein* to its unhomely home: the call of conscience is one which "calls us back in calling us forth" (Heidegger 325). If we apply Heidegger's concept of the uncanny to the issue of narrative, the uncanniness of discovering that one has repeated a "primordial" narrative can be potentially liberating, because it frees us from the illusion that our "normal," everyday lives are our true home. Reveka must relinquish her above-ground plans and her dreams of breaking the curse for reward money (which would allow her the freedom to have her own herbary at a convent); only then can she find a way to both waken the sleepers and to exercise healing and growing powers over the entire Underworld as its Queen. Relinquishing control over her narrative, while still retaining the power of ethical choice, opens Reveka's life to new possibilities (albeit ones that may echo pre-existing narratives). To put it another way, "the authentic capacity for being oneself, which in Heidegger replaces self-determination, is an involuntary submission to letting oneself be determined" by "socially and culturally preformed possibilities for action" (Seel 85). Reveka's relationship to Persephone's narrative could be described in this way.

These pre-existing narratives can also be used as crutches to prevent one from exploring other options, and this pattern of behavior can entrap male characters just as easily as female ones, as *The Princess Curse* shows. Dragos also refers to Hades and Persephone, not in order to suggest any decision to Reveka, but to explain the choices he made in regard to the twelve princesses. "Hades got Persephone through kidnapping!" he reminds Reveka. "My choices came down to lying or extortion" (Haskell, *Princess* 267). Dragos, more than Reveka, is trapped within the narrative frames he knows, and Reveka calls him to task for it, saying, "I told you this when we first met! It's stupid to take the only choices offered, if they aren't any good" (267). While here Reveka seems an uncomplicated advocate for free will and narrative self-determination, Haskell later adds other layers through a confrontation between Reveka and one of the princesses, in which Reveka becomes defensive about her own apparent lack of options. When Princess Lacrimora tries to convince Reveka that she should not be bound to her promise, since it was a "forced oath," Reveka responds angrily, "Why does a forced oath mean less?" (Haskell, *Princess* 273). Her decision is no less moral because of the narrowed range of options presented to her: choice is still possible, and deserves merit when made for the right reasons. "I had a choice! I made the bargain and gave my word," Reveka insists (Haskell, *Princess* 274). Through her time in the *unheimlich* Underworld, Reveka matures in her view of preexisting narratives, gradually understanding that they both restrict choice and make it possible. As Martin Seel argues, "The individual who is not in some respect determined would be incapable of determining anything whatsoever, for there would be no counter-weight against which self-determination could have any leverage. Being determined is a constitutive *basis* of self-determination" (86–87). The narrowing of Reveka's options can form a clear background against which she can define herself through her choices—if she chooses to see it this way.

Reveka's ultimate decision to eat of the food of the Underworld is one she makes consciously, but it is crucial, for Haskell's themes, that Reveka does not know the full range of consequences of her choice; nor is she aware, at the moment, of how her decision echoes, with some key differences, the story of Persephone. Also, despite Reveka's earlier protes-tations, her crucial decision ultimately boils down to two options: "Maybe in a thousand years I could save the sleepers, but I didn't know how right then. I had to choose: heal the land that I knew I could heal so simply, or stick like a leech to dwindling hope and lose both the sleep-ers and Thonos" (Haskell, *Princess* 299). Reveka makes this choice in the dark, so to speak. Even though she knows the myth of Hades and Persephone, in this moment she seems unaware of the significance of choosing to eat pomegranate seeds: they are simply near at hand. Once Reveka eats the seeds, the darkness literally recedes, and she learns that it has always been light in Thonos: she simply has been unable to see it as it truly is. That this revelation and insight comes after her choice, not before, might be taken by some readers as evidence that Reveka lacks the metafictional insight she should possess and that she is a less empow-ered heroine than she could be. In truth, Reveka's "blind" decision is all the more courageous for its lack of certainty: her true self-determination lies in finally relinquishing the narrative she had clung to and fully embracing the unknown, the *unheimlich*, represented by the Underworld itself. Once she opens herself to the possibility of other narratives, the darkness—and the fear accompanying it—is transformed.

In resigning her attachment to the narrative Reveka thought should be hers, in unconsciously mirroring the story of Persephone, she gains control and power, even over the narratives of others. The nymph of the river Alethe explains to her, "You did not eat just any fruit in this world—you ate the pomegranate, the fruit that makes indissoluble marriage, and the fruit that the dead consume in order to be reborn. You became the Intercessor of Souls in that moment, the true Queen of Thonos"

(Haskell 307). Even with this power, Reveka still wrestles with the sus-
picion that it came about through chance or fate, rather than choice; she
replies incredulously, "And all because I ate a pomegranate, instead of
... a fig?" (Haskell, *Princess* 308). Though she has come around to
acknowledge that her options may not be entirely open, she still advocates for the moral significance of choice. When the nymph replies, "If
you choose to believe that, certainly; some would argue that it was your
fate," Reveka shoots back, "Fate is for people too lazy to make choices"
(308). The nymph concludes, "Maybe that's true. In another life, I made
my choices and did not wait for fate—though that's not how they tell it
in the stories" (308). The nymph's last ambiguous comment becomes
clearer when readers know that she is Persephone herself: Haskell, in
response to an email query, makes explicit that she is not merely repeating but also revising the Hades and Persephone myth: "I view Persephone as having been ultimately sympathetic to Hades, knowingly
choosing to eat the pomegranate seeds in the end" ("Re: Untold stories").
Persephone, then, in the world of *The Princess Curse*, was not ravished
against her will, but, like Reveka, made her own choices (though those
choices may not have been entirely free).

Reading, Adolescence and Narrative Control

The nymph's/Persephone's comment foreshadows that, though
Reveka has some control over her choices, she cannot exercise universal
control over the way her story is told by others (who may not even see
it as her story). She finds this to be the truth when she returns, for a
time, to the world above: "Somehow, Pa got most of the public credit
for breaking the curse ... [e]ven though all the princesses knew very
well that it was my promise to marry Lord Dragos that had freed them"
(Haskell, *Princess* 314). Reveka is not concerned with the way the story
is told, though readers will recognize the fictional "origin story" behind
"The Twelve Dancing Princesses" as we know it, in which a male hero
rescues the princesses and marries one of them as his reward. Reveka
seems to feel slightly resentful that the princesses do not publicly recognize her role, but she does not believe that she has to make sure everyone is aware of the "correct" version of the story. In this aspect of *The
Princess Curse*, as well as in the treatment of free will, Haskell deals with

darker aspects of metanarrative than many feminist-applauded fairy tale revisions. Of course, an even darker twist would be to depict a Persephone figure as having control over her own narrative even if she is subject to extremely disturbing circumstances—like a literal rape, for example. Haskell has evaded sexual subject matter, except at the metaphorical level (the level at which fairy tales have often dealt with "adult" content). Though metaphorizing rape is always a fraught endeavor, G. B. Stewart hints at the connection to loss of narrative control when she writes of rape as an "unhappy shift from a belief in one's autonomy to an image of oneself as victim of a brutal force" (131). Merrie Haskell is hardly the first writer for young readers to use the Persephone narrative to address some of these fears, albeit in a symbolic way. Late nineteenth and early twentieth-century children's classics such as George MacDonald's *The Princess and the Goblin* and J. M. Barrie's *Peter and Wendy* also draw on elements from the myth of Persephone and Hades to address the transition to adolescence and adulthood. Kiera Vaclavik argues that there are "clear undertones of Persephone and her abduction by Hades in [MacDonald's] text, since the goblin populations live in the subterranean caverns beneath the princess's castle" (190). The Goblin Queen desires the Princess Irene to marry her son, but, with the guidance of maternal figures like Irene's grandmother—upon whose spindle Irene pricks her finger, drawing blood symbolic of the onset of puberty (Patterson 176)—the underworld in this tale ultimately functions as a transition stage to lead Irene back to the overworld and eventual marriage with Curdie: "the descent to the underworld is itself a kind of death, a death of girlhood" (Patterson 179). Holly Blackford makes a similar argument about the use of the Persephone myth in *Peter and Wendy*, Barrie's later novelization of his play *Peter Pan*.

Peter Pan is a construct of the female psyche and a transitional object between mother and daughter. He represents a site of struggle between Wendy's desire to fly the nursery and Mrs. Darling's desire to keep Wendy young, which is finally resolved by their bargain to share her, Wendy visiting Peter Pan during spring cleaning and sending her daughters and daughter's daughters when she gets too old. The myth of Persephone prevails in the ending Barrie chose for his novel, proposing a solution to the paradox of desiring connection and separation, the paradox of mother-daughter desire. In the common logic of novels of female development, argues Adrienne Gavin, girls must die to become women (135), which, thanks to Peter and a harem of boys who build her a house and make her Queen of the underworld, Wendy does (117–118). In Barrie's and MacDonald's tales, the Underworld is a transitional stage, from which a young woman eventually emerges to join the adult world. Haskell, while using a transitional stage to represent adolescence, does not depict the Underworld as something to be ultimately left behind. Reveka, at age thirteen, is too young to carry through with marriage to Dragos, even in her medieval-esque setting: Haskell is careful to explain, through Reveka, that only the nobility married this early during the time period, while "peasants and guildsmen, sensibly, marry later" (*Princess* 190). However, Reveka sets her own terms for the significance of the five pomegranate seeds she ate, promising to return permanently to the Underworld in five years, as well as making visits every five days in the interim. Like Persephone, she suffers consequences from eating the seeds, but she frames their symbolism so that they allow her a transitional stage. Though the transition of adolescence is inevitable, Reveka can choose her own approach to it. In this respect, though she wisely relinquishes the attempt to manage how others tell her story, she maintains control over her passage to adulthood. At the end of that period, too, the Underworld will become her true home, which reinforces Haskell's theme of the importance of accepting the *unheimlich*. Adolescence, *The Princess Curse* implies, can be a time not just to be survived, but a time of exploration and discovery, a time for processing narrative possibilities, even if one is not fully sure of the course one's story will take. Though Haskell gives enough resolution to satisfy readers, she also deliberately leaves several loose ends—loose ends, like Dragos's still-mysterious backstory, of which Reveka herself is aware. As a character looking forward to unraveling narrative dilemmas, Reveka suggests the possibilities of adolescence as a time of reading: of learning to read the stories surrounding her, perhaps doing so more carefully and observantly than she has up to this point.

Haskell, in an email response, clarifies that Dragos's backstory is, in fact, another intertextual reference, to more obscure portions of the legends surrounding Vlad the Impaler ("Re: Untold stories"). Many adult readers, let alone adolescent ones, will not recognize these allusions, just as some young readers might not know the myth of Hades and Persephone. The reader of *The Princess Curse* occupies a position similar to that of Reveka within the tale: she may not recognize intertextual gestures, and younger readers in particular may be captivated at the level of plot and character, without considering the author as a figure who shapes the narrative. As Appleyard writes, "Younger children scarcely know authors' names or think of them as no more than labels to identify books they like" (119). Adolescents begin to develop an awareness of authors, siding with them as fan-worthy friends or against them as controlling authorities.[3] In between these two stages, many middle-grade readers are only beginning to establish a critical distance from their reading material, but this does not mean that they are powerless. Simultaneously capable of childlike surrender to a text but also beginning to view authority as sinister, they are open to reading as *unheimilich* experience. *The Princess Curse* constructs its readers as, like Reveka, capable of choice within the options presented to them, even if they do not grasp how a single narrative connects to other, external narratives. As metafiction, Haskell's novel allegorizes not only adolescence, as classic works of children's literature have done, but specifically adolescent reading. *The Princess Curse* is particularly apt as an allegory of postmodern adolescent reading because it can aid young readers as they transition from a view of the author as irrelevant, to a view of the author as an authority, to a view of the author as an intersection of texts. Especially if readers discover that Haskell herself did not plan *The Princess Curse* as a rewriting of "Beauty and the Beast," they may reconsider simplistic visions of authorial intent, instead accepting that the author is more like the center point of a web of overlapping narratives.

The Princess Curse may somewhat resemble other contemporary fairy tale retellings in its gestures toward metafiction and intertextuality, but, unlike them, it forces the reader to experience narrative uncertainty as Haskell switches from one fairy tale frame to another. Like Reveka in the Underworld, readers must relinquish their grasp on previous narratives, though this does not rob them of agency. Haskell's novel also shares similarities with classic children's literature in its use of the Persephone/Underworld motif to deal with issues of narrative control in adolescence, but ultimately it departs from these models in depicting the narrative uncertainty of adolescence and the Underworld as something that both transforms and can be transformed by a protagonist who willingly embraces it. As Reveka herself points out, a situation does not have to be accepted as either/or—even without seeing the clear shape of the story, a character can find a third way. Some narrative frames, Haskell suggests, cannot be changed—or even recognized ahead of time—yet this does not render one powerless over one's own story. A protagonist, even without knowing the shape of her narrative, can make ethical choices based upon her desire to help others. If these choices end up mirroring the shape of another, preexisting story, that does not diminish the significance of her decisions. Through surrendering attachment to preexisting narrative frames and fully embracing the *unheimlich*, without surrendering responsibility for ethical choice, a fairy tale heroine—or a reader—can reframe the darkness around her as light.

Notes

1. Haskell writes, "Like most writers, I started out as a little kid with a big imagination, and while I would have gladly embraced the chance to visit another world– as a long lost princess-wizard-dragon-tamer, preferably—I never, ever, ever, EVER wanted to visit the Underworld. Any version of it. Not the Christian Hell, for certain; I was super-scared of that on a visceral level. But I also hated Hades, Avernus, Annwn, and any other variant I ran across. I imagined the dead as a passive zombie horde, at best. And the monster under my bed not only had long, Grim Reaper fingers, but a portal to the Underworld" ("The Big Idea").

2. I am using "metafiction" here in the context of Jessica Tiffin's definition specific to contemporary fairy tales, which invoke "a notion of geometric form which self-consciously presents itself in precisely those fixed terms recognized by structuralist analysis" (*Marvelous* 2). These fixed patterns may be questioned or revised within the fairy tale narrative, but, "radical inquiry and reinterpretation notwithstanding, the structures of fairy tale must be invoked with sufficient power to be recognizable, to identify the text as fairy tale within the context of the structural tradition" (*Marvelous* 3).

3. Appleyard further describes the transition from juvenile to adolescent reading: "Thinking about the implications of a story may seem to be at the opposite pole from being wrapped up in the experience of it, but the connection between the two responses lies in the adolescent's new way of making the world meaningful. The adolescent has become what the juvenile was not, an observer and evaluator of self and others, so it is an easy step from involvement in the story to reflecting about it" (101).

Works Cited

Appleyard, J. A. *Becoming a Reader: The Experience of Fiction from Childhood to Adulthood*. New York: Cambridge University Press, 1991. Print.

Bernstein, Susan. "It Walks: The Ambulatory Uncanny." *MLN* 118.5 (Dec. 2003): 1111–1139. *JSTOR*. Web. 17 Jan. 2013.

Blackford, Holly. "Mrs. Darling's Scream: The Rites of Persephone in *Peter and Wendy* and *Wuthering Heights*." *Studies in the Humanities* 32.2 (2005): 116–144. *MLA International Bibliography*. Web. 16 Jan. 2013.

Byatt, A. S. "The Story of the Eldest Princess." *The Djinn in the Nightingale's Eye: Five Fairy Stories*. 1994. New York: Vintage, 1998. 39–71. Print.

Doughty, Amie A. "'I Think You Are Not Telling Me All of This Story': Storytelling, Fate, and Self-Determination in Robin McKinley's Folktale Revisions." *Fairy Tales Reimagined: Essays on New Retellings.* Ed. Susan Redington Bobby. Jefferson, NC: McFarland, 2009. 85–97. Print.

Gibson, Jeffrey K. "'And the Princess, Telling the Story': A. S. Byatt's Self-Reflexive Fairy Stories." *Fairy Tales Reimagined: Essays on New Retellings.* Ed. Susan Redington Bobby. Jefferson, NC: McFarland, 2009. 85–97. Print.

Haskell, Merrie. "The Big Idea: Merrie Haskell." Interview with John Scalzi. *Whatever.* 7 Sept. 2011. Web. 19 Jan. 2013.

_____. *The Princess Curse.* New York: Harper, 2011. Print.

_____. "Re: Untold stories in *The Princess Curse.*" Message to the author. 12 Jan. 2013. Email.

_____. "A Timeless Romance: Merrie Haskell on *Beauty: A Retelling of Beauty and the Beast.*" *Los Angeles Review of Books.* 11 Oct. 2012. Web. 19 Jan. 2013.

_____. "The Writing Process and Mer Haskell." Interview by Catherine Schaff-Stump. *Writer Tamago.* 12 Dec. 2012. Web. 19 Jan. 2013.

Heidegger, Martin. *Being and Time.* New York: Harper & Row, 1962. Print.

Patterson, Nancy-Lou. "Kore Motifs in *The Princess and the Goblin.*" *For the Childlike: George MacDonald's Fantasies for Children.* Ed. Roderick McGillis. Metuchen, NJ: The Children's Literature Association and Scarecrow Press, 1992. 169–182. Print.

Seel, Martin. "Letting Oneself Be Determined: A Revised Concept of Self-Determination." *Philosophical Romanticism.* Ed. Nikolas Kompridis. New York: Routledge, 2006. 81–96. Print.

Stewart, G. B. "Mother, Daughter, and the Birth of the Female Artist." *Women's Studies* 6.2 (1979): 127–145. *MLA International Bibliography.* Web. 16 Jan. 2013.

Tiffin, Jessica. "Ice, Glass, Snow: Fairy Tale as Art and Metafiction in the Writings of A. S. Byatt." *Marvels & Tales* 20.1 (2006): 47–66. *MLA International Bibliography.* Web. 16 Jan. 2013.

_____. *Marvelous Geometry: Narrative and Metafiction in Modern Fairy Tale.* Detroit: Wayne State University Press, 2009. Print.

Tolkien, J. R. R. *The Two Towers.* 1954. New York: Ballantine, 1965. Print.

Vaclavik, Kiera. "Undermining Body and Mind? The Impact of the Underground in Nineteenth-Century Children's Literature." *Histoires de la Terre: Earth Sciences and French Culture, 1740–1940.* Ed. Louise Lyle and David McCallam. Amsterdam: Rodopi, 2008. 187–201. Print.

Warner, Marina. *From the Beast to the Blonde: On Fairy Tales and Their Tellers.* New York: Farrar, Straus and Giroux, 1994. Print.

About the Contributors

Joseph **Abbruscato** is a high school English teacher in Arizona. He specializes in the study of young adult literature, fairy tales and mythologies (both classic and contemporary). His lifelong love of comic books, pop culture, and science fiction provides a great intersection of research interests.

Carys **Crossen** is a graduate teaching assistant in the University of Manchester's Department of English and American Studies. Her main research interests include the Gothic, psychoanalytic criticism, Monster Theory, Victorian literature, young adult fantasy and horror fiction, feminist theory and anything with werewolves.

Eileen **Donaldson** is a senior lecturer in the Department of English Studies at the University of South Africa. Her publications include articles on Joanna Russ, Ursula Le Guin and Roald Dahl. Her scholarly interests converge on the examination of the relationship between the hero and the monster.

Tanya **Jones** is a former high school English teacher and department chairperson in Charlotte, North Carolina. Her scholarly interests lie in Gothicism, children's and adolescent literature, fairy tales, Celtic and Nordic folk tales and the paradox between science and the supernatural in literature.

Erin Wyble **Newcomb** teaches at the State University of New York at New Paltz; courses include writing, American literature, and young adult literature. Feminism, religion and young adult literature are among her reseach interests.

Rhonda **Nicol** teaches courses in English studies, gender in the humanities, introductory women's and gender studies and both introductory and advanced composition at Illinois State University. Her recent academic work focuses on issues of gender, power and identity in contemporary fantasy.

Lisa K. **Perdigao** is an associate professor of English at the Florida Institute of Technology where she teaches twentieth and twenty-first century American literature, children's and adolescent literature and popular culture. Her recent research has focused on television series like *Grimm*, *Once Upon a Time*, adaptations of *Alice in Wonderland*, and *Glee*.

Tim **Sadenwasser** is an associate professor of English at Augusta State University, where he teaches, among other things, Victorian and modern literature, detective literature, children's literature and freshman composition. He also directs the university's Honors Program.

Carissa Turner **Smith** is an assistant professor of English at Charleston Southern University. She writes about place and spirituality in American literature and is working on a project dealing with American spiritual autobiographies that resist an upwardly mobile, progress-driven narrative.

Sarah R. **Wakefield** is an associate professor of English at Prairie View A&M University in Prairie View, Texas. Her research interests in women, gender and the fantastic led her to write *Folklore in British Literature: Naming and Narrating in Women's Fiction, 1750 to 1880* (Peter Lang, 2006). Recent projects involve the work of Sandra Cisneros and Stephenie Meyer.

Index

Index

Index

Trites, Roberta Seelinger 103, 12, 172,
178, 180
"The Twelve Dancing Princesses" 186,
188, 194

uncanny 11, 14, 49–50, 55, 61–62, 102–
104, 121, 169, 182, 191
unheimlich 111, 181–182, 189, 191–193,
196, 198
utopia 47, 50–51, 59, 63–64

Vaclavik, Kiera 195, 199
Valiant: A Modern Tale of Faerie 166,
175–176, 178–179
Verdi, Giuseppe 123
victim 8, 32, 89, 92–93, 98, 100, 135,
139, 173; child 30, 43, 45–46, 125,
131, 134, 152; incest 85, 90, 96; rape
90, 176, 195
The Vile Village 135, 144; see also
A Series of Unfortunate Events;
Snicket, Lemony
violence 4, 7, 38, 48–51, 53, 55–56, 58,
62–63, 75, 95, 127, 160; see also murder
von Franz, Marie Louise 70, 80, 82,
101, 103, 145, 147, 163

Warner, Maria 31, 36–37, 40, 45–46,

63–64, 128, 144, 147, 152, 156, 163–
164, 189, 199
Waugh, Patricia 118, 122
The Wee Free Men 148–149, 160, 163
The Wicked Lovely Series 165–168, 171,
173–174, 178–180; see also Darkest
Mercy; Fragile Eternity; Ink
Exchange; Radiant Shadows
The Wide Window 130–132, 144; see
also A Series of Unfortunate Events;
Snicket, Lemony
Wild Hunt 166, 172–174
Williams, Anne 15, 29
The Wintersmith 145, 148, 158–159,
163
wish 4, 20, 27, 40, 52–53, 59, 76, 80–
81, 112, 127, 132, 135, 171; fulfillment
3, 54, 56, 81
witch 7–9, 30, 32, 34–37, 75–76, 78,
89, 114, 123–126, 129, 137, 145, 148–
154, 157–161; as mother 32, 34–36,
152
Wonderland 103–104, 106–108, 111–
112, 116, 121

Zipes, Jack 18, 22–23, 25, 28–29, 40,
46, 50, 56–57, 64, 66, 81–82, 104–
105, 121–122, 145, 149, 164–165, 180
zmeu 186–188

208